Performance of Manufacturing Firms in Africa

Performance of Manufacturing Firms in Africa

An Empirical Analysis

Hinh T. Dinh and George R. G. Clarke
Editors

THE WORLD BANK
Washington, D.C.

Contents

Chapter 3   **Manufacturing Firms in Africa**   **47**
                George R. G. Clarke

Chapter 4   **The Binding Constraint on the Growth
of Firms in Developing Countries**   **87**
                *Hinh T. Dinh, Dimitris A. Mavridis,
and Hoa B. Nguyen*

Figures

Tables

Foreword

After stagnating for most of the past 45 years, economic performance in Sub-Saharan Africa is at a turning point. From 2001 to 2010, the region's gross domestic product grew at an average of over 5 percent a year compared with an average of −0.4 percent in the 1990s. However, this growth has not been accompanied by a structural transformation that lifts workers from low-productivity jobs in the informal sector to higher-productivity activities in the formal sector. Such a transformation has yet to take place in Sub-Saharan Africa; a large part of the growth of the last decade was fueled by booming prices among commodities that Sub-Saharan Africa mostly exports.

Labor-intensive manufacturing has led the economic transformation of most successful developing countries, especially in Asia, in their low-income stage of development, but it has not fared well in Sub-Saharan Africa. Sub-Saharan Africa's share of global light manufacturing has continually declined (to less than 1 percent), and preferential access to markets in the European Union and the United States has not made much of a difference. Without structural transformation, Sub-Saharan Africa is unlikely to catch up with more prosperous countries, such as the Asian countries, particularly China, which, in the 1980s, was not so different from Sub-Saharan Africa now. In addition to increasing the productivity of medium and large formal firms, Sub-Saharan Africa has to raise the

productivity and encourage the upgrading and expansion of small enterprises, mostly in the informal sector.

This book presents empirical evidence on manufacturing firm performance in Africa based on two sources of data. The first is the well-known
World Bank Enterprise Survey, which, using almost identical questionnaires and sampling methods, covers over 100 low- and middle-income
countries, including most countries in Sub-Saharan Africa. The second
data source is a new, one-time quantitative survey conducted for the
World Bank by Oxford University's Centre for the Study of African
Economies. This survey provides in-depth information on formal and
informal manufacturing firms, including firms with only one or two
employees, in three countries in Africa and two countries in Asia.
Together, these two data sources form a comprehensive basis on which
analytical studies can be conducted to gain an understanding of the performance of manufacturing firms.

The studies based on the Enterprise Survey show that most African
firms are small and that few are exporters. Because of their institutional
environment, their labor productivity is low, and their labor costs also
tend to be low. Key constraints to firm growth vary by country, by sector,
and by firm size. The binding constraints for most large formal firms in
Africa are access to finance and to electricity. The binding constraints for
small firms tend to be access to finance and competition from foreign
firms. After controlling for differences in firm characteristics, geography,
infrastructure, political and institutional factors, business environment,
and finance, the authors show that African manufacturing actually has a
conditional advantage in productivity and sales growth. Political and institutional factors (especially party monopoly), access to finance, and the
nature of the business environment are keys to explaining the disadvantage of African countries in firm performance relative to countries at
similar levels of income in which firms perform better.

The results of the new survey conducted by the Oxford group shed
light on manufacturing firm performance in Africa in relation to that in
Asian countries such as China. The survey results suggest that, whatever
the reason for China's success relative to Africa, it is unlikely to be less
regulation. Indeed, China seems to have more stringent registration
requirements and labor laws. It is also unlikely to be corruption, lower
labor or land costs, or social networks: Chinese firms report fewer links
with banks and politicians and fewer business friends. There also are no
strong differences across the countries in the rate at which individual
firms innovate and invest. The dimensions along which Chinese firms are

at an advantage appear to be finance, competition, information about innovations, and educational attainment. Asian workers and entrepreneurs have more schooling. Nonetheless, education is not a good predictor of how quickly production workers can become fully active in firm operations.

We hope that the book, part of the knowledge creation and dissemination fostered by the Bank, will contribute in a practical way to spur the development of productive jobs in Sub-Saharan Africa.

Justin Yifu Lin
Senior Vice President and Chief Economist
Development Economics
World Bank
April 2012

Acknowledgments

This book is a product of the project on Light Manufacturing in Africa[1] conducted by a core team consisting of Hinh T. Dinh (Lead Economist and Team Leader), Vincent Palmade (Lead Economist and Co-Team Leader), Vandana Chandra (Senior Economist), Frances Cossar (Junior Professional), Tugba Gurcanlar (Finance Specialist), Ali Zafar (Senior Economist), Kathleen Fitzgerald (Consultant), and Gabriela Calderon Motta (Program Assistant). The work has been carried out with the support and guidance of Oby Ezekwesili (Vice President, Africa Regional Vice Presidency, World Bank) and Justin Yifu Lin (Former Senior Vice President and Chief Economist, World Bank), Shanta Devarajan (Chief Economist, Africa Regional Vice Presidency, World Bank), and Zia Qureshi (Director, Operations and Strategy Department, Development Economics Vice Presidency, World Bank).

Throughout the preparation of the project, the team has received valuable advice and guidance from an external advisory committee consisting of Yaw Ansu (African Center for Economic Transformation), Augusto Luis Alcorta (United Nations Industrial Development Organization), William Lewis (Founding Director, McKinsey Global Institute), Howard Pack (University of Pennsylvania), Jean-Philippe Platteau (University of Namur, Belgium), Kei Otsuka (National Graduate Institute for Policy

Studies, Tokyo), John Sutton (London School of Economics), and Alan Gelb and Vijaya Ramachandran (Center for Global Development).

The report was edited by a team headed by Robert Zimmermann. Financial support from the Bank-Netherlands Partnership Program and the Japan Policy and Human Resources Development Fund is gratefully acknowledged.

---

[1] Dinh, Hinh T., Vincent Palmade, Vandana Chandra, and Frances Cossar. 2012. *Light Manufacturing in Africa: Targeted Policies to Enhance Private Investment and Create Jobs*. Washington, DC: World Bank. http://elibrary.worldbank.org/content/book/9780821389614.

Contributors

George R. G. Clarke is the Killam Distinguished Associate Professor of Economics at the A. R. Sanchez, Jr. School of Business at Texas A&M International University in Laredo, Texas. Before joining Texas A&M International in August 2009, he was a Senior Private Sector Development Specialist at the World Bank. He received his BA in mathematics and economics from Cornell University and his PhD in economics from the University of Rochester.

Hinh T. Dinh is Lead Economist, Office of the Senior Vice President and Chief Economist of the World Bank. Previously, he served in the Africa Region, the Finance Complex, and the Middle East and North Africa Region at the Bank. He received his undergraduate degrees in economics and mathematics from the State University of New York, and his MA in economics, MS in industrial engineering, and PhD in economics from the University of Pittsburgh.

Marcel Fafchamps is Professor of Development Economics at Oxford University and Deputy Director of the Centre for the Study of African Economies, Oxford. He has also taught at Stanford University and worked for the International Labour Organization. His research focuses on market institutions and social networks in Sub-Saharan Africa.

Professor Fafchamps holds a PhD from the University of California, Berkeley, and degrees in law and in economics from Université Catholique de Louvain, Belgium. His regional interests are Africa and South Asia.

Ann E. Harrison is Professor of Multinational Management at the Wharton School, University of Pennsylvania; a Research Associate at the National Bureau of Economic Research, Cambridge, MA; and an affiliate of the International Growth Centre in London. She has also taught at Columbia Business School, the University of California, Berkeley, the Kennedy School of Government at Harvard University, and the University of Paris. Before joining the Wharton School, Professor Harrison spent two years in Washington, DC, as the Director of Development Policy at the World Bank. She holds a PhD in economics from Princeton University.

Justin Yifu Lin is Professor of Economics at Peking University. He was Senior Vice President and Chief Economist of the World Bank from 2008–12. Prior to joining the Bank, he served for 15 years as Professor and Founding Director of the China Center for Economic Research at Peking University. He was a Deputy of China's People's Congress and Vice Chairman of the All-China Federation of Industry and Commerce. He is the author of 23 books and the recipient of numerous academic prizes and awards. He received his PhD in economics from the University of Chicago.

Dimitris Mavridis is a PhD candidate in economics at the Paris School of Economics, where he works on labor and development economics. He holds a BA in economics from Université Paris 1 Panthéon-Sorbonne and an MA from the Paris School of Economics. From 2009 to 2011, he was a Junior Professional Associate at the World Bank, where he worked in the Office of the Senior Vice President and Chief Economist and in the Development Research Group.

Hoa B. Nguyen is a Senior Economist in the Division of Model, Mission, and Research at Freddie Mac. Previously, she worked for the World Bank as a consultant in the Development Research Group. She holds a PhD in economics from Michigan State University. Her research interests cover econometrics and applied microeconomic topics such as the housing market, labor economics, and economic development.

Simon Quinn is an Examination Fellow at All Souls College, Oxford University, where he is doing research in development economics. His work focuses on firms in developing economies, with particular emphasis on the use of survey data. He holds undergraduate degrees in economics and in law from the University of Queensland, Brisbane, and a D. Phil in economics from Oxford University. His doctoral thesis dealt with the access of Moroccan manufacturing firms to bank credit.

Lixin Colin Xu is a Lead Economist in the Development Research Group of the World Bank. After studying at Peking University (BA and MA) and the University of Chicago (PhD), he joined the Research Group of the World Bank, in 1996. His current research is focused on applied micro-economics topics such as development, empirical industrial organization, corporate governance, political economy, labor and household economics, income distribution, and the Chinese economy in transition. He has published widely in many economic journals.

Abbreviations

GDP	gross domestic product
HLX	Harrison, Lin, and Xu (2011)
HRV	Hausmann, Rodrik, and Velasco (2005)
MSMEs	micro, small, and medium enterprises
OECD	Organisation for Economic Co-operation and Development
PPP	purchasing power parity

Note: All dollar amounts are U.S. dollars unless otherwise indicated.

CHAPTER 1

Overview

George R. G. Clarke and Hinh T. Dinh

Introduction

Although most low-income countries in Sub-Saharan Africa have many unskilled workers, few have been successful in export-oriented light manufacturing. Manufacturing accounts for only about 13 percent of gross domestic product (GDP) in Sub-Saharan Africa, a smaller share than in any other region except the Middle East and North Africa (figure 1.1, table 1.1). Furthermore, the most successful countries are middle-income countries in southern Africa (Lesotho, Mauritius, South Africa, and Swaziland). Manufacturing accounted for over 15 percent of GDP in only two other countries between 2005 and 2009: Cameroon and Côte d'Ivoire.

Given the small size of the manufacturing sector in most countries, it is not surprising that manufacturing exports are not an important source of export earnings in most African countries. Manufacturing accounts for only about one-quarter of exports in Sub-Saharan Africa, lower than in any region except the Middle East and North Africa (see figure 1.1; table 1.2). Other than the middle-income countries in southern Africa and the middle-income island economies, manufacturing accounts for over 30 percent of exports only in Kenya, Madagascar, Senegal, and Zimbabwe.

Figure 1.1   Few African Countries Have Been Successful in Export-Oriented Manufacturing

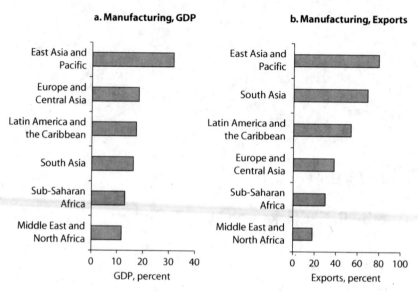

a. Manufacturing, GDP

b. Manufacturing, Exports

Source: World Development Indicators (database), World Bank, Washington, DC (accessed 2011), http://data .worldbank.org/data-catalog/world-development-indicators.
Note: Percentages are regional weighted averages for each year between 2005 and 2009. Manufacturing exports are expressed as a percentage of merchandise exports. GDP = gross domestic product.

The importance of manufacturing in the economic development of Africa has been studied in a previous volume. The chapters in this volume look at the barriers that manufacturing firms in Africa face.[1] They compare firms in Sub-Saharan Africa with firms in other regions, focusing on comparisons with successful manufacturing economies in East Asia such as China and Vietnam. The goal is to identify constraints to firm performance and growth that prevent African firms from entering export-oriented light manufacturing.

The chapters use data from two main sources. Chapters 2–4 use data from the World Bank's Enterprise Survey program.[2] The Enterprise Surveys provide information on representative weighted samples of formal firms in each country. Surveys have been completed in over 100 low- and middle-income countries, including most countries in Sub-Saharan Africa. Since 2006, the surveys have used almost identical questionnaires and sampling methods. They cover manufacturing firms with more than five employees in two to five cities in each country.[3] Because firms are sampled from lists provided by government statistical agencies,

Table 1.1   Manufacturing as a Share of GDP

percent

Region or country	Average, 2005–09	Region or country	Average, 2005–09
Regions (developing countries only)		Gabon	4.01
East Asia and Pacific	31.46	Gambia, The	4.97
Europe and Central Asia	18.26	Ghana	8.74
Latin America and the Caribbean	17.39	Guinea	4.26
Middle East and North Africa	11.92	Guinea-Bissau	—
South Asia	16.24	Kenya	10.10
Sub-Saharan Africa	13.18	Lesotho	19.74
East Asia (exporters)		Liberia	13.05
China	33.03	Madagascar	14.90
Indonesia	27.93	Malawi	14.06
Malaysia	27.70	Mali	3.13
Philippines	22.15	Mauritania	5.05
Thailand	34.86	Mauritius	19.84
Vietnam	20.74	Mozambique	14.90
Sub-Saharan Africa		Namibia	14.92
Angola	4.79	Niger	—
Benin	7.51	Nigeria	2.71
Botswana	3.69	Rwanda	5.23
Burkina Faso	14.10	São Tomé and Príncipe	6.37
Burundi	8.83	Senegal	13.83
Cameroon	17.00	Seychelles	12.23
Cape Verde	6.73	Sierra Leone	—
Central African Republic	7.52	Somalia	—
Chad	5.92	South Africa	16.89
Comoros	4.24	Sudan	6.38
Congo, Dem. Rep.	6.09	Swaziland	43.28
Congo, Rep.	3.92	Tanzania	6.87
Côte d'Ivoire	18.13	Togo	10.14
Equatorial Guinea	11.15	Uganda	7.67
Eritrea	5.90	Zambia	11.39
Ethiopia	4.61	Zimbabwe	13.52

Source: World Development Indicators (database), World Bank, Washington, DC (accessed 2010), http://data
.worldbank.org/data-catalog/world-development-indicators.
Note: Averages for regions are weighted. Averages across years and unweighted averages for each country
are for available years for that country. GDP = gross domestic product, — = not available.

company registrars, and other official agencies and because of the size
limit, the Enterprise Surveys focus on formal firms.

Chapter 5 (Fafchamps and Quinn) uses data from the Quantitative
Entrepreneur Survey, one-time surveys of small and medium firms in food
processing, garments, leather, metal products, and wood products. The
surveys were conducted in the largest cities of three countries in Africa

Table 1.2   Manufacturing Exports as a Share of Merchandise Exports
percent

Region or country	Average, 2005–10	Region or country	Average, 2005–10
Regions		Gabon	4
East Asia and Pacific	79	Gambia, The	21
Europe and Central Asia	38	Ghana	25
Latin America and the Caribbean	53	Guinea	14
Middle East and North Africa	16	Guinea-Bissau	0
South Asia	69	Kenya	35
Sub-Saharan Africa	30	Lesotho	—
East Asia (exporters)		Liberia	—
China	93	Madagascar	53
Indonesia	42	Malawi	11
Malaysia	68	Mali	15
Philippines	86	Mauritania	0
Thailand	76	Mauritius	61
Vietnam	54	Mozambique	6
Sub-Saharan Africa		Namibia	46
Angola	—	Niger	10
Benin	12	Nigeria	4
Botswana	79	Rwanda	7
Burkina Faso	9	São Tomé and Príncipe	5
Burundi	14	Senegal	41
Cameroon	7	Seychelles	5
Cape Verde	39	Sierra Leone	—
Central African Republic	24	Somalia	—
Chad	—	South Africa	51
Comoros	11	Sudan	0
Congo, Dem. Rep.	—	Swaziland	68
Congo, Rep.	—	Tanzania	23
Côte d'Ivoire	15	Togo	65
Equatorial Guinea	—	Uganda	22
Eritrea	—	Zambia	7
Ethiopia	8	Zimbabwe	37

Source: World Development Indicators (database), World Bank, Washington, DC (accessed 2010), http://data .worldbank.org/data-catalog/world-development-indicators.
Note: Averages for regions are weighted. Averages across years and unweighted averages for each country are for available years for that country. — = not available.

(Ethiopia, Tanzania, and Zambia) and two countries in East Asia (China and Vietnam). Unlike the Enterprise Surveys, these surveys included informal and semiformal firms, as well as formal firms. Given that informal firms account for most employment in Africa and that these firms face unique challenges, chapter 5 complements the analysis of formal firms in the other chapters.

Characteristics of African Manufacturing Firms

Before addressing the binding constraints on sector growth, this section draws on the results in chapters 2–5 to discuss the characteristics of firms in Africa and how they are different from and similar to firms in other regions.

Informality: A Dual Labor Market in Most Countries in the Region

One striking characteristic of African economies is the importance of informal firms. Although it is difficult to estimate the size of the informal sector, Schneider, Buehn, and Montenegro (2011) estimate that the informal sector accounts for about 38 percent of GDP in Sub-Saharan Africa. This is a higher share than in any other region. By comparison, the informal sector accounts for only about 18 percent in East Asia and Pacific.

Nonetheless, this underestimates the importance of the informal sector in Sub-Saharan Africa. Informal firms are far less productive than formal firms in most countries in the region, meaning that they account for a greater share of employment than they do of output.[4] For example, about 88 percent of the employed in Zambia work for enterprises with less than five employees (Clarke and others 2010). Almost all micro and small firms in Zambia are unregistered, even with local authorities (Clarke and Kim 2011). Because of this, in Africa, most people either own or work for informal or semiformal enterprises.

A first question is why do firms remain small and informal rather than growing and becoming formal? One reason emphasized in previous studies is that informal firms avoid the costs associated with paying taxes and complying with regulations (Schneider and Enste 2000). In Tanzania, it has been reported that the 6 percent payroll tax was responsible for many firms becoming informal. Although avoiding taxes benefits the informal firms, it has a negative impact on government revenue. Moreover, it is difficult for government to regulate informal firms, undermining the government's ability to achieve social and other goals.

Although, as discussed below, the burden of regulation is often heavy in Africa, Fafchamps and Quinn (this volume) argue that it is not a binding constraint. In particular, they note that Chinese firms face stricter registrations requirements and heavier labor regulations than firms in the three African countries in their study. And, they note, there are fewer tiny informal firms in China than in the three African countries.

Informal micro and small firms may avoid the cost of paying taxes and complying with regulations, but being informal can create problems for the firms. One problem is that these firms can only remain informal for as long as they remain small and out of sight. Because this is difficult for large productive firms, unregistered firms have only limited opportunities for expansion and growth.[5] Remaining informal also makes it more difficult for micro and small firms to use government services. Having a fixed location and obtaining utility services at that location make the firm more visible, and it will therefore be more difficult for the firm to remain informal.[6]

One of the goals of this volume is to look at the constraints facing small firms that prevent them from growing and becoming formal. Although the three chapters that use Enterprise Survey data do not look at the constraints facing informal firms, Fafchamps and Quinn (this volume), which includes these firms in their analysis, provide details on this topic.

Firm Size: African Firms Are Smaller than Firms in Other Regions

Not surprisingly, most informal firms are small. Given the size of the informal sector, it is therefore not surprising that firms in Africa tend to be small. It is not, however, only informal firms that are small in Africa. As discussed in this volume, an important difference between manufacturing firms in Africa and similar firms in East Asia is that African firms—even formal firms—are much smaller than their East Asian counterparts. The Enterprise Surveys use a standardized sampling methodology to try to examine representative samples of formal firms with at least five employees within the major cities in each country. Dinh, Mavridis, and Nguyen (chapter 4) show that Africa has the largest share of micro and small formal firms, while other regions have more medium and large firms. This can be seen by looking at the average size of manufacturing firms. In Sub-Saharan Africa, the average size is about 47 employees (table 1.3). In comparison, the average size of a firm in the Enterprise Survey was about 171 employees in Malaysia, 195 employees in Vietnam, 393 employees in Thailand, and 977 employees in China.

Other evidence from the chapters in this volume support the analysis of the Enterprise Survey data. Fafchamps and Quinn (this volume) note that their original goal in their survey was to collect data only on firms with between 2 and 40 permanent employees. In practice, they note, it was difficult to find enough large firms in Tanzania and Zambia, and they

Table 1.3 Average and Median Number of Employees, Weighted Enterprise Survey Samples

number of employees

Region or country	Median	Mean	Region or country	Median	Mean
Africa, low income	16	47	Nigeria	11	17
Angola	11	16	Rwanda	39	187
Benin	5	43	Senegal	12	58
Burkina Faso	13	33	Sierra Leone	8	13
Burundi	9	20	Tanzania	15	43
Cameroon	22	83	Togo	6	41
Chad	11	41	Uganda	14	56
Congo, Dem. Rep.	11	23	Zambia	33	81
Congo, Rep.	20	28	*Africa, middle income*	17	149
Eritrea	15	24	Botswana	17	59
Gabon	12	49	Cape Verde	15	23
Gambia, The	14	28	Lesotho	10	695
Ghana	12	48	Mauritius	10	45
Guinea	9	24	Namibia	14	30
Guinea-Bissau	8	18	South Africa	27	73
Côte d'Ivoire	7	27	Swaziland	24	116
Kenya	58	147	*East Asia, exporters*	91	311
Liberia	8	12	China	258	977
Madagascar	27	122	Indonesia	6	28
Malawi	45	203	Malaysia	57	171
Mali	10	23	Philippines	30	101
Mauritania	12	24	Thailand	134	393
Mozambique	11	25	Vietnam	63	195
Niger	14	21			

Source: Enterprise Surveys (database), World Bank, Washington, DC, http://www.enterprisesurveys.org/.
Note: Regional averages are simple averages for all countries with available data. Country averages are weighted averages for manufacturing firms based on the Enterprise Survey samples.

therefore included one-person firms in these countries. In contrast, they were unable to find enough small firms in China and, therefore, raised the upper limit there to 100 employees.

Globalization: There Are Few Manufacturing Firms in the Region, and Few of These Export

Another feature that makes Sub-Saharan Africa different from other regions is that, as noted in Clarke (chapter 3), few enterprises in most countries in Sub-Saharan Africa export. Fewer than one in five exports anything in most countries (figure 1.2). This suggests that poor export performance does not reflect simply the small size of the manufacturing sector; it also reflects the fact that few of these firms export. Fafchamps and Quinn (this volume) find similar results in their sample of firms.

Moreover, even in successful countries such as Kenya, manufacturing firms that export do so mostly to neighboring countries rather than to Europe or other high-income economies. Although the most recent Enterprise Surveys do not collect information on the destination of exports, earlier Enterprise Surveys did. In the Enterprise Surveys conducted between 2002 and 2004, firms in most countries were more likely to export to neighboring countries than to more distant markets (table 1.4). For example, Uganda and Tanzania were the most important export destinations for Kenyan firms, with 74 and 61 percent of exporters exporting to these countries, respectively. In comparison, only 8 percent exported to the United Kingdom, the biggest overseas export market. This is true for both landlocked countries (for example, Uganda and Zambia) and countries with access to the sea (for example, Kenya and Tanzania).

Figure 1.2   Share of Firms That Export, by Region

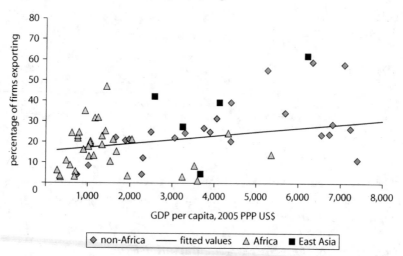

Source: Calculations based on data of Enterprise Surveys (database), World Bank, Washington, DC, http://www
.enterprisesurveys.org/.
Note: See table 1.5 for additional notes on data construction. East Asia is China, Indonesia, the Philippines, Thailand, and Vietnam. Africa is Sub-Saharan Africa only. Data are for all Enterprise Surveys conducted since 2006 with at least 50 firms. Countries with per capita GDP over US$8,000 are excluded for presentational purposes. Fitted values is the line from log-log regression. GDP = gross domestic product, PPP = purchasing power parity .

Table 1.4   Export Destinations for Enterprises Included in the Investment Climate Surveys of the Early 2000s

percentage of responses

	% of exporters who report that the destination is important	
Country	Most important export destinations	Most important industrialized export destination
Ethiopia	Italy (55), United Kingdom (29), Germany (19)	Italy (55)
Kenya	Uganda (74), Tanzania (61), Rwanda (19)	United Kingdom (8)
Mali	Burkina Faso (63), Guinea (53), Niger (38)	France (9)
Senegal	Gambia, The (39); Mali (36); Mauritania (31)	France (18)
Tanzania	Kenya (38), Malawi (14), Uganda (12), United Kingdom (12), Zambia (12)	United Kingdom (12)
Uganda	Rwanda (49); Congo, Dem. Rep. (33); Kenya (18)	United Kingdom (16)
Zambia	Congo, Dem. Rep. (38); Malawi (22); Germany (21)	Germany (21)

Source: Data of Enterprise Surveys (database) (2002–04), World Bank, Washington, DC, http://www.enterprisesurveys.org/.
Note: Enterprises were asked to list their three most important export destinations. Countries are ranked on the basis, the number of enterprises that ranked each country among the top three. Not all enterprises reported three destinations.

Labor Productivity is Low in Africa, but This is a Function of the Institutional Environment

Although the best performing firms in most African countries are productive even by international standards, and firms in some sectors are as productive as those in East Asia (Dinh and others 2012), the average manufacturing firm in Sub-Saharan Africa is less productive than the average firm in the best performing East Asian countries (table 1.5). Clarke (this volume) shows that the average firm in Sub-Saharan Africa produces about US$3,300 of output per worker in 2005 dollars. In comparison, the average firm in the successful East Asian exporting economies (China, Indonesia, Malaysia, the Philippines, Thailand, and Vietnam) produces about US$6,500 of output per worker. The results in Fafchamps and Quinn (this volume) are also consistent with this: they find that firms in China are more productive than firms in Vietnam and that the latter, in turn, are more productive than firms in the three African countries they study.

Although these comparisons are useful, it is important to note that African firms face a more challenging business environment than firms in other regions.[7] On average, physical infrastructure and the institutional

Table 1.5 Differences in Productivity, by Region (Firm-Level Regressions)

Indicator or region	Value added per worker, 2005 US$	Labor costs per worker, 2005 US$	Monthly wage production workers, 2005 US$	Unit labor costs
Observations	26,340	29,112	27,431	27,497
Sector dummies	included	included	included	included
Per capita GDP (log)	0.846*** (7.91)	0.813*** (7.46)	0.641*** (6.54)	−0.046 (−0.74)
Region dummies[a]				
Asia and Pacific, manufacturing only	−0.142 (−0.47)	−0.890*** (−4.58)	−0.434** (−2.22)	−0.783*** (−4.05)
Asia and Pacific, other	−0.547 (−1.60)	−0.550* (−1.85)	−0.861*** (−6.26)	−0.347** (−2.38)
Eastern Europe and Central Asia	−0.640** (−2.06)	−0.607** (−2.33)	−0.075 (−0.29)	−0.056 (−0.36)
Latin America and the Caribbean	−0.216 (−0.82)	−0.269 (−1.24)	0.102 (0.46)	−0.079 (−0.56)
South Asia	−0.499*** (−3.26)	−0.209* (−1.75)	0.020 (0.16)	−0.125 (−0.61)
Africa, middle income	0.034 (0.10)	0.091 (0.23)	0.172 (0.61)	0.130 (0.61)
Constant	1.318* (1.74)	0.745 (0.94)	−0.448 (−0.64)	−0.492 (−1.06)
R^2	0.26	0.35	0.51	0.15

Source: Author calculations based on data of Enterprise Surveys (database), World Bank, Washington, DC, http://www.enterprisesurveys.org/.

Note: The model includes sector dummies for textiles, garments, food and beverage, chemicals, construction materials, wood and furniture, metal products, paper, plastics, machinery, electronics, cars, and other manufacturing. Outliers more than 3 standard deviations from the country-level averages are excluded. Value added is calculated by subtracting intermediate inputs and energy costs from sales from manufacturing. Workers include permanent and temporary full-time workers. Labor cost is the total cost of wages, salaries, allowances, bonuses, and other benefits for both production and nonproduction workers. Unit labor costs are labor costs divided by value added. GDP = gross domestic product.

a. The omitted dummy is the dummy for Sub-Saharan Africa.

Significance level: * = 10 percent, ** = 5 percent, *** = 1 percent. Robust *t*-statistics are clustered at the country level in parentheses.

environment are worse in Africa than in other regions.[8] Business regulation is also more burdensome.[9] And corruption is more costly (see Clarke, this volume). Furthermore, the external environment affects worker quality and capital intensity. If education is better, workers have higher human capital. And, if the financial sector is more well developed, firms will find it easier to finance investment and training.

After accounting for these differences, our authors find that firms in Sub-Saharan Africa appear more, not less, productive than firms in other regions. Clarke (this volume) shows that, after he controls for per capita GDP, which is used as a proxy for the quality of the investment climate, firms in Sub-Saharan Africa are more productive, on average, than firms in East Asia, Eastern Europe and Central Asia, and Latin America. In a more detailed analysis that explicitly controls for differences in infrastructure, regulation, access to credit, and other political and geographical differences, Harrison, Lin, and Xu (chapter 2) also show that firms in Africa perform better, on average, than firms in other regions. This suggests that improving the business environment could allow firms to improve their performance.

However, given the pervasive distortions in the business environment and the limited resources at the disposal of most African countries, what is the best way to move forward? Based on their finding that the binding constraints vary by country, by sector, and by firm size, Dinh and others (2012) suggest that policy makers could identify the most promising sectors as well as the binding constraints in these sectors by firm size, and proceed to remove the constraints one by one.

Although labor productivity is lower in Africa than in other countries, at least before one controls for the institutional environment, firms appear to perform well in other ways. Even before controlling for the institutional environment, Harrison, Lin, and Xu (this volume) show that the difference in sales growth between Africa and other regions is small and statistically insignificant. Similarly, Fafchamps and Quinn (this volume) show that median growth is similar in the three African countries and the two Asian countries in their study.

Fafchamps and Quinn also show that there is little difference in terms of innovation. Although few firms in Tanzania innovate, the differences between China, Ethiopia, Vietnam, and Zambia are small. Moreover, large firms tend to innovate more than small firms. After one controls for this, firms in China appear to innovate less, not more, than firms of similar size in the three African countries.

Labor Costs Are Low, although, in Part, this Reflects Low Productivity

Although productivity affects whether firms can compete in competitive markets, unproductive firms can compete with more productive firms if their labor costs are low. It is possible that Africa's problems with exporting might reflect high labor costs rather than low productivity.

This does not appear to be the case. Clarke (this volume) notes that labor costs, like labor productivity, are low in Africa. Per worker labor costs are about US$1,059 in 2005 dollars for the median firm in low-income and lower-middle-income countries in the region. For the successful manufacturing economies in East Asia, per worker labor costs are about US$1,629 per worker. In part, African firms might be able to remain competitive because of their low labor costs. Fafchamps and Quinn (this volume) report similar results for the five countries in their study. They note that labor costs are lower in Ethiopia and Tanzania than in Vietnam or Zambia and that labor costs are lower in all of these countries than in China. This is also consistent with the results in Dinh and others (2012).

As Clarke (this volume) discusses, low wages could reflect either that the African firms are relatively competitive or that workers in African firms are not productive. It is therefore useful to look at the ratio of wages to value added (unit labor costs). If unit labor costs are high, this suggests that wages are outstripping productivity. Clarke (this volume) shows that, for the most part, unit labor costs are comparable in Africa and other regions: the average for Africa is about 34 percent, compared with 38 percent in Eastern Europe and Central Asia and 37 percent in Latin America. They are, however, higher in Africa than in East Asia.

Binding Constraints on Growth for Formal Firms

The previous section discusses the characteristics of firms in Africa and how these firms are similar to and differ from firms in other regions. As noted above, low productivity appears to at least partly reflect the difficult business environment. It is therefore useful to look at what the main constraints are to firm performance and growth.

Although the business environment is difficult for firms in Africa, it is important to note that firms in other regions also face challenges. Even in countries such as China and Vietnam that have been successful in light manufacturing, firms face serious challenges. For example, Fafchamps and Quinn (this volume) show that corruption appears to be a more binding constraint in Vietnam than in the three African countries they look at and that the burden of regulation might be even greater in China.

Perhaps the most common approach to assessing the binding constraints to firm performance and growth in a country is to ask managers what they consider the biggest obstacles. The World Bank Enterprise Surveys include two types of questions about the perceptions of managers. First, managers are asked to rank a series of investment climate constraints on a 5-point scale ranging from "no obstacle" to a "very severe obstacle." Typically, firms are asked to rate about 15 different areas on this scale in most Enterprise Surveys.[10] Second, managers are asked which constraints are the most serious for the firm. For the second type of question, managers usually either note only the most serious obstacle or the top three obstacles.

Dinh, Mavridis, and Nguyen (this volume) use these data together with objective measures of the business environment to examine the key constraints to the growth of a firm. Figure 1.3 shows the number of countries in Africa in which firm managers were most likely to say that each

Figure 1.3   Firm Managers in Africa Say Electricity and Access to Finance Are the Biggest Problems They Face

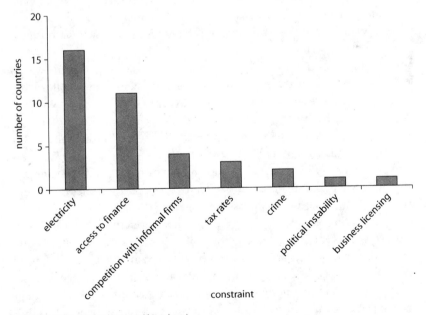

Source: Dinh, Mavridis, and Nguyen (this volume).
Note: Biggest constraint is based upon ranking (biggest constraint), not ratings (the seriousness of a constraint).

of the 15 constraints was the biggest constraint they faced. By far the most common concerns are electricity (top constraint in 16 countries with available data) and access to finance (top constraint in 11 countries). In the other 11 countries, however, five additional constraints ranked as the top constraint, emphasizing that there is considerable heterogeneity in perceptions across the continent.

Not surprisingly, the top concerns vary across countries. For example, firms in Zambia were most likely to say that access to finance, competition from informal firms, and tax rates were major or very severe problems (World Bank 2009a). Relatively few Zambian firms were concerned about electricity. The top concerns of Ethiopian firms were similar to those of Zambian firms: access to finance, competition from informal firms, and tax rates (World Bank 2009b). In contrast, for Tanzanian firms, the most serious constraint was electricity.

Key Constraints Vary by Country, Sector, and Firm Size

Dinh, Mavridis, and Nguyen (this volume) show that the biggest reported obstacles differ across regions and countries. They also find that different sectors confront different obstacles. For example, in the manufacturing sector, access to finance, informal sector competition, tax rates, and labor regulations matter the most, while in the sales and services sectors, only access to finance and informal sector competition are negatively and significantly correlated with firm growth. They find that objective business conditions vary systematically across firms of different sizes and ages, and good business conditions favor smaller firms, especially microfirms. Micro and small firms gain the most from access to finance ranging from the simple to the more sophisticated, from a loan or overdraft facility to sales credit to external finance for investment. This finding holds not only globally, but also for different regions, including Africa. While sales credit is important only for micro and small firms, having a loan or overdraft facility and receiving external finance for investment promote employment growth among firms of all sizes across regions. And sales credit and external finance matter for firms of all ages.

Their findings have several implications for developing countries. First, because the constraints faced by firms differ across countries and, within countries, across sectors and firm size, policies to promote firm growth need to be tailored to each country and sector and according to firm size. Second, finance appears to be the most binding constraint across sectors and countries, suggesting that reforms in this area could yield broad benefits, including by helping to address the problem of the missing middle in developing countries. Third, reforms in finance take time, and a quicker development strategy could involve identifying the binding constraints in a specific sub-sector and trying to address them through market-based measures and selected government interventions.

The Burden of Regulation Is High, But Does Not Appear to Be a Binding Constraint on Firms

The burden of regulation is relatively heavy in most countries in the region. In 2012, the average country in Sub-Saharan Africa ranked 137th in the *Doing Business* rankings, worse than any other region (World Bank 2011). Despite this, regulation does not appear to be a significant burden on most firms in the region. As noted above, although the Enterprise Surveys ask about regulation, most firms do not report regulation among the top constraints that they face (see figure 1.3).

The results of Fafchamps and Quinn (this volume) are consistent with this. As noted above, they find that firms need more licenses to start a business in China than in any of the three African countries in their study. Similarly, although Africa compares with other regions unfavorably with respect to labor regulation, Fafchamps and Quinn note that few firms in any of the three African countries report that they would lay off workers if there were no restrictions that prevented them from doing so.

The results in Dinh, Mavridis, and Nguyen (this volume) and Harrison, Lin, and Xu (this volume) also suggest that regulation is not the most bind-ing constraint in Sub-Saharan Africa. Harrison, Lin, and Xu find that firm growth is slower in countries where firing costs are higher, but also find that labor productivity and investment are higher in these countries. This could be because tough labor regulations encourage firms to substitute capital for labor. Dinh, Mavridis, and Nguyen include several measures of regulation in their regressions, but do not find consistent and significant results for any of the regulatory variables they include.

Access to Finance Is a Constraint, Especially for Small Firms

One of the most robust results is that access to finance is a serious con-straint for firms in Africa and is especially serious for small firms. As noted above, access to finance is the area that African firms were second most likely to say is the biggest problem they face (see figure 1.3). Fafchamps and Quinn (this volume) find that firms in China and Vietnam have bet-ter access to credit than firms in Ethiopia, Tanzania, and Zambia. Firms in the East Asian countries were more likely to purchase inputs on credit, were more likely to finance investment with bank loans, and were more likely to use bank credit than firms in Africa. Chinese firms were also more likely to have an overdraft facility, pay lower interest rates, and face lower collateral requirements than African firms.

The econometric analysis in the chapters in this volume is consistent with the idea that credit is an important constraint for firms in Africa. Dinh, Mavridis, and Nguyen (this volume) find that access to finance is more consistently correlated with firm growth than any of the other constraints that they look at. The results in Harrison, Lin, and Xu (this volume) are also consistent with the idea that finance is important in explaining firm performance.[11]

The results also suggest the important role that both trade credit and bank credit play for firms. Harrison, Lin, and Xu (this volume) find that more productive firms are more likely to have both trade credit and bank credit. Firms with trade credit also invest and export more than other firms do. Similarly, Dinh, Mavridis, and Nguyen (this volume) find that trade and bank credit are both associated with firm growth.

For the most part, access to credit appears to be a greater constraint for small firms than for large firms. Past studies have found that managers of small firms are more likely to say access to finance is a serious constraint and that the growth of small firms is more constrained by lack of credit.[12] Small firms are also less likely to have loans or overdraft facilities than other firms, are more likely to be credit constrained, less likely to have trade credit, and more likely to have external finance. The results in Dinh, Mavridis, and Nguyen (this volume) are consistent with this. Relative to large firms, small firms gain more if they have a loan or overdraft and if they have trade credit.

Infrastructure Is also Poor

Another way that African firms are disadvantaged is by poor infrastructure. As noted by Dinh, Mavridis, and Nguyen (this volume), firms in more countries in Africa say electricity is the biggest constraint they face relative to any of the other potential constraints. Clarke (this volume) also shows that power outages impose a large cost on firms in Africa. The median firm reports that outages result in losses equal to about 5 percent of sales in Africa. In comparison, the median firm in East Asia reports losses equal to less than 1 percent of sales. Similarly, Fafchamps and Quinn (this volume) note that power outages are less common in China than in the three African economies they look at.

Although firm managers are most concerned about electricity, other areas of infrastructure might also constrain firm performance in

Africa. Eifert, Gelb, and Ramachandran (2008) show that, in particular, transportation and communication costs are high in Sub-Saharan Africa. Perhaps because of this, relative to firms in China, African firms appear to focus more on customers in the same city or region (Fafchamps and Quinn, this volume).

Despite the relevant concern among African firms, Dinh, Mavridis, and Nguyen (this volume) and Harrison, Lin, and Xu (this volume) do not find a strong link between electricity constraints and firm growth. One possible explanation is that most firms in the subsectors that require electricity somehow cope with the shortage by having their own generators. Harrison, Lin, and Xu do, however, find that a broader measure of infrastructure quality that reflects the overall development of trade and transportation infrastructure is correlated with higher firm productivity and more rapid growth.

In contrast to access to finance, large firms appear to be more concerned than smaller firms about poor infrastructure. In particular, in Namibia, Tanzania, and Uganda, large firms were significantly more likely than small firms to say that power was a serious constraint.[13] This might reflect the fact that large firms tend to be more capital intensive than small firms and that they are less able to cope with irregular power than smaller, less capital-intensive firms.

Education Is a Constraint

Another important constraint is the quality of human capital. Fafchamps and Quinn (this volume) note that Chinese and Vietnamese workers and entrepreneurs have more formal schooling than workers and entrepreneurs in Ethiopia, Tanzania, or Zambia. In China and Vietnam, only a small number of workers have less than nine years of schooling, which was not the case in the three African countries. Consistent with this, Clarke (this volume) notes that both labor productivity and labor costs are low in Africa, which would be consistent with low levels of human capital.

Fafchamps and Quinn note, however, that there is less evidence that Chinese entrepreneurs have greater experience in other ways than African entrepreneurs. In particular, they find that Chinese entrepreneurs have traveled less, have fewer foreign friends, and are more likely to come from an agricultural family than entrepreneurs in Africa.

For the most part, worker skills and education appear to be a greater concern for large firms than for small firms. Both Gelb and others (2006) and Hallward-Driemeier and Aterido (2009) find that managers of large firms are more concerned about worker education and skills than managers of small firms are. In the individual country studies, however, there is little evidence that this is the case.[14] This could be because there are differences across countries or because samples in the individual country studies are too small to find statistically significant results consistently.

Trade Logistics

Several earlier studies have noted that high transportation costs discourage firms in Africa from exporting.[15] The results in this volume are mostly consistent with this. Clarke (this volume) notes that, although formal barriers to trade have fallen over time, natural and policy barriers to trade remain.[16] As a result, it is expensive for African firms to export. The World Bank's *Doing Business* report notes that it takes an average of 32 days to complete all procedures to import manufactured goods into Sub-Saharan Africa. This is as least as long as in any other region. It is also expensive to do so. It costs an average of US$2,000 to export a standard container from Sub-Saharan Africa. This is far more than in any other region; for example, it costs less than US$900, on average, in East Asia. Dinh et al. (2012) noted that the high trade logistics costs in Africa result from four broad factors; i) higher inland trasport costs; ii) port and terminal handling fees; iii) higher customs cleareance, and technical control fees; and iv) higher costs of document preparation and letters of credit, among others.

Note that while this survey covers only five countries (see annex 5.1), the in-depth questionnaire provides richer information than the Enterprise Survey.

As noted above, Harrison, Lin, and Xu (this volume) find some results consistent with the idea that poor trade logistics constrain firms. In particular, they find that firms export less and invest less if transportation costs are higher.

Binding Constraints for Small Firms

As discussed above, African firms appear to be smaller than similar firms in other countries. Because the Enterprise Surveys only include firms with at least five employees, the three chapters that use Enterprise Survey data do not provide much information on the specific constraints facing small firms. Fafchamps and Quinn (this volume), however, include firms with as few as one or two employees in their analysis, thereby allowing us to look at the specific constraints that face micro, small, and medium enterprises (MSMEs). While this survey covers only five countries (annex 5.1), the in-depth questionnaire provides richer information than the Enterprise Survey.

Figure 1.4   MSMEs Were Less Likely to Be Registered in the Three African Countries Relative to China or Vietnam

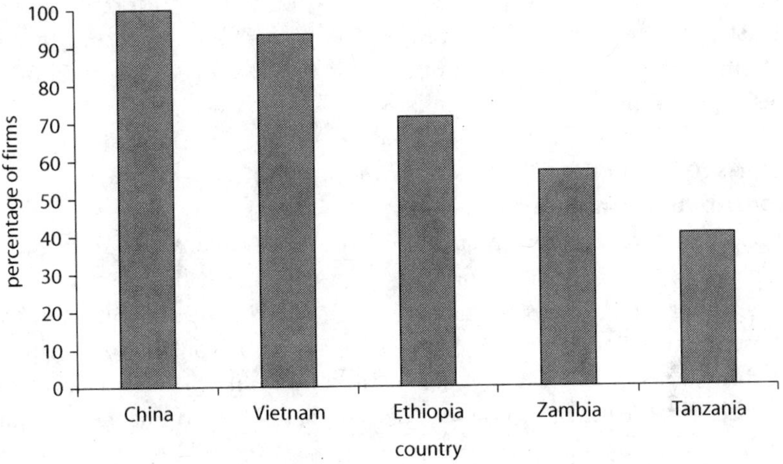

Source: Fafchamps and Quinn (this volume).
Note: MSME = micro, small and medium enterprise.

Registration

Fafchamps and Quinn (this volume) include registered and unregistered firms in their analysis (figure 1.4). One notable difference between China, Vietnam, and the three African countries is that firms were less likely to report that they were registered in the three African countries. Whereas almost all MSMEs in China and more than 90 percent of MSMEs in Vietnam were registered, only about half of the MSMEs in Tanzania and Zambia were registered. This is likely caused by the political system of the two Asian countries, which is stricter than that of the African countries.

In practice, this is likely to underestimate the prevalence of informality in Africa. As discussed in Fafchamps and Quinn (this volume), the sample was selected in ways that would exclude many informal microenterprises. Samples were drawn from firms in the main urban centers, and the focus was on firms with between 2 and 40 employees.[17] Given that informality is more common among small firms, among firms in agriculture and retail trade, and among firms in rural areas, this will exclude many informal firms.[18]

Informal firms do not appear to pay large penalties for operating without registering. Except in Tanzania, few respondents said that they had to pay a penalty for operating without registering. Even in

Tanzania, where the proportion of positive responses nears 10 percent, the proportion of penalized firms is well below the proportion of unregistered businesses. This suggests that the enforcement of registration and license requirements is present in the three African countries in our sample, but not so strong as to prevent informal business operations.

Access to Finance Is a Particularly Binding Constraint for Small Firms

As noted above, access to finance is a problem for many African firms. It is, however, a particularly binding constraint for MSMEs. Several recent Investment Climate Assessments in Africa have included analyses of the constraints facing microenterprises.[19] One common finding is that microenterprise managers are consistently more likely than managers of formal firms in the same countries to say that access to finance is a constraint to firm operations.[20]

The results in Fafchamps and Quinn (this volume) are consistent with this: MSMEs in general and microenterprises in particular were less likely than similar firms in China to have bank accounts, overdraft facilities, and loans from banks and equipment suppliers on the same continent. For example, most Chinese MSMEs—even small firms—had a current account and a savings account. African MSMEs, particularly in Tanzania and Zambia, were far less likely to have these. The gap is especially large among microenterprises. Whereas medium firms in the three African countries were almost as likely to have a current account as corresponding firms in China, small firms were far less likely to have such an account.

Small African firms were also far less likely to have access to credit. For example, Fafchamps and Quinn (this volume) note that, whereas 63 percent of Chinese MSMEs with a bank account have an overdraft facility, firms in the three African countries were far less likely to have one: less than 1 percent of MSMEs in Ethiopia, 6 percent of MSMEs in Tanzania, and 19 percent of MSMEs in Zambia.

Competition from Foreign Firms

Fafchamps and Quinn (this volume) note that another way in which MSMEs in Africa are different is that they face greater competition from imports than do MSMEs in China and Vietnam. About 94 percent of Chinese MSMEs said that they do not compete with any foreign firms. By comparison, only 60 and 53 percent of firms in landlocked Ethiopia and Zambia said the same, respectively. In Tanzania, which is not land-locked, only 18 percent of respondent said that they faced no competi-tion from imports.

Fafchamps and Quinn (this volume) note that it is possible that Chinese and Vietnamese firms are more competitive and that, therefore, foreign firms do enter these markets. Consistent with this, they note that many of the African respondents listed China as the major source of competing imports. The proportions of respondents who cite China as the source of foreign competition are large: 93 percent in Ethiopia and 84 percent in Tanzania. Respondents in Zambia mentioned China less frequently (only 56 percent of respondents mentioned it), but it remained one of the main sources of competing imports even in Zambia.

Conclusion

Drawing on two data sources, the studies included in this book shed light on the characteristics of formal and informal manufacturing firms in Africa by comparing them with firms in other regions. The share of manufacturing in GDP and in exports in Africa is very low. Most African manufacturing firms are informal, perhaps because the enforcement of registration and licensing regulations is not strict. They are also smaller than firms in other regions and few export. Labor productivity is low in Africa relative to other regions, but this may be because of the more chal-lenging environment, including the lack of physical infrastructure, the heavy burden of business regulation, and other issues. After accounting for these differences, the authors find that firms in Sub-Saharan Africa appear more, not less, productive than firms elsewhere.

This analysis suggests that improving the business environment might allow firms to enhance their performance. However, given the pervasive distortions in the business environment and the limited resources at the disposal of most African countries, Africa cannot and should not wait until the business environment becomes healthier before growing a more viable manufacturing sector. The book shows that binding constraints vary by country, by sector, and by firm size. Therefore, countries should identify the binding constraints in the most promising sectors and adopt policies designed specifically to remove these constraints.

African firms already perform well in other ways. There is little differ-ence in sales growth between Africa and other regions, and, at least rela-tive to East Asia, there is little difference in the level of innovation. Similar to the situation in labor productivity, labor costs are low in Africa.

For the most part, unit labor costs are comparable with other regions except East Asia.

Of all the constraints, access to finance appears to be the most binding for African firms, especially those firms that are small in size. The studies highlight the important role that trade credit and bank credit play among African firms. Other constraints—the regulatory burden, the poor electricity grids, the limited quality in human capital, the complicated trade logistics—represent additional disadvantages for African firms, but they are not insurmountable.

Notes

1. Chapters 2–5 were originally background papers for *Light Manufacturing in Africa: Targeted Policies to Enhance Private Investment and Create Jobs* (Dinh and others 2012).

2. Enterprise Surveys (database) World Bank, Washington, DC, http://www .enterprisesurveys.org/.

3. The surveys also cover some services and the retail and wholesale trade. The chapters in this volume, however, mostly focus on manufacturing (group D in the International Standard Industrial Classification of All Economic Activities, revision 3.1).

4. Several studies have noted that, in Africa, informal micro and small firms tend to be far less productive than registered formal firms of similar size or larger (Gelb and others 2009; La Porta and Shleifer 2011). Clarke and Kim (2011), for example, note that the average registered micro and small firm in Zambia produces almost four times as much output per worker as the average unregistered firm: about K 17.2 million (US$4,600 in 2008) per worker compared with about K 3.3 million (US$900) per worker.

5. La Porta and Shleifer (2011) find that representatives of firms in Kenya, Madagascar, and Mauritius that had recently registered said they did so because they were becoming too large. Consistent with this, Gelb and others (2009) find that larger firms are more likely to be registered in six of seven countries in Sub-Saharan Africa.

6. This is especially the case if the firm needs to have direct contact with local authorities to access utility connections. For example, firms in Lusaka that are not close enough to power lines need to procure an excavation permit from the Lusaka City Council for a connection from ZESCO, the state power company ("Getting Electricity in Zambia," World Bank, Washington, DC, http:// www.doingbusiness.org/data/exploreeconomies/zambia/getting-electricity/).

7. Similarly, Zeufack (2002) argues that neither the endowment ratio nor observable and unobservable skills explains the poor export performance of textile

and garment firms in Ghana and Kenya relative to similar firms in India. Rather, he argues that weak institutions explain much of the difference.

8. See, for example, Eifert, Gelb, and Ramachandran (2008), who show that indirect costs related to infrastructure and services account for a relatively high share of the costs of firms in poor African countries and pose a competitive burden on African firms.

9. In 2012, the average country in Sub-Saharan Africa ranked 137th in the *Doing Business* rankings: worse than any other region (World Bank 2011).

10. In the most recent set of surveys, managers rank 16 obstacles: (a) electricity; (b) telecommunications; (c) transport; (d) customs and trade regulation; (e) practices of competitors in the informal sector; (f) access to land; (g) crime, theft, and disorder; (h) access to finance; (i) tax rates; (j) tax administration; (k) business licensing and permits; (l) political instability; (m) corruption; (n) courts; (o) labor regulation; and (p) inadequately educated workers. The list of constraints and how the constraints are defined have varied considerably across Enterprise Surveys.

11. Although Harrison, Lin, and Xu do not find a statistically significant link between credit and growth for their sample, they do find that it is linked to labor productivity and total factor productivity.

12. Using data from 105 countries in all regions, Hallward-Driemeier and Aterido (2009) find that managers of small firms are more likely than managers of large firms to say that access to finance is a serious constraint. Using data from 26 African countries, Gelb and others (2006) find similar results. Beck, Demirgüç-Kunt, and Maksimovic (2005) find that the growth of small firms is particularly affected by lack of credit. Other studies that have looked only at access to finance have found similar results. In particular, Beck, Demirgüç-Kunt, and Maksimovic (2005) and Clarke, Cull, and Martínez Pería (2006), who use data from the World Business Environment Survey, a World Bank– European Bank for Reconstruction and Development initiative that preceded the Enterprise Surveys, also find that small firms were more likely to say that access to finance was a more serious problem for small enterprises in some model specifications. In contrast, Aterido and Hallward-Driemeier (2010) find that employment growth is more rapid among small firms in Sub-Saharan Africa if access to finance is more difficult, perhaps because they face less competition from larger firms if the access to finance is more difficult.

13. See World Bank (2008, 2009c, 2009d). Neither Gelb and others (2006) nor Hallward-Driemeier and Aterido (2009) find this for their large cross-country samples. It is possible that this is because electricity only becomes a constraint for large firms under specific circumstance (for example, power crises). Consistent with this, two of the countries noted above were going through major power crises as the Enterprise Survey was ongoing, and firms were suffering outages most working days (World Bank 2009c, 2009d).

14. See World Bank (2007, 2009a, 2009c, 2009d).

15. Clarke (2009), Iwanow and Kirkpatrick (2009), and Yoshino (2008) show that problems with trade regulation and customs administration make exporting difficult for firms in Africa. Djankov, Freund, and Pham (2010) show that increasing the number of days required to export by one day has an impact on trade equivalent to the addition of a distance of 70 kilometers in a gravity model of trade.

16. Most countries in the region took steps toward liberalizing trade by eliminating export taxes and reducing tariffs during the 1990s and 2000s. Mbaye and Golub (2003) note that Senegal had eliminated most export taxes by 1985. Similarly, Grenier, McKay, and Morrissey (1999) note that export duties had become uncommon by the mid-1990s in Tanzania. Milner, Morrissey, and Rudaheranwa (2000) make a similar point for Uganda. According to data of the World Bank, the average weighted tariff in the manufacturing sector fell from about 15–18 percent at the beginning of the 1990s to about 8 percent by 2008 (World Development Indicators [database], World Bank, Washington, DC, http://data.worldbank.org/data-catalog/world-development-indicators).

17. As they note, the size restriction was relaxed in Tanzania and Zambia.

18. See, for example, Clarke and Kim (2011) for a discussion of Zambia.

19. For several African countries, additional small surveys were conducted using area sampling of microenterprises. Because these have not been consistently implemented, it is difficult to make cross-country comparisons.

20. See, for example, the recent Investment Climate Assessments for Botswana, Namibia, Tanzania, and Uganda (World Bank 2007, 2009a, 2009c, 2009d).

References

Aterido, Reyes, and Mary Hallward-Driemeier. 2010. "The Impact of the Investment Climate on Employment Growth: Does Sub-Saharan Africa Mirror Other Low-Income Regions?" Policy Research Working Paper 5218, World Bank, Washington, DC. http://go.worldbank.org/KDAS6GU2L0.

Beck, Thorsten, Asli Demirgüç-Kunt, and Vojislav Maksimovic. 2005. "Financial and Legal Constraints to Firm Growth: Does Firm Size Matter?" *Journal of Finance* 60 (1):137–77.

Clarke, George R. G. 2009. "Beyond Tariffs and Quotas: Why Do African Manufacturers Not Export More?" *Emerging Markets Finance and Trade* 45 (2): 44–64.

Clarke, George R. G., Robert Cull, and María Soledad Martínez Pería. 2006. "Foreign Bank Participation and Access to Credit across Firms in Developing

Countries." *Journal of Comparative Economics* 34 (4): 774–95. http://dx.doi
.org/doi:10.1016/j.jce.2006.08.001.

Clarke, George R. G., and YoungJun Kim. 2011. "Why Do Microenterprises
Remain Informal?" Texas A&M International University, Laredo, TX.

Clarke, George R., Juliet Munro, Roland V. Pearson Jr., Manju Kedia Shah, and
Marie Sheppard. 2010. "The Profile and Productivity of Zambian Businesses."
World Bank, Lusaka, Zambia.

Dinh, Hinh T., Vincent Palmade, Vandana Chandra, and Frances Cossar. 2012.
*Light Manufacturing in Africa: Targeted Policies to Enhance Private Investment
and Create Jobs.* Washington, DC: World Bank. http://elibrary.worldbank.org/
content/book/9780821389614.

Djankov, Simeon, Caroline Freund, and Cong Pham. 2010. "Trading on Time."
Review of Economics and Statistics 92 (1): 166–73.

Eifert, Benn, Alan Gelb, and Vijaya Ramachandran. 2008. "The Cost of Doing
Business in Africa: Evidence From Enterprise Survey Data." *World Development*
36 (9): 1531–46.

Gelb, Alan, Taye Mengistae, Vijaya Ramachandran, and Manju Kedia Shah. 2009.
"To Formalize or Not to Formalize? Comparisons of Microenterprise Data
from Southern and East Africa." CGD Working Paper 175, Center for Global
Development, Washington, DC.

Gelb, Alan, Vijaya Ramachandran, Manju Kedia Shah, and Ginger Turner. 2006.
"What Matters to African Firms? The Relevance of Perceptions Data." Policy
Research Working Paper 4446, World Bank, Washington, DC.

Grenier, Louise, Andrew McKay, and Oliver Morrissey. 1999. "Exporting,
Ownership, and Confidence in Tanzanian Enterprises." *World Economy* 22 (7):
995–1011.

Hallward-Driemeier, Mary, and Reyes Aterido. 2009. "Comparing Apples with . . .
Apples: How to Make (More) Sense of Subjective Rankings of Constraints to
Business." Policy Research Working Paper 5054, World Bank, Washington, DC.

Iwanow, Tomasz, and Colin Kirkpatrick. 2009. "Trade Facilitation and Manufactured
Exports: Is Africa Different?" *World Development* 37 (6): 1039–50.

La Porta, Rafael, and Andrei Shleifer. 2011. "The Informal Economy in Africa."
NBER Working Paper 16821, National Bureau of Economic Research,
Cambridge, MA.

Mbaye, Ahmadou Aly, and Stephen Golub. 2003. "Unit Labour Costs, International
Competitiveness, and Exports: The Case of Senegal." *Journal of African
Economics* 11 (2): 219–48.

Milner, Chris, Oliver Morrissey, and Nicodemus Rudaheranwa. 2000. "Policy and
Non-Policy Barriers to Trade and Implicit Taxation of Exports in Uganda."
Journal of Development Studies 37 (2): 67–90.

Schneider, Friedrich, Andreas Buehn, and Claudio E. Montenegro. 2011. "Shadow Economies All Over the World: New Estimates for 162 Countries from 1999 to 2007." In *Handbook on the Shadow Economy*, ed. Fredrich Schneider, 9–77. Cheltenham, U.K.: Edward Elgar.

Schneider, Friedrich, and Dominik H. Enste. 2000. "Shadow Economies: Size, Causes and Consequences." *Journal of Economic Literature* 38 (1): 77–114. http://dx.doi.org/DOI:10.1257/jel.38.1.77.

World Bank. 2007. "An Assessment of the Investment Climate in Botswana." Regional Program on Enterprise Development, Africa Private Sector Group, World Bank, Washington, DC.

———. 2008. "An Assessment of the Investment Climate in Namibia." Regional Program on Enterprise Development, Africa Private Sector Group, World Bank, Washington, DC.

———. 2009a. "An Assessment of the Investment Climate in Zambia." Regional Program on Enterprise Development, Africa Private Sector Group, World Bank, Washington, DC.

———. 2009b. "Toward the Competitive Frontier: Strategies for Improving Ethiopia's Investment Climate." Report 48472-ET, Finance and Private Sector Development, Africa Region, World Bank, Washington, DC. http://siteresources.worldbank.org/INTETHIOPIA/Data%20and%20Reference/22432643/Et-ICA-10-June-09.pdf.

———. 2009c. "An Assessment of the Investment Climate in Tanzania." Regional Program on Enterprise Development, Africa Private Sector Group, World Bank, Washington, DC.

———. 2009d. "An Assessment of the Investment Climate in Uganda." Regional Program on Enterprise Development, Africa Private Sector Group, World Bank, Washington, DC.

———. 2011. *Doing Business 2012: Doing Business in a More Transparent World.* Washington, DC: World Bank. http://www.doingbusiness.org/~/media/fpdkm/doing%20business/documents/annual-reports/english/db12-fullreport.pdf.

Yoshino, Yutaka. 2008. "Domestic Constraints, Firm Characteristics, and Geographical Diversification of Firm-Level Manufacturing Exports in Africa." Policy Research Working Paper 4575, World Bank, Washington, DC.

Zeufack, Albert. 2002. "Export Performance in Africa and Asia's Manufacturing: Evidence from Firm-Level Data." *Journal of African Economies* 10 (3): 258–81.

CHAPTER 2

Performance of Formal Manufacturing Firms in Africa

Ann E. Harrison, Justin Yifu Lin, and L. Colin Xu

Introduction

Although Africa experienced slow growth between 1970 and 2000, with per capita gross domestic product (GDP) increasing at an average rate of 0.5 percent per year (Collier and Gunning 1999a), its economic performance has improved recently. Between 2000 and the recent financial crisis, GDP growth averaged 5.9 percent per year (World Economic Forum 2009). How can Africa keep growing? And what are the most important policies that affect Africa's economic performance? A recent study by Harrison, Lin, and Xu (2011) (HLX hereafter) looks at these questions using firm-level data from the World Bank's Enterprise Surveys and other cross-country data on politics, geography, and the business environment.

To achieve sustainable economic growth, developing countries might need to upgrade industry according to their comparative advantage (Lin 2009; Maddison 2001). Sub-Saharan Africa might need to develop manufacturing, especially light manufacturing industries with low capital needs. Using measures of static efficiency (for example, labor productivity) and dynamic efficiency (for instance, sales growth), HLX compare the performance of formal manufacturing firms in Africa with the performance of similar firms in other countries with per capita GDP below US$3,000 (2005 dollars). The analysis encompasses many explanatory variables, including firm characteristics, geography, infrastructure, access to finance, political and institutional factors, and other characteristics of the business environment (such as labor flexibility, corruption, international competition, domestic competition, and crime).[1] Having this comprehensive list allows us to quantify the relative importance of determinants in accounting for African manufacturing performance.

The Enterprise Surveys cover manufacturing firms of all sizes and ownership types. The detailed quantitative measures allow HLX to measure firm performance such as labor productivity and sales growth. Equally importantly, the Enterprise Surveys produce detailed objective and subjective information on the political, institutional, and business environment constraints that firms face, including infrastructure, regulation, corruption, crime, and access to finance. HLX also look at additional cross-country data on the political and business environment, including information on telecommunications, infrastructure quality, the transportation costs of export, the incidence of domestic conflicts, and political competition.

One concern is that the business environment variables may be endogenous to performance, that is, they might be correlated with omitted determinants of firm performance. HLX handle this in several ways. First, instead of using subjective measures of the business environment, they use objective measures (Dethier, Hirn, and Straub 2011). Subjective measures may be affected by firm performance and country-specific factors such as exposure to open media and development history. We therefore use subjective measures only if objective measures are not available. Second, rather than directly using the answers of firms, we use city-industry-size averages to represent the local business environment. This allows us to avoid the reverse causality associated with firm-level responses. Recent studies suggest there are large differences in the business environment within a country and that what matters for firms is the de facto rather than the de jure business environment (Hallward-Driemeier, Khun-Jush, and Pritchett 2010; Hallward-Driemeier and Pritchett 2011).

Before one controls for any variable, formal African manufacturing firms have a slight disadvantage in labor productivity, but similar sales growth relative to firms in other regions. After one holds firm characteristics, geography, infrastructure, the political and institutional environment, access to finance, and the business environment constant, however, Africa leads in sales growth and productivity. Thus, the slight disadvantage of African firms can be traced to the political, policy, and business environments.

HLX also explain the main causes of Africa's disadvantage relative to better performing countries at similar income levels.[2] The largest problems are political and institutional factors, access to finance, and the business environment. These represent the basic roles of the government: property rights protection, a well-developed financial sector, and a sound business environment. In contrast, geography, infrastructure, and firm characteristics are less important.

Data and Measurements

The main data source for HLX is the World Bank's Enterprise Surveys. Since the focus is on the manufacturing sector, the analysis only uses the 12,000 manufacturing firms covered in the surveys. The analysis includes data from 33 Sub-Saharan African countries and 89 countries overall.

The Enterprise Surveys contain rich information on the business environment, including corruption, infrastructure, regulation, and access to finance. This makes it possible to control simultaneously for multiple aspects of the business environment and thus reduces the likelihood that omitted variables will drive the results. While the surveys contain both objective and subjective measures of the business environment, HLX primarily rely on objective measures to avoid endogeneity of firm responses. If a firm reports perceived obstacles, this reflects both the objective level of services, which is a focus of interest, and the marginal value of good service, which is a confounding factor that differs by firm type. In addition, the perceived obstacle may depend on the openness of information and the history of performance, both of which vary across countries. As Bigsten and others (2003) illustrate, firms in Sub-Saharan Africa that complain vigorously about infrastructure appear to be the most productive firms and the exporters: the marginal benefits of infrastructure are the greatest for these productive firms. However, contaminated measures are likely better than no measures at all. For any particularly important aspect that is not associated with proper objective measures (for example, crime), HLX rely on subjective measures.

For indicators of the business environment, HLX do not directly employ individual answers because they are likely endogenous. As an example, firms might lose sales because of electricity outages for two distinct reasons. One is that electricity access imposes a strong constraint on the firm. But another is that electricity has higher marginal benefits for productive firms, resulting in reverse causality. Following the literature of the business environment (Dollar, Hallward-Driemeier, and

Mengistae 2005; Xu 2011), HLX use the local average of the business environment answers as a proxy of the local business environment. In other words, HLX rely on a city-industry-size cell as the basic unit for measuring the business environment.[3] Because the business environment has been shown to differ greatly across regions, this allows for the city-specific dimension. Given that different industries exhibit varying needs in licensing, permits, and infrastructure and may deal with different regulators and levels of competition, this also accommodates the industry-specific business environment. Because firms of various sizes face different business environments, in particular, small firms are particularly vulnerable to expropriation (Beck, Demirgüç-Kunt, and Maksimovic 2005), HLX allow the business environment to differ by size. To implement this, a firm is defined as small (large) if the firm has fewer (more) employees than the median firm in the city-industry cell.[4] Because it is difficult for an individual firm to alter the local business environment directly, relying on local business environment indicators mitigates the problem of reverse causality.

Because many important dimensions of political, macro, and policy environments cannot be measured at the firm level, HLX use cross-country data on geography, infrastructure, the political and institutional environment, and macroeconomic policies. To be comprehensive, HLX combine measures of the business environment from the Enterprise Surveys with country-level measures of the political, institutional, and business environments.

Here, we describe how HLX measure the key variables.

Infrastructure is captured by four main measures. Two capture the extent of modern communications infrastructure: telephone density (from World Development Indicators) and the local (that is, city-industry-size) share of firms using websites for their businesses (based on the Enterprise Surveys). The third measure is the general infrastructure index from the Logistics Performance Index of the World Bank (Arvis and others 2010), which proxies the general quality of infrastructure covering ports, roads, railroads, and information technology. The final measure is the cost (in U.S. dollars) of exporting a standard container (from *Doing Business*), which captures the soundness of the infrastructure devoted to integration into the international market. These four measures thus capture the basic infrastructure that facilitates domestic and international trade.[5]

A small complication is that telephone density and local web intensity are closely correlated, and they both measure the use of modern telecommunications. Thus, HLX use factor analysis to obtain their principal factor and call it *Telecom*. After conditioning on telecom, the general infrastructure index captures the quality of other aspects of infrastructure.

Geography. Leading authorities on African development (Collier and Gunning 1999a; Sachs and Warner 1997) have suggested that geography is an important reason for Africa's lack of development. Indeed, there are more landlocked countries in Africa than in other regions, heightening the need for coordination among neighboring countries. Because of the higher trade costs associated with borders, being landlocked impedes international trade.

Another important aspect of geography for Africa is the small population relative to the vast scale of the continent. The low fertility of land and other aspects of geography mean that African countries are sparsely populated and have low population density. To measure the geographical elements above, HLX employ two variables: a dummy variable indicating that a country is landlocked and domestic market size as measured by population.

Political and institutional factors include three political and institutional factors that might affect firm performance. Many scholars argue that ethnic fractionalization is a defining characteristic that might affect many formal and informal institutions in Africa (Easterly and Levine 1997). Ethnic fractionalization is starkly greater in Africa than in other regions, which is not surprising given that Africa is the birthplace of humanity and that humans have been evolving in Africa throughout human history. Ethnic fractionalization has been put forth as an important explanation for poor African performance. Collier and Gunning (1999b) suggest that ethnic fractionalization is a potential barrier to social interactions. Easterly and Levine (1997) provide evidence that ethnic fractionalization accounts for one-third of Africa's growth shortfall, and even this may only reflect the direct effects. We thus include this measure of ethnic diversity as a potential explanation for firm performance.

The second component is basic property rights protection, which likely affects many formal and informal institutions in Africa. Property rights protections affect whether investors are willing to commit to investment projects without fearing expropriation. Consistent with this view, cross-country evidence suggests that countries with a worse record on property rights have lower aggregate investment, worse access to finance, and slower economic growth (Acemoglu, Johnson, and Robinson 2000; Knack and Keefer 1995; North 1990). Some new firm-level evidence also highlights the importance of property rights (Johnson, McMillan, and Woodruff 2002; Cull and Xu 2005) and the adverse effects of corruption (Fisman and Svensson 2007; Cai, Fang, and Xu 2005).

HLX rely on political competition to capture the protection of property rights: the number of years that the ruling party has been in power (from the Database of Political Institutions, based on Beck and others 2001 and Keefer 2007). The reasoning is that the longer a ruling party has been in power, the more absolute power the ruling party has and the greater the risk of unconstrained government expropriation.

The third political and institutional component is whether a country has experienced any armed domestic conflict in the previous 10 years. For domestic and foreign firms to invest and grow, they need to enjoy a safe environment in which their factories will not be damaged by war and other armed conflicts. This simple prerequisite is not, however, the reality in many countries. Many are afflicted by wars and armed conflicts because of weak governments that cannot control domestic disorder and, in some cases, governments that instigate the armed conflicts. To capture basic domestic safety, HLX construct a dummy variable of the experience of domestic armed conflicts in the past 10 years based on Gleditsch and others (2002) and updates of UCDP and PRIO (2010).

Business environment. There are two intuitive definitions of the business environment. The narrowly defined business environment measures the rights of firm owners to keep the proceeds of the firm, the discretion for firm managers in factor adjustments, and the competitive pressure faced by firms. The broadly defined concept of the business environment, embraced by the World Bank (2004) and many others, would include the narrowly defined business environment and much more, including infrastructure, macropolicies, political and institutional factors, and access to finance. For expositional convenience, because HLX distinguish carefully between different categories of policies and environments, we use the narrow definition of the business environment.

The first aspect of the business environment is the extent to which firms are expropriated by government officials and common criminals. Whatever the causes of expropriation, firms are less well off. On the government side, HLX measure the extent of corruption using the Enterprise Survey measure of corruption: the local average of bribes to the government over sales. This has the advantage of being directly comparable across countries and avoids some of the flaws of subjective measures of corruption (Dethier, Hirn, and Straub 2011). Previous research has shown that firms in developing countries (such as China and Uganda) are hurt more by corruption than by taxation (Cai, Fang, and Xu 2005;

Fisman and Svensson 2007). On the expropriation of firms by criminals, HLX do not have good measures of the objective burden of crime. However, firms are asked about the seriousness of the obstacle of crime with respect to their development. HLX thus construct *Obstacle_crime*, which is the local share of firms that view crime as a moderate or major constraint.

Labor market flexibility, the second element of the business environment, captures how much discretion firm managers have in adjusting labor inputs. Some recent microstudies suggest that strict labor regulations have serious adverse effects. For instance, cumbersome labor regulations are associated with smaller firm size, more informality, and higher unemployment in Brazil and India (Almeida and Carneiro 2009; Amin 2009a). These regulations also affect technological choices in India and lead to lower productivity and investment in Brazil (Almeida and Carneiro 2005; Amin 2009b). Minimum wages negatively affect employment in Indonesia (Harrison and Scorse 2010). In Chile, higher firing costs have been found to increase the gap between wages and the marginal products of labor (Petrin and Sivadasan 2006). Labor inflexibility is also found to have indirect effects by reducing returns to infrastructure and access to finance in India (Li, Mengistae, and Xu 2011).

For labor market flexibility, HLX rely on Botero and others (2004) and use an index of toughness for firing workers at the country level (*Firing difficulty*). This measures the cost of firing 20 percent of a standardized firm's workers (10 percent are fired for redundancy, and 10 percent without cause). The cost of firing a worker is calculated as the sum of the severance pay and any mandatory penalties established by law or by mandatory collective agreements for a worker with three years of tenure with the firm.

The third ingredient of the business environment captures domestic and international product market competition. Product market competition is widely viewed as important in developing countries. Product market competition is important for employment, productivity, entry, turnover, and growth. However, because most of the literature does not simultaneously control for other basic country characteristics such as political risk, infrastructure, geography, and access to finance, it remains to be seen whether product market competition is still important once we control for other basic business environment elements.

Because product market competition is multifaceted, we employ several measures to capture such competition. The first is the country-industry-year import tariff, a high level of which entails lower international competition for domestic producers. Related to this, a larger presence of foreign firms also represents stronger competition from the international front. Foreign firms in developing countries tend to be more productive. HLX thus also rely on the country-industry-year average of foreign ownership as another measure of foreign competition. It is useful to note that this measure entails two effects: the competitive (or market-stealing) effects and the productivity spillover effect (Aitken and Harrison 1999). The third measure captures the level of domestic country-industry competition (*Competition_ind*), as measured by $(1-\text{markup}_{CI})$ (Aghion and others 2005). Markup_{CI} is the country-industry average of firm-level markup, that is, (value added–labor costs)/sales. A higher value of *Competition_ind* implies more competition.

Access to finance. A large literature suggests there is a causal link between access to finance and economic development (see Levine 1997). While most of this literature focuses on access to formal finance such as bank loans and overdraft facilities, a growing literature examines the impact of access to informal finance (Cull and Xu 2005; Fisman 2001). Following this literature, HLX include access to both formal and informal finance and examine whether these have distinct impacts and which looms larger. Access to formal finance is measured as the city-industry-size share of firms with access to overdraft facilities, and access to informal finance is measured as the city-industry-size share of firms that grant trade credit (to other firms).[6]

How Do African Firms Compare with Firms in Other Countries?

In HLX, African manufacturing performance is measured by both static performance and dynamic performance. To see how firms in Africa stack up against firms in other regions, HLX look at labor productivity (in logarithm), which is measured as sales (in constant 2005 U.S. dollars) over the number of employees. To examine Africa's dynamic momentum, HLX look at sales growth among African firms.

For sales growth, HLX use growth during a three-year period because they only have such data. Following Davis and Haltiwanger (1995), they compute the sales growth rate as (sales this year–sales three years ago)/ their average, which is bound between –2 and 2, and successfully contains the outlier problem. With the conventional way of measuring growth, the growth rate could exceed 1000 percent, even though the mean is often in single digits. The results will then be unnecessarily influenced by a few outliers.

Because HLX aim to uncover what hinders poor countries in Sub-Saharan Africa from having a successful manufacturing sector, the definition of Africa excludes the four richest countries, Botswana, Mauritius, Namibia, and South Africa, which have per capita GDP higher than US$3,000 (2005 dollars). The sample therefore consists of all Sub-Saharan African sample countries where per capita GDP is lower than US$3,000 (2005 dollars) at the time of each country's survey. However, the key conclusions about Africa do not hinge on whether these four successful Sub-Saharan African countries are included or excluded.

In evaluating African economic performance, HLX have to compare countries in Africa with other countries. They thus construct two comparison groups for Africa. The first, *the average comparison group*, consists of non-Sub-Saharan African countries with per capita GDP lower than US$3,000 (2005 dollars). The second, *the better comparison group*, consists of the top half of the average comparison group in terms of performance. Country performance is measured in the following way. HLX first standardize each of the five performance measures—labor productivity, total factor productivity, sales growth, export share in sales, and investment rate (that is, investment over sales)—so that each now has a mean of zero and a standard deviation of 1.[7] They then add up the five standardized measures to form an aggregate performance measure. Countries showing a mean aggregate performance ranking in the top half of the average comparison group are defined as members of the better comparison group.

Differences in firm performance. For the average comparison group, Africa manufacturing shows a slightly worse firm performance. Log labor productivity in Africa is lower by 5.4 log points (statistically significant). Sales growth is slightly lower, but the difference is not statistically significant. The difference with the better comparison group is more pronounced. The labor productivity lag is significant at 31 log points, and the sale growth difference remains insignificant. Thus, the growth and productivity performance of formal manufacturing firms in African countries is adequate relative to firms in countries with similar income.

Difference in key explanatory variables. African manufacturing firms are three to five years younger than firms in the two comparison groups. They have lower rates of state ownership, but higher foreign ownership by 6 (3) percentage points relative to the average (better) comparison group. They also feature higher ownership concentration, with the largest owner taking 82 percent of firm ownership, higher than the average (better) comparison group by 8 (11) percentage points. African manufacturing firms are much smaller: the log of the number of employees is lower than the average (better) comparison groups by 70 (102) log points.

African countries have a greater tendency to be landlocked and have a smaller domestic market. African countries are slightly more likely to be landlocked than countries in the average comparison group (although the difference is statistically insignificant), but significantly more likely to be landlocked than the countries in the better comparison group (25 versus 14 percent). African countries also have smaller populations, with the population of the average country lower by 60 (133) log points than the population of countries in the average (better) comparison group. Furthermore, even with the same upper bound in income, African countries (excluding the top four richest countries) still have much lower per capita GDP (US$488), about US$1,000 lower than the average and the better comparison groups.

Africa displays a stronger level of political monopoly: the logarithm of the number of years that the ruling party in an African country has been in power is greater by 46 (15) log points than the case in the average (better) comparison group. In addition, African firms face violence and crime to a greater extent. In terms of the incidence of major or minor domestic conflicts in the previous 10 years, Africa has a greater tendency than the average comparison group (50 versus 41 percent). Surprisingly, the better-performing group actually has a greater past history of domestic conflict (53 percent). In a related issue, Africa exhibits the highest level of ethnic diversity. Ethnic fractionalization (or diversity) in Africa, at 0.716, is much greater than the diversity in the average (better) comparison group by 0.316 (0.369).

Infrastructure in Africa is worse, an outcome consistent with Africa's low income level. In particular, both the telecom index and the general infrastructure index are much lower in Africa than in the two comparison groups. The transportation costs of exporting a standard container is also significantly higher in Africa: about 10 (25) percent higher than in the average (better) comparison groups.

The overall business environment is worse in Africa than in either comparison group. To begin with, African firms have to pay larger bribes to get things done. The average share of bribes to government (over sales), 2.9 percent, is significantly higher among African firms than among the average comparison group or the better comparison group, by 1.3 and 1.8 percentage points, respectively. While the subjective perception of crime as a moderate or severe obstacle is similar in Africa and in countries of similar income, the better comparison group reports significantly lower perceived crime. Africa also features lower labor flexibility because firing costs are higher there than in either comparison group. African firms face less fierce competition, both domestically and internationally. The average industry-level tariff rate, for instance, is about 60 percent higher in Africa than in either comparison group. The country-industry level index of competition is also significantly lower in Africa than in either comparison group.

African firms have less access to formal and informal finance. The local average share of firms with overdraft facilities is 23 percent, which is 22 (12) percentage points lower than in the average (better) comparison group. The better comparison group actually shows less access to formal finance than the average comparison group, suggesting that access to formal finance may not be crucial for firm performance in countries at low income levels. Equally important, African firms have less access to trade credit: the local share of firms granting trade credit is 27 percent, which is 27 percentage points lower than in the average comparison group and 30 percentage points lower than in the better comparison group. The fact that the rank order of trade credit prevalence corresponds to the order of firm performance suggests that trade credit may play an important role in explaining regional economic performance, a conjecture confirmed below.

Determinants of Firm Performance

HLX investigate how the business environment affects firm performance and how Africa compares with other regions. The empirical specification is as follows:

$$Y_{icj} = Firm_i\alpha + Geography_c\beta_1 + infrastructure_{cj}\beta_2 + PoliInst_c\beta_3$$
$$+ busiEnvi_{cj}\beta_3 + finance_{cj}\beta_4 + \varepsilon_{icj}, \tag{2.1}$$

where Y is the firm performance indicator, and i, c, and j represent firm, country, and local levels, respectively. Y could be log labor productivity or the sales growth rate. $Firm$ is basic firm-level controls, including firm age, state and foreign ownerships, and the ownership share of the largest owner. For the sales growth rate equation, we control for the initial level (that is, sales three years ago) to allow for regression toward the mean. $Geography$ includes log country population and the landlocked dummy. $Infrastructure$ includes the infrastructure index, the logarithm of the transportation costs of shipping a standard container to the nearest port, and the telecom index (measured at the local, that is, the city-industry-size level). *PoliInst* represents the category of political and institutional factors and includes log party years, any conflict in the past 10 years, and ethnic fractionalization. *BusiEnvi* indicates the business environment, consisting of average country-industry foreign ownership, firing difficulty, the local average bribe, country-industry tariff levels, the country-industry competition index, and the average perceived level of crime at the local level. *Finance* includes the local share of firms having access to overdraft facilities and the local average of firms having access to trade credit. The error term captures unobserved variables and any measurement error.

As mentioned above, to avoid the endogeneity associated with the fact that some of the business environment variables may be choice variables among firms, such as telecommunications use, bribes, and access to overdraft facilities, HLX use the city-industry-size average of these variables as proxies of the local business environment. An important caveat is that some local variables may have been omitted.

HLX obtain the following detailed findings. The most important finding is that, after they control for firm characteristics and the business environment, the coefficient on the Africa dummy is positive and large for labor productivity (212 log points) and the sales growth rate (23 percent). Thus, if one holds constant the conditioning variables, Africa not only does not lag behind other regions in terms of productivity and growth, but is, rather, ahead of them. Taken at face value, if one fixes this daunting list of geography, infrastructure, political, and institutional factors, the business environment, and access to finance to the levels in other countries, Africa possesses an inherent advantage (that is, the African dummy variable) compared with other regions.

Firm characteristics matter a great deal in explaining firm performance. First, younger firms tend to have lower labor productivity. The positive correlation between age and labor productivity is consistent with the conjecture of entrants learning in the initial years. Younger firms also have higher growth rates. Entry therefore proves to be important for growth. Second, state ownership is, surprisingly, positively associated with labor productivity and sales growth, in sharp contrast to a large literature suggesting that private ownership is superior in delivering firm performance. But there are also papers suggesting that concentrated state ownership could outperform dispersed private ownership if there is no strong monitoring mechanism associated with dispersed private ownership. There is always the possibility that the state will control elite businesses and grant monopoly power to them. The positive effect might therefore reflect selection rather than causal effects (that is, better corporate governance, higher efforts, better chief executives). Similarly, and easier to interpret, foreign ownership has positive effects both on productivity and on growth. This can reflect better access to finance or technological and managerial expertise. Finally, a large ownership share of the largest owner is negatively related to labor productivity and sales growth. A plausible interpretation is that these firms are unable to obtain external financing for expansion and therefore have to resort to their own resources for expansion, leading to lower growth. An additional reason may be the heightened possibility of the expropriation of minority shareholders by the largest shareholder.

Geography. The landlocked dummy and the measure of transportation costs are uncorrelated with both productivity and growth. Firms in larger countries show slightly greater productivity, although the difference is statistically insignificant. This is consistent with the conjecture that larger countries can facilitate larger firms because of greater demand.

Infrastructure matters little for our two performance measures. The general infrastructure index is insignificantly associated with greater labor productivity. The telecom index is also positively, but insignificantly, associated with labor productivity and sales growth.

Political and institutional factors. Government expropriation seems to hurt firm performance. The number of years that the ruling party has been in power is negatively associated with labor productivity and sales growth. These negative effects likely reflect the fear of entrepreneurs in expanding and investing as expropriation risks increase. The negative correlation of party monopoly with productivity is consistent with the notion that fear of government expropriation may shift firms to engage in low-productivity businesses.[8] In the same vein, countries that experienced domestic conflict in the previous 10 years tend to have lower labor productivity (significantly) and sales growth (insignificantly). This makes sense given that the danger of domestic conflict shortens the horizon for entrepreneurs to reap returns on investments, causing them to reduce their investments (and thus lower productivity) and expand more slowly. While it has been suggested that ethnic fractionalization has an important impact on macro-outcomes (Collier and Gunning 1999a; Easterly and Levine 1997), HLX do not find that ethnic fractionalization is significantly associated with micro-outcomes. They cannot, of course, rule out the possibility that ethnic fractionalization affects these outcomes *through* the policy or environmental variables we control for.

Business environment. What firms can take away (net of expropriations and crime) seems to have significant effects on firm performance. The local share of bribe payments in sales is negatively related to sales growth. Though statistically insignificant, this result is consistent with results in other studies in developing countries (Cai, Fang, and Xu 2005; Fisman and Svensson 2007). In addition, local areas with strong concerns about crime have significantly lower sales growth.

What firm managers can decide without government interference also matters a great deal. One of the key components of managerial discretion—firing costs—is associated with higher labor productivity, which likely reflects the substitution of capital (including human capital) for labor because of higher labor adjustment costs. Nonetheless, firing costs are also associated with lower sales growth, possibly reflecting the fact that firms are less willing to expand if factor costs are rising.

Foreign presence in an industry—proxied by the share of foreign ownership within a country-industry cell—is negatively related to labor productivity. This may reflect the market-stealing effects of foreign entry (Aitken and Harrison 1999). Foreign presence is also presumed to have spillover effects, which we do not find with sales growth rates. While many would suspect that tariff rates, as a measure of protection from international import competition, may be important, we find in our sample that this variable is statistically insignificant. Finally, the industry competition variable, HLX's measure of domestic competition, does not affect firm performance. There are thus no strong indications that the proxies of competition matter much.

Financial access. Both access to bank finance (that is, overdraft facilities) and the prevalence of *trade credit* are positively correlated with labor productivity, providing support to the macrofinance-growth literature (Levine 1997). The result for trade credit is consistent with Fisman (2001), who uses data from five African countries and finds that supplier credit is positively associated with capacity utilization, even after being instrumented by supplier characteristics. Fisman provides evidence that access to supplier credit allows for better inventory management and lowers the chance of inventory shortage.

Explaining Africa's Disadvantage Relative to the Better Comparison Group

The results in HLX can explain quantitatively why Africa falls behind the better comparison group by reporting

$$100^* \beta_X (X_{\text{Africa}} - X_{\text{better}})/\Delta y, \qquad (2.2)$$

the percentage of outcome differences due to each element. Here, X stands for an explanatory variable; y for the outcome variable; and *better* for the better comparison group. β_X refers to the coefficient of a generic variable X. The coefficients are drawn from their base specifications. X_{Africa} and X_{better} refer to the mean for Africa and the mean for the better comparison group, and Δy refers to the outcome difference between Africa and the better comparison group. The results show that the key factors explaining Africa's disadvantage are political and institutional factors (especially party monopoly), access to finance, and the business environment. In contrast, geography, infrastructure, and firm characteristics explain relatively little about Africa's disadvantage.

The political and institutional factors exert large negative effects on firm performance in Africa. These factors explain 711 percent of the sales growth shortage of Africa (of only 0.8 percentage points), being the number 1 explanatory category. The key variable is party monopoly, which accounts for all the difference.

While infrastructure does not matter much for productivity and sales growth, access to finance contributes importantly to Africa's disadvantage, especially informal finance. It is the number 1 explanatory category for labor productivity (252 percent of the labor productivity disadvantage). Collier and Gunning (1999b) suggest that a lack of financial depth may be a reason behind Africa's growth shortfall; the HLX accounting results suggest that, if finance matters, informal finance likely matters more for Africa.

The business environment matters only marginally for labor productivity, but importantly for sales growth. It explains 9 percent of the Africa labor productivity disadvantage (number 3), but 275 percent of the Africa sales growth disadvantage (number 2). Geography does not matter at all for HLX's two performance measures, that is, the evidence does not support the notion that geography is important in explaining Africa's performance disadvantage. Similarly, firm characteristics do not matter much.

Conclusion

HLX use comprehensive cross-country firm-level data to understand how formal African manufacturing firms compare with firms in other regions in terms of performance. They also look at whether Africa's business environment can explain the performance shortfalls (if any) and what the key factors are in explaining Africa's performance shortfalls. They find that formal African manufacturing firms show a slight disadvantage in labor productivity, but similar sales growth. More importantly, after they control for differences in firm characteristics, geography, infrastructure, political and institutional factors, business environment, and finance, they find that Africa manufacturing actually has a *conditional advantage* in productivity and sales growth.[9] Key factors explaining Africa's disadvantage in firm performance relative to better-performing countries of similar income are political and institutional factors (especially party monopoly), access to finance, and the business environment. In contrast, infrastructure, geography, and firm characteristics do not matter much.[10] The key explanations for Africa's disadvantage represent the basic roles of the government: property rights protection, a sound business environment, and adequate access to finance.

Notes

We are grateful for the useful comments, discussions, help, and criticisms of Yaw Ansu, Jing Cai, Hinh T. Dinh, Weili Ding, Luosha Du, Li Gan, Philip Keefer, Steve Lehrer, Dimitris Mavridis, Vincent Palmade, and Jean-Philippe Platteau. Helen Yang offered superb research assistance. This study has been financed through the Japanese Population and Human Resources Development Trust Fund TF 096317 and the Bank Netherlands Partnership Program on Capacity Building Trust Fund TF 097170, along with financing of the Africa Region of the World Bank.

1. See Xu (2011) for a survey of this growing literature.

2. The comparison group is to be defined precisely later.

3. In computing the mean for a firm, the observation for the firm itself is excluded to avoid endogeneity.

4. If the city-industry-size cell has fewer than five observations, we replace the cell mean with the city-industry mean as a proxy of the local business environment.

5. A glaring omission in our measure of infrastructure is the lack of road network data. While World Development Indicators has data on paved roads, the data are unreliable. For instance, India is said to have a longer road network than China, a possibility that is instantly dismissed by anyone who has traveled to both countries. The World Development Indicators road data simply do not capture the quality of roads well. In contrast, the measures we adopt here make more sense in our judgment.

6. We have also tried using the local share of firms *receiving* trade credit. These two variables are, not surprisingly, closely correlated. This fact, coupled with the fact that the latter measure is associated with significantly fewer observations, leads us to use the former trade credit measure in our empirical analysis.

7. While we look only at two firm performance measures in this chapter, HLX look more comprehensively at the five performance measures. Because the additional three measures also capture key aspects of firm capacity and performance, we have opted to use these five measures to construct the better comparison group.

8. While we interpret the number of years that the ruling party has been in power as a measure of government expropriation, we must point out that this holds only on average and does not imply that every government having a long-running ruling party is an expropriating government. Under some institutional setups, long-running ruling parties can be conducive to development for several reasons. First, sometimes a country happens to feature a strong party, combined with benevolent and strong leaders (such as Lee Kuan Yew of Singapore and Deng Xiaoping of China). Second, sometimes, accountability to the citizens is built within a monopoly party system for some path-dependent reasons (Gehlbach and Keefer 2011a, 2011b), and some accountability holds the party in check so that it helps deliver good economic performance. Finally, it is useful to keep in mind that the longer the party is in monopoly, the more stable the system is. Stability itself is conducive to private investment.

9. HLX show that the conditional advantage remains intact when they control for business environment factors, deal with multicollinearity, use only the similar income sample, or examine a certain size category or a technology class. Moreover, the conditional advantage of Africa is greater in small firms compared with large and medium firms, in low-technology manufacturing compared with high-technology manufacturing, and in manufacturing relative to services.

10. Infrastructure does matter a lot for export share and investment rate for the African disadvantage in these two aspects, according to HLX.

References

Acemoglu, Daron, Simon Johnson, and James A. Robinson. 2000. "The Colonial Origins of Comparative Development: An Empirical Investigation." NBER Working Paper 7771, National Bureau of Economic Research, Cambridge, MA. http://www.nber.org/papers/w7771.pdf?new_window=1.

Aghion, Philippe, Nick Bloom, Richard Blundell, Rachel Griffith, and Peter Howitt. 2005. "Competition and Innovation: An Inverted-U Relationship." *Quarterly Journal of Economics* 120 (2): 701–28.

Aitken, Brian J., Ann E. Harrison. 1999. "Do Domestic Firms Benefit from Direct Foreign Investment? Evidence from Venezuela." *American Economic Review* 89 (3): 605–18.

Almeida, Rita, and Pedro Carneiro. 2005. "Enforcement of Regulation, Informal Labor and Firm Performance." IZA Discussion Paper 1759, Institute for the Study of Labor, Bonn.

————. 2009. "Enforcement of Labor Regulation and Firm Size." *Journal of Comparative Economics* 37 (1): 28–46.

Amin, Muhammad. 2009a. "Labor Regulation and Employment in India's Retail Stores." *Journal of Comparative Economics* 37 (1): 47–61.

————. 2009b. "Are Labor Regulations Driving Computer Usage in India's Retail Stores?" *Economics Letter* 102 (1): 45–48.

Arvis, Jean-François, Monica Alina Mustra, Lauri Ojala, Ben Shepherd, and Daniel Saslavsky. 2010. *Connecting to Compete 2010: Trade Logistics in the Global Economy; The Logistics Performance Index and Its Indicators.* Washington, DC: World Bank. http://siteresources.worldbank.org/INTTLF/Resources/LPI2010_for_web.pdf.

Beck, Thorsten, George R. G. Clarke, Alberto Groff, Philip Keefer, and Patrick Walsh. 2001. "New Tools and New Tests in Comparative Political Economy: The Database of Political Institutions." *World Bank Economic Review* 15 (1): 165–76.

Beck, Thorsten, Asli Demirgüç-Kunt, and Vojislav Maksimovic. 2005. "Financial and Legal Constraints to Growth: Does Firm Size Matter?" *Journal of Finance* 60 (1): 137–77.

Bigsten, Arne, Paul Collier, Stefan Dercon, Marcel Fafchamps, Bernard Gauthier, Jan Willem Gunning, Abena Oduro, Remco Oostendorp, Cathy Pattillo, Mans Söderbom, Francis Teal, and Albert Zeufack. 2003. "Risk Sharing in Labor Markets." *World Bank Economic Review* 17 (3): 349–66.

Botero, Juan C., Simeon Djankov, Rafael La Porta, Florencio López-de-Silanes, and Andrei Shleifer. 2004. "The Regulation of Labor." *Quarterly Journal of Economics* 119 (4): 1339–82.

Cai, Hongbin, Hanming Fang, and Lixin Colin Xu. 2005. "Eat, Drink, Firms, Government: An Investigation of Corruption from Entertainment and Travel Costs of Chinese Firms." NBER Working Paper 11592, National Bureau of Economic Research, Cambridge, MA. http://www.nber.org/papers/w11592.pdf?new_window=1.

Collier, Paul, and Jan Willem Gunning. 1999a. "Why Has Africa Grown Slowly?" *Journal of Economic Perspectives* 13 (3): 3–22.

————. 1999b. "Explaining African Economic Performance." *Journal of Economic Literature* 37 (1): 64–111.

Cull, Robert, and Lixin Colin Xu. 2005. "Institutions, Ownership, and Finance: The Determinants of Investment among Chinese Firms." *Journal of Financial Economics* 77 (1): 117–46.

Davis, Steven J., and John Haltiwanger. 1995. "Employer Size and the Wage Structure in U.S. Manufacturing." NBER Working Paper 5393, National Bureau of Economic Research, Cambridge, MA. http://www.nber.org/papers/w5393.pdf?new_window=1.

Dethier, Jean-Jacques, Maximilian Hirn, and Stephane Straub. 2011. "Explaining Enterprise Performance in Developing Countries with Business Climate Survey Data." *World Bank Research Observer* 26 (2): 258–309.

Dollar, David, Mary Hallward-Driemeier, and Taye Mengistae. 2005. "Investment Climate and Firm Performance in Developing Economies." *Economic Development and Cultural Change* 54 (1): 1–31.

Easterly, William, and Ross Levine. 1997. "Africa's Growth Tragedy: Policies and Ethnic Divisions." *Quarterly Journal of Economics* 112 (4): 1203–50.

Fisman, Raymond. 2001. "Trade Credit and Productive Efficiency in Developing Economies." *World Development* 29 (2): 311–21.

Fisman, Raymond, and Jacob Svensson. 2007. "Are Corruption and Taxation Really Harmful to Growth? Firm Level Evidence." *Journal of Development Economics* 83 (1): 63–75.

Gehlbach, Scott, and Philip Keefer. 2011a. "Private Investment and the Institutionalization of Collective Action in Autocracies: Ruling Parties and Legislatures." World Bank, Washington, DC.

———. 2011b. "Investment without Democracy: Ruling Party Institutionalization and Credible Commitment in Autocracies." *Journal of Comparative Economics* 39 (2): 123–39.

Gleditsch, Nils Petter, Peter Wallensteen, Mikael Eriksson, Margareta Sollenberg, and Håvard Strand. 2002. "Armed Conflict 1946–2001: A New Dataset." *Journal of Peace Research* 39 (5): 615–37.

Hallward-Driemeier, Mary, Gita Khun-Jush, and Lant Pritchett. 2010. "Deals Versus Rules: Policy Implementation Uncertainty and Why Firms Hate It." NBER Working Paper 16001, National Bureau of Economic Research, Cambridge, MA. http://www.nber.org/papers/w16001.pdf?new_window=1.

Hallward-Driemeier, Mary, and Lant Pritchett. 2011. "How Business Is Done and the 'Doing Business' Indicators: The Investment Climate When Firms Have Climate Control." Policy Research Working Paper 5563, World Bank, Washington, DC.

Harrison, Ann E., Justin Yifu Lin, and Lixin Colin Xu. 2011. "Explaining Africa's (Dis)Advantage." In *Background Papers*, vol. 3 of *Light Manufacturing in Africa*. Washington, DC: World Bank. http://econ.worldbank.org/africa manufacturing.

Harrison, Ann E., and Jason Scorse. 2010. "Multinationals and Anti-Sweatshop Activism." *American Economic Review* 100 (1): 247–73.

Johnson, Simon, John McMillan, and Christopher Woodruff. 2002. "Property Rights and Finance." *American Economic Review* 92 (5): 1335–56.

Keefer, Philip. 2007. "DPI2006 Database of Political Institutions: Changes and Variable Definitions." Development Research Group, World Bank, Washington, DC.

Knack, Stephen, and Philip Keefer. 1995. "Institutions and Economic Performance: Cross-Country Tests Using Alternative Institutional Measures." *Economics and Politics* 7 (3): 207–27.

Levine, Ross. 1997. "Financial Development and Economic Growth: Views and Agenda." *Journal of Economic Literature* 35 (2): 688–726.

Li, Wei, Taye Mengistae, and Lixin Colin Xu. 2011. "Diagnosing Development Bottlenecks: China and India." *Oxford Bulletin of Economics and Statistics* 73 (6): 722–52.

Lin, Justin Yifu. 2009. *Economic Development and Transition: Thought, Strategy, and Viability*. New York: Cambridge University Press.

Maddison, Angus. 2001. *The World Economy: A Millennial Perspective*. Paris: Organisation for Economic Co-operation and Development.

North, Douglass C. 1990. *Institutions, Institutional Change and Economic Performance*. New York: Cambridge University Press.

Petrin, Amil, and Jagadeesh Sivadasan. 2006. "Job Security Does Affect Economic Efficiency: Theory, a New Statistic, and Evidence from Chile." NBER Working Paper 12757, National Bureau of Economic Research, Cambridge, MA. http://www.nber.org/papers/w12757.pdf?new_window=1.

Sachs, Jeffrey D., and Andrew M. Warner. 1997. "Sources of Slow Growth in African Economies." *Journal of African Economies* 6 (3): 335–76.

UCDP (Uppsala Conflict Data Program) and PRIO (International Peace Research Institute, Oslo). 2010. "UCDP/PRIO Armed Conflict Dataset Codebook." Version 4–2010, Department of Peace and Conflict Research, Uppsala University, Uppsala, Sweden; Centre for the Study of Civil War, International Peace Research Institute, Oslo. http://www.pcr.uu.se/research/ucdp/datasets/ucdp_prio_armed_conflict_dataset/.

World Bank. 2004. *World Development Report 2005: A Better Investment Climate for Everyone*. Washington, DC: World Bank; New York: Oxford University Press.

World Economic Forum. 2009. *The Africa Competitiveness Report 2009*. Geneva: World Economic Forum.

Xu, Lixin Colin. 2011. "The Effects of Business Environments on Development: A Survey of New Firm-Level Evidence." *World Bank Research Observer* 26 (2): 310–40.

CHAPTER 3

Manufacturing Firms in Africa

Some Stylized Facts about Wages and Productivity

George R. G. Clarke

Introduction

Few countries in Sub-Saharan Africa have been successful in export-oriented manufacturing. On average, manufacturing accounted for only about 13 percent of gross domestic product (GDP) between 2005 and 2009 for countries in the region, lower than the share in developing countries in any other region except North Africa and the Middle East (table 3.1). As a result, African countries mostly export agricultural goods and natural resources (Collier 1998). Diversifying into labor-intensive manufacturing would reduce vulnerability to terms-of-trade shocks and allow for more rapid and steadier growth.

Despite the failure to diversify, manufacturing firms in the region are relatively productive. Using data from the World Bank's Enterprise Surveys, we show that, although productivity is low, it is higher, on average, than in other countries at similar levels of development. However, wages are also high, possibly stopping these relatively productive firms from being competitive in international markets.[1]

This chapter discusses possible reasons for the high wages and high productivity. One possibility is that the difficult business environment in

Table 3.1   Manufacturing as a Share of GDP

percent

Region or country	Average, 2005–09	Region or country	Average, 2005–09
Regions (developing countries only)		Gabon	4.01
East Asia and Pacific	31.46	Gambia, The	4.97
Europe and Central Asia	18.26	Ghana	8.74
Latin America and the Caribbean	17.39	Guinea	4.26
Middle East and North Africa	11.92	Guinea-Bissau	—
South Asia	16.24	Kenya	10.10
Sub-Saharan Africa	13.18	Lesotho	19.74
East Asia (exporters)		Liberia	13.05
China	33.03	Madagascar	14.90
Indonesia	27.93	Malawi	14.06
Malaysia	27.70	Mali	3.13
Philippines	22.15	Mauritania	5.05
Thailand	34.86	Mauritius	19.84
Vietnam	20.74	Mozambique	14.90
Sub-Saharan Africa		Namibia	14.92
Angola	4.79	Niger	—
Benin	7.51	Nigeria	2.71
Botswana	3.69	Rwanda	5.23
Burkina Faso	14.10	São Tomé and Príncipe	6.37
Burundi	8.83	Senegal	13.83
Cameroon	17.00	Seychelles	12.23
Cape Verde	6.73	Sierra Leone	—
Central African Republic	7.52	Somalia	—
Chad	5.92	South Africa	16.89
Comoros	4.24	Sudan	6.38
Congo, Dem. Rep.	6.09	Swaziland	43.28
Congo, Rep.	3.92	Tanzania	6.87
Côte d'Ivoire	18.13	Togo	10.14
Equatorial Guinea	11.15	Uganda	7.67
Eritrea	5.90	Zambia	11.39
Ethiopia	4.61	Zimbabwe	13.52

Source: World Development Indicators (database), World Bank, Washington, DC (accessed 2010), http://data
.worldbank.org/data-catalog/world-development-indicators.
Note: Averages for regions are weighted. Averages across years and unweighted averages for each country are
for the available years for that country. GDP = gross domestic product, — = not available.

Africa causes even productive firms to struggle to be profitable. High taxes,
failing infrastructure, and weak governance mean that indirect costs are
high (Eifert, Gelb, and Ramachandran 2005, 2008). Because labor and total
factor productivity do not take these extra costs into account, some productive firms might find that high indirect costs make them unprofitable.

Although high taxes and high indirect costs could explain why surviving firms are productive, they do not explain why wages are high, that is, if indirect costs and taxes drive profits downward, they should also drive wages downward. The high wages paid by formal firms are especially puzzling given that many unskilled workers earn subsistence wages working for informal firms. This pool of underemployed workers should force wages in the formal sector down and allow formal firms that use unskilled labor, including those in light manufacturing, to expand. A different explanation, which could clarify both the high wages and the high productivity, is that limited competition results in high profits. Firms might then share these high profits with their workers.

Exporting by African Manufacturing Firms

Most African manufacturing firms sell all or most of their output domestically. Many do not export at all, and those that do mostly export to neighboring countries. Using firm-level data, this section discusses the export performance of manufacturing firms in the region.

The firm-level data come from the World Bank's Enterprise Surveys (see annex 3.1 for details). The Enterprise Surveys cover formal firms with over five employees and omit microenterprises and informal enterprises. Although separate microenterprise surveys that include informal enterprises were conducted in some countries in Sub-Saharan Africa, similar surveys have not been conducted in other regions. This omission is not serious, however, because, although some microenterprises are light manufacturers, few export.[2]

Manufacturing enterprises in most, but not all, African countries focus on internal markets. In most countries, fewer than one enterprise in five exports (figure 3.1). Given the small size of the manufacturing sector in most countries, this means that manufacturing exports are small in most economies in the region.

Although manufacturing enterprises have been unsuccessful in export markets in many African countries, there are significant differences across countries. For example, Kenyan firms are more successful exporters than firms in other African countries. Even in successful countries such as Kenya, however, firms mostly export to neighboring countries rather than to Europe or other high-income economies. Although the most recent Enterprise Surveys do not collect information on the destination of exports, earlier Enterprise Surveys did. In the Enterprise Surveys conducted between 2002 and 2004, firms were more likely to export to

Figure 3.1   Share of Firms That Export, by Region

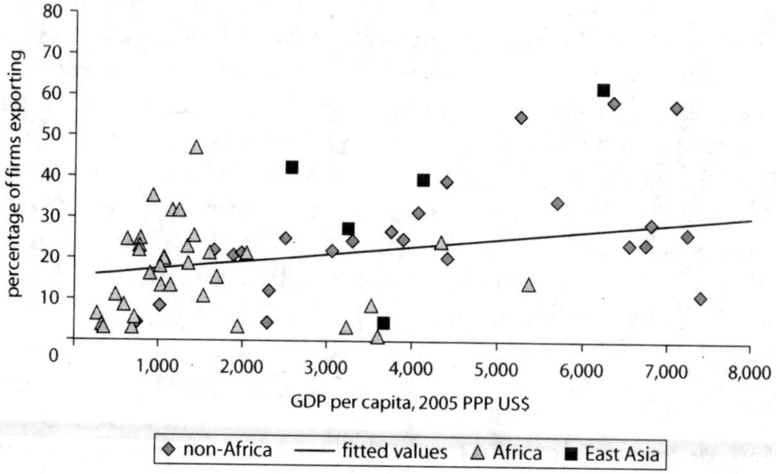

Source: Author calculations based on data of Enterprise Surveys (database), World Bank, Washington, DC, http://www.enterprisesurveys.org/.

Note: See table 3.4 for additional notes on data construction. East Asia is China, Indonesia, the Philippines, Thailand, and Vietnam. Africa is Sub-Saharan Africa only. Data are for all Enterprise Surveys conducted since 2006 with at least 50 firms. Countries with per capita GDP over US$8,000 are excluded for presentational purposes. Fitted values is the line from log-log regression. GDP = gross domestic product, PPP = purchasing power parity.

Table 3.2   Export Destinations for Enterprises Included in the Investment Climate Surveys of the Early 2000s

percentage of responses

Country	% of exporters who report that the destination is important	
	Most important export destinations	Most important industrialized export destination
Ethiopia	Italy (55), United Kingdom (29), Germany (19)	Italy (55)
Kenya	Uganda (74), Tanzania (61), Rwanda (19)	United Kingdom (8)
Mali	Burkina Faso (63), Guinea (53), Niger (38)	France (9)
Senegal	Gambia, The (39); Mali (36); Mauritania (31)	France (18)
Tanzania	Kenya (38), Malawi (14), Uganda (12), United Kingdom (12), Zambia (12)	United Kingdom (12)
Uganda	Rwanda (49); Congo, Dem. Rep. (33); Kenya (18)	United Kingdom (16)
Zambia	Congo, Dem. Rep. (38); Malawi (22); Germany (21)	Germany (21)

Source: Data of Enterprise Surveys (database) (2002–04), World Bank, Washington, DC, http://www.enterprisesurveys.org/.

Note: Enterprises were asked to list their three most important export destinations. Countries are ranked on the basis of number of enterprises that ranked each country among the top three. Not all enterprises reported three destinations.

neighboring countries than to more distant markets (table 3.2). For example, Uganda and Tanzania were the most important export destinations for Kenyan firms, with 74 and 61 percent of exporters exporting to these countries, respectively. In comparison, only 8 percent exported to the United Kingdom, the biggest overseas export market. This is true for both landlocked countries (for example, Uganda and Zambia) and countries with access to the sea (for example, Kenya and Tanzania).[3]

Stylized Facts about Firm Performance in Sub-Saharan Africa

Why do so few African firms export? One possibility is that firms are unproductive. Natural and policy barriers to trade might make it difficult for exports to enter African markets, allowing poorly performing domestic firms to survive. These unproductive firms, however, might be unable to overcome natural and policy barriers of other countries to trade and, so, are unable to compete in competitive foreign markets.[4]

Firm Productivity in Sub-Saharan Africa[5]

Consistent with this, labor productivity (value added per worker) is lower, on average, in Sub-Saharan Africa than in any region other than South Asia.[6] In the average country in Sub-Saharan Africa, median labor productivity is US$4,734 per worker measured in 2005 dollars.[7] Labor productivity is especially low in the low-income and lower-middle-income economies in the region (US$3,316 per worker). In comparison, labor productivity is US$6,713 per worker in the average country in East Asia that has a strong manufacturing base.

So why is labor productivity low in Africa? One possibility is that this outcome mostly reflects problems at the firm level. Internal factors such as capital intensity, the educational attainment and skill levels of workers, and firm organization affect productivity. Management quality is also important: firms with more highly educated managers are more productive than other firms.[8] Poor performance might, therefore, partly reflect problems at the firm level.

But external factors also matter. On average, physical infrastructure and the institutional environment are worse in Africa than in other regions.[9] Business regulation is also more burdensome.[10] Furthermore, the external environment affects worker quality and capital intensity, both of which are internal to the firm. If their educational attainment is greater, workers have higher human capital. And if the financial sector is more well developed, firms find it easier to finance investment and training.

Although per capita GDP is not perfectly correlated with external factors that affect firm performance, many of these factors vary with income. Institutional quality, for example, is lower in poor countries.[11] Thus, corruption is more extensive in low-income countries; the rule of law is less well protected; and government efficiency is lower.[12] To control for these differences, figure 3.2 graphs value added per worker against GDP per capita. Although the fit is not perfect, value added per worker is usually lower in poor countries.

If one takes income into account, value added per worker is not consistently lower in Sub-Saharan Africa than in other regions. In fact, more African countries lie above the regression line than below it. This suggests that, all else equal, value added per worker is higher in Africa than would be expected given relative income levels.

It is interesting to compare Africa with successful exporters of manufactured goods in East Asia: China, Indonesia, the Philippines, Thailand, and Vietnam.[13] Per capita GDP and value added per worker are higher in these countries than in most countries in Sub-Saharan Africa. These countries do not consistently lie above or below the line either (see figure 3.2).

Figure 3.2   Value Added per Worker in Firms in Africa and Other Regions

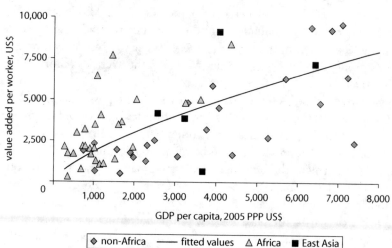

Source: Author calculations based on data of Enterprise Surveys (database), World Bank, Washington, DC, http://www.enterprisesurveys.org/.
Note: See table 3.4 for additional notes on data construction. East Asia is China, Indonesia, the Philippines, Thailand, and Vietnam. Africa is Sub-Saharan Africa only. Data are for all Enterprise Surveys conducted since 2006 with at least 50 firms. Countries with GDP over US$8,000 are excluded for presentational purposes. Fitted values is the line from log-log regression. GDP = gross domestic product, PPP = purchasing power parity.

China lies significantly above the line: value added per worker is higher than would be expected given income levels. Indonesia lies significantly below the line: value added per worker is lower than would be expected. The other three countries lie close to the fitted line: labor productivity is about what would be expected given the income levels.

Labor Costs in Sub-Saharan Africa

Although productivity affects how competitive firms are, unproductive firms can survive and compete with more productive firms if the labor costs of the unproductive firms are low. To assess whether African firms can compete in export markets, we therefore also have to look at labor costs.

Labor costs, similar to labor productivity, are low in Africa (table 3.3). Per worker labor costs are about US$1,059 for the median firm in low-income and lower-middle-income countries in the region. For the successful manufacturing economies in East Asia, per worker labor costs are about US$1,629 per worker. This suggests that African firms might be able to remain competitive because of their low labor costs.

So, why are labor costs low in Sub-Saharan Africa? One possibility is that the quality or quantity of human capital is low. More highly educated workers are more productive and command higher wages. Thus, low wages and low labor productivity might both reflect that workers are poorly educated.

Characteristics other than education affect wages, however. Investment climate constraints that reduce the marginal productivity of labor also reduce wages. If, for example, poor-quality infrastructure or institutions reduce the marginal productivity of labor, wages will be lower in countries with poor infrastructure and weak institutions. It is therefore useful to control for income. As discussed above, although per capita income does not completely control for the quality of the business environment, it is highly correlated with many aspects of this environment.

Figure 3.3 shows labor costs per worker plotted against per capita GDP. Not unsurprisingly, the cost of labor, like labor productivity, is higher in countries where income is higher. This could be because high-income countries have more human capital, stronger institutions, or better infrastructure.

As with labor productivity, labor costs are high in most African countries. Of 31 countries in Africa on which data are available, labor costs were higher than would be predicted based on per capita income in 19 of them. For many of the remaining countries, labor costs were close to the predicted values. This suggests that labor costs are high for formal

Table 3.3 Labor Costs in Africa and Other Regions

Region	Observations	Labor cost per worker, US$		Value added per worker, US$		Unit labor costs, %	
		Mean	Median	Mean	Median	Mean	Median
Africa	37	1,464	887	4,734	3,210	33.5	32.6
Low and lower-middle income	32	1,059	873	3,316	2,462	33.9	33.9
Upper-middle income	5	4,056	2,818	13,811	14,967	30.7	28.8
East Asia	12	1,733	1,246	6,631	5,192	31.7	31.9
Nonmanufacturing	6	1,837	1,800	6,713	4,064	33.4	34.6
Manufacturing	6	1,629	1,246	6,548	5,684	30.0	28.1
Eastern Europe and Central Asia	30	4,046	2,869	10,297	7,741	37.7	37.5
Latin America and the Caribbean	14	3,241	2,795	8,890	7,884	36.6	37.2
South Asia	2	817	817	1,483	1,483	39.9	37.5

Source: Author calculations based on data of Enterprise Surveys (database), World Bank, Washington, DC, http://www.enterprisesurveys.org/.

Note: Means and medians are unweighted country-level means and medians for all countries in the region. The country-level data are weighted medians for that country. Table 3A.1 shows a list of countries in each region.

Figure 3.3   Labor Costs per Worker in Firms in Africa and Other Regions

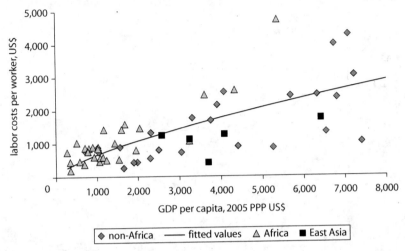

Source: Author calculations based on data of Enterprise Surveys (database), World Bank, Washington, DC, http://www.enterprisesurveys.org/.

Note: See table 3.4 for additional notes on data construction. East Asia is China; Indonesia, the Philippines, Thailand, and Vietnam. Africa is Sub-Saharan Africa only. Data are for all Enterprise Surveys conducted since 2006 with at least 50 firms. Countries with GDP over US$8,000 are excluded for presentational purposes. Fitted values is the line from log-log regression. GDP = gross domestic product, PPP = purchasing power parity.

manufacturing firms in Africa compared with the case in other countries at similar levels of development.

One concern is that labor costs may be high because firms pay high wages to skilled workers such as managers and professional staff. If there are shortages of these workers in Africa, firms might face high labor costs because wages are high for these categories rather than because they are high for production workers.

The Enterprise Survey also asks managers about the wages that they pay production workers. These data are less reliable than accounting data; managers will find it easier to lie and to make mistakes if they cannot check their accounts. However, because wages for managers and professional staff do not affect these data, they offer a more direct measure of wages for workers. Furthermore, because they come from a different source (that is, managers do not report the data directly from company accounts), they provide a useful robustness check.

The results are similar if we focus on this measure of wages rather than on labor costs from firm balance sheets (figure 3.4). Monthly wages were higher than would be expected given income levels in 18 of the 26 countries

Figure 3.4   Average Monthly Wages for Production Workers in Firms in Africa and Other Regions

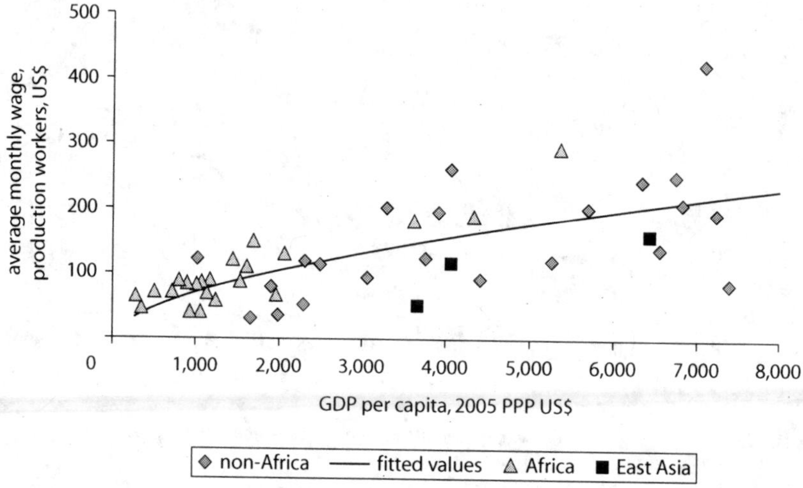

Source: Author calculations based on data of Enterprise Surveys (database), World Bank, Washington, DC, http://www.enterprisesurveys.org/.
Note: See table 3.4 for additional notes on data construction. East Asia is China, Indonesia, and Thailand. Africa is Sub-Saharan Africa only. Data are for all Enterprise Surveys conducted since 2006 with at least 50 firms. Countries with GDP over US$8,000 are excluded for presentational purposes. Fitted values is the line from log-log regression. GDP = gross domestic product, PPP = purchasing power parity.

in Sub-Saharan Africa on which there are data. In comparison, among three successful exporters in East Asia, monthly wages were lower than would be expected given the income levels. This suggests that high labor costs do not reflect only high wages for skilled workers and managers. Rather, wages are also high for production workers.

Unit Labor Costs in Sub-Saharan Africa

If labor costs are high because workers are productive (for example, because they are highly skilled or well educated), then firms can remain competitive while paying high wages. The ratio of value added to labor costs—which we refer to as unit labor costs—allows us to see whether this is the case.[14] Although this ratio does not measure competitiveness perfectly (for example, it does not take capital use into account), it is a better measure than labor costs alone.

Unit labor costs are not especially high in Sub-Saharan Africa: they average 34 percent in low-income and lower-middle-income econo- mies. This is less than in Eastern Europe and Central Asia (38 percent),

Latin America (37 percent), or South Asia (40 percent). It is, however, slightly higher than in the manufacturing economies of East Asia (28 percent). This remains true after one controls for per capita income (figure 3.5). Unlike labor productivity and labor costs, there is not a strong relationship between income and unit labor costs.

Although unit labor costs are not especially high in Africa, they are higher than would be predicted by per capita income alone. Of 31 countries in Sub-Saharan Africa on which there are data available, 18 have higher unit labor costs than would be predicted. In contrast, with the notable exception of Indonesia, the East Asian countries that have been successful in manufacturing have low unit labor costs. Although unit labor costs are not exceptionally high in Sub-Saharan Africa, they are higher there than in most successful exporters in East Asia.

Econometric Analysis

Although the graphical analysis is suggestive, it is useful to analyze the data formally. This will allow us to see whether the differences between Sub-Saharan Africa and other regions are statistically significant.

Figure 3.5   Unit Labor Costs in Firms in Africa and Other Regions

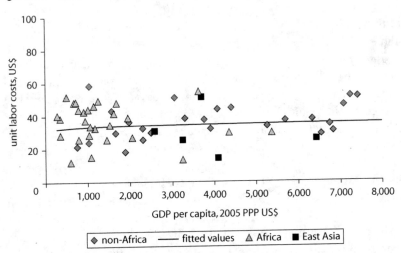

Source: Author calculations based on data of Enterprise Surveys (database), World Bank, Washington, DC, http://www.enterprisesurveys.org/.
Note: See table 3.4 for additional notes on data construction. East Asia is China, Indonesia, the Philippines, Thailand, and Vietnam. Africa is Sub-Saharan Africa only. Data are for all Enterprise Surveys conducted since 2006 with at least 50 firms. Countries with GDP over US$8,000 are excluded for presentational purposes. Fitted values is the line from log-log regression. GDP = gross domestic product, PPP = purchasing power parity.

Models

To see whether the differences between firms in Sub-Saharan Africa and firms in East Asia and Pacific and other regions are statistically significant after controlling for differences in income, we estimate models of the following form:

$$\text{Performance}_{ij} = \alpha + \beta \text{ per capita GDP}_j + \gamma \text{region}$$
$$\text{dummies}_j + \lambda \text{ sector dummies}_{ij} + \varepsilon_{ij} \qquad (3.1)$$

Productivity and wages for firm i in country j are regressed on per capita income, a set of region dummies, and a set of sector dummies.[15] As discussed above, the regressions include per capita GDP to control for institutional and other differences between low- and middle-income countries that might affect wages and productivity. The regressions do not include a region dummy for Africa. The coefficients on the other region dummies, γ, therefore represent the average difference in productivity and wages between firms in Sub-Saharan Africa and firms in other regions.[16] Because labor costs and productivity vary across subsectors of manufacturing, the regressions include subsector dummies. This means that any observed performance differences will not have arisen because firms in Africa are in different subsectors relative to firms in other regions.

Empirical Results

Table 3.4 shows the results of the base regression.

Per capita income. Consistent with the graphical analysis, value added per worker, labor costs per worker, and monthly wages for production workers increase as per capita income increases. For labor productivity and costs, the point estimates of the coefficients are close to 1, that is, labor productivity and labor costs increase at about the same rate as per capita income.[17] A 1 percent increase in per capita income is associated with a 0.85 percent increase in labor productivity and a 0.81 percent increase in per worker labor costs. The coefficient on monthly wages for production workers is smaller: a 1 percent increase in per capita income is associated with a 0.64 percent increase in monthly wages. The coefficient on per capita income is statistically insignificant and small in the regression for unit labor costs. This suggests that unit labor costs are not consistently higher or lower in countries with higher per capita income. This is also consistent with the graphical analysis.

Region dummies. As noted above, the regressions do not include a region dummy for Sub-Saharan Africa. The coefficients can therefore be

Table 3.4　Differences in Productivity, by Region (Firm-Level Regressions)

Indicator or region	Value added per worker, 2005 US$	Labor costs per worker, 2005 US$	Monthly wage production workers, 2005 US$	Unit labor costs
Observations	26,340	29,112	27,431	27,497
Sector dummies	included	included	included	included
Per capita GDP (log)	0.846*** (7.91)	0.813*** (7.46)	0.641*** (6.54)	−0.046 (−0.74)
Region dummies[a]				
Asia and Pacific, manufacturing only	−0.142 (−0.47)	−0.890*** (−4.58)	−0.434** (−2.22)	−0.783*** (−4.05)
Asia and Pacific, other	−0.547 (−1.60)	−0.550* (−1.85)	−0.861*** (−6.26)	−0.347*** (−2.38)
Eastern Europe and Central Asia	−0.640** (−2.06)	−0.607** (−2.33)	−0.075 (−0.29)	−0.056 (−0.36)
Latin America and the Caribbean	−0.216 (−0.82)	−0.269 (−1.24)	0.102 (0.46)	−0.079 (−0.56)
South Asia	−0.499*** (−3.26)	−0.209* (−1.75)	0.020 (0.16)	−0.125 (−0.61)
Africa, middle income	0.034 (0.10)	0.091 (0.23)	0.172 (0.61)	0.130 (0.61)
Constant	1.318* (1.74)	0.745 (0.94)	−0.448 (−0.64)	−0.492 (−1.06)
R^2	0.26	0.35	0.51	0.15

Source: Author calculations based on data of Enterprise Surveys (database), World Bank, Washington, DC, http://www.enterprisesurveys.org/.

Note: The model includes sector dummies for textiles, garments, food and beverage, chemicals, construction materials, wood and furniture, metal products, paper, plastics, machinery, electronics, cars, and other manufacturing. Outliers more than 3 standard deviations from the country-level averages are excluded. Value added is calculated by subtracting intermediate inputs and energy costs from sales from manufacturing. Workers include permanent and temporary full-time workers. Labor cost is the total cost of wages, salaries, allowances, bonuses, and other benefits for both production and nonproduction workers. Unit labor costs are labor costs divided by value added. GDP = gross domestic product.

a. The omitted dummy is the dummy for Sub-Saharan Africa.

Significance level: * = 10 percent, ** = 5 percent, *** = 1 percent. Robust t-statistics are clustered at the country level in parentheses.

interpreted as the average difference between countries in other regions and countries in Sub-Saharan Africa. For the most part, the coefficients in the first three regressions are negative and are often statistically significant. This suggests that, after one takes per capita income differences into account, labor productivity, labor costs, and monthly wages for production workers are higher in Sub-Saharan Africa than in countries at similar levels of development in other regions. The coefficients are mostly statistically significant for the dummy variables for countries in East Asia and Pacific and countries in Eastern Europe and Central Asia. In contrast, the coefficients are mostly statistically insignificant for the dummy variables for Latin America.

The results indicate that, after one takes income differences into account, labor productivity is about 14 percent lower in the manufacturing economies of East Asia than in Sub-Saharan Africa; labor costs are about 89 percent lower; and wages for production workers are about 43 percent lower. The large difference in wages and the more modest difference in productivity suggest that it will be difficult for firms in Sub-Saharan Africa to compete with East Asian firms unless productivity can be improved.

In contrast, the coefficients on most of the dummy variables are statistically insignificant in the regressions for unit labor costs. This suggests that unit labor costs are similar in Sub-Saharan Africa to corresponding costs in other regions. The exceptions are the coefficients on the dummy variable indicating that the country is in East Asia. For countries there, the coefficient is statistically significant and negative. This is consistent with the previous results, which suggest that the difference in wages between East Asia and Africa is larger than the difference in productivity.

Omitting per capita GDP. In the above analysis, the high productivity and high labor costs in Africa are considered relative to other countries at the same level of development. As discussed above, before one controls for income, productivity and wages appear relatively low in Sub-Saharan Africa (table 3.4). This can also be seen by excluding per capita income from the previous regressions.

After per capita income is excluded, the coefficients on most of the dummies become positive in the regressions for labor productivity (table 3.5). The coefficients on the dummies for Eastern Europe and Central Asia and for Latin America, in particular, are positive and statistically significant, indicating that wages and productivity are higher in these regions, on average, than in Africa before one controls for income differences. The coefficient on the dummy variable indicating that the country is an East Asian exporter is also positive and is statistically significant.

Table 3.5 Differences in Productivity, by Region, with GDP Omitted (Firm-Level Regressions)

Indicator or region	Value added per worker, 2005 US$	Labor costs per worker, 2005 US$	Monthly wage, production workers, 2005 US$	Unit labor costs
Observations	26,568	29,401	27,730	27,735
Sector dummies	Yes	Yes	Yes	Yes
Region dummies[a]				
Asia and Pacific, manufacturing only	0.744*** (2.79)	−0.034 (−0.28)	0.255** (2.36)	−0.833*** (−4.73)
Asia and Pacific, other	0.141 (0.35)	−0.141 (−0.58)	−0.370* (−1.90)	−0.538*** (−2.92)
Eastern Europe and Central Asia	0.991*** (4.37)	0.983*** (4.81)	1.166*** (6.51)	−0.134 (−1.46)
Latin America and the Caribbean	1.208*** (7.99)	1.112*** (7.57)	1.166*** (10.30)	−0.157** (−2.05)
South Asia	−0.533*** (−2.59)	−0.406*** (−5.76)	0.268 (0.75)	−0.203 (−1.07)
Africa, middle income	1.639*** (8.05)	1.651*** (5.34)	1.380*** (9.36)	0.042 (0.26)
Constant	7.405*** (81.71)	6.576*** (75.10)	4.172*** (53.65)	−0.838*** (−10.82)
R^2	0.19	0.25	0.40	0.15

Source: Author calculations based on data of Enterprise Surveys (database), World Bank, Washington, DC, http://www.enterprisesurveys.org/.

Note: GDP = gross domestic product.

a. The omitted dummy is the dummy for Sub-Saharan Africa.

Significance level: * = 10 percent, ** = 5 percent, *** = 1 percent.

In the regression for unit labor costs, the results are similar to the results when per capita GDP is included. This is not surprising given that unit labor costs do not appear to vary consistently with income. For the most part, unit labor costs do not appear to be excessively high, on average, in Sub-Saharan Africa. The only region with lower unit labor costs is East Asia.

In summary, the econometric analysis confirms many of the previous results from the graphical analysis. Most notably, firms in Sub-Saharan Africa appear to be productive and to have high labor costs in comparison with firms in low-income countries in other regions. The differences are largest and most statistically significant in the comparison between firms in Sub-Saharan Africa and firms in East Asia and in Eastern Europe and Central Asia. The differences in wages between Africa and East Asia appear larger than the difference in productivity, suggesting that it might be difficult for African firms to remain competitive.

For the most part, unit labor costs are no different in Sub-Saharan Africa than in other regions. Unit labor costs are, however, significantly higher than in East Asia (China, Indonesia, Malaysia, the Philippines, Thailand, and Vietnam). This also suggests that it will be difficult for firms in Sub-Saharan Africa to compete with firms in East Asia.

The High Cost of Doing Business in Sub-Saharan Africa

Given their poor export performance, it is surprising that firms in Africa are more productive than firms in other countries at similar stages of development. One possible explanation is that standard measures of productivity fail to account for some aspects of performance that affect competitiveness. Eifert, Gelb, and Ramachandran (2008), in particular, note that labor productivity does not take indirect costs into account. This section discusses two types of indirect costs—high indirect costs related to the weak institutional environment and high tax rates on formal firms—that might affect whether firms can export.

High Indirect Costs

Standard measures of productivity take the cost of intermediate inputs, raw materials, and the cost of energy and fuel into account.[18] As Eifert, Gelb, and Ramachandran (2008) point out, this ignores other costs that affect profitability, such as transport, communications, and security costs. Using data from 17 Enterprise Surveys between 2002 and 2005, they show that indirect costs are higher in Africa than in other regions. After considering these, they show that African firms are less productive than firms in other regions.

High indirect costs reduce profitability. Firms that are relatively productive before one takes indirect costs into account might become unprofitable after one takes them into account. If indirect costs are high, therefore, only the most productive firms survive. This could result in a small, but relatively productive manufacturing sector, which is seen in Sub-Saharan Africa.

Because the information collected in the Enterprise Surveys has changed significantly over time, it is not possible to perform calculations identical to those in Eifert, Gelb, and Ramachandran (2008) for the more recent surveys. However, the available evidence from the newer surveys is consistent with Eifert, Gelb, and Ramachandran (2008). Figure 3.6 and table 3.6 show bribe payments, the cost of power outages, losses during

Figure 3.6   Indirect Costs as a Percentage of Sales, by Region

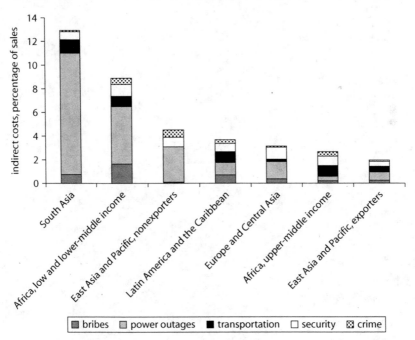

Source: Author calculations based on data of Enterprise Surveys (database), World Bank, Washington, DC, http://www.enterprisesurveys.org/.
Note: Regional averages are unweighted averages across countries in which data are available in that region. Costs are only for manufacturing firms.

Table 3.6   Indirect Costs as a Share of Sales, by Region
percent

Country	Bribes	Power outages	Losses during transport	Security	Crime	Regional total
Africa, low and lower-middle income	1.6	4.8	0.9	1.0	0.5	8.9
Angola	2.6	2.9	0.5	0.9	0.2	
Benin	3.1	6.8	—	1.2	0	
Burkina Faso	0	2.3	0.1	0.7	0	
Burundi	3.3	8.1	0.1	0.6	0.5	
Cameroon	3.0	4.3	2.0	1.4	0.9	
Cape Verde	0	2.8	—	0.7	0.8	
Chad	1.4	1.9	—	0.9	1.6	
Congo, Dem. Rep.	3.5	6.1	0.3	0.3	0.5	
Congo, Rep.	2.6	13.2	—	2.1	0.2	
Côte d'Ivoire	3.6	1.8	0.3	0.3	0.2	
Eritrea	0	0	—	0.3	0	
Gambia, The	2.0	8.9	0.9	2.6	1.0	
Ghana	1.5	5.3	0.8	0.5	0.2	
Guinea	3.6	14.0	0.7	0.2	0.7	
Guinea-Bissau	4.3	1.3	0.6	0.8	0.5	
Kenya	2.2	4.3	1.6	0.7	0.5	
Lesotho	0.1	2.1	—	2.2	1.1	
Liberia	0.6	0.5	—	2.3	1.7	
Madagascar	1.8	7.9	1.0	1.1	0.4	
Malawi	0	7.9	—	4.7	1.6	
Mali	0.5	0.8	0.6	0.3	0.1	
Mauritania	3.4	0.9	0.5	0.5	0	
Mozambique	0.5	0.9	0.9	0.5	1.0	
Niger	1.6	1.4	—	0.5	0.1	
Nigeria	0.9	8.8	2.4	1.3	0.2	
Rwanda	0.9	6.5	1.0	0.6	0.3	
Senegal	0.8	6.2	0.6	0.5	0.1	
Sierra Leone	0.3	5.4	—	0.9	0.8	
Swaziland	0.7	1.0	0.8	0.8	0.4	
Tanzania	2.3	7.7	1.4	1.4	0.6	
Togo	0	6.3	—	0.9	0.2	
Uganda	2.7	8.9	1.0	0.7	0.3	
Zambia	0.2	2.3	0.7	1.0	0.4	
Africa, upper-middle income	0.2	0.4	0.9	0.8	0.4	2.6
Botswana	0.2	0.3	1.3	1.0	0.5	
Gabon	0.5	0.7	—	0.8	0.2	
Mauritius	0	0.5	0.2	0.8	0.1	

(continued next page)

Table 3.6 (continued)

percent

Country	Bribes	Power outages	Losses during transport	Security	Crime	Regional total
Namibia	0.1	0	0.8	0.6	0.6	
South Africa	0.1	0.4	1.3	1.0	0.5	
East Asia and Pacific, exporters	0.2	0.7	0.5	0.4	0.1	1.9
Indonesia	0.1	0.1	0.6	0.1	0	
Philippines	0.3	0.6	0.7	0.7	0.3	
Vietnam	0.3	1.3	0.2	0.4	0	

Source: Author calculations based on data of Enterprise Surveys (database), World Bank, Washington, DC, http://www.enterprisesurveys.org/.

Note: — = not available.

transport, the cost of security, and losses because of crime and theft.[19] These specific indirect costs are equal to about 9 percent of sales in Sub-Saharan Africa. In comparison, they are equal to only 2 percent of sales in the exporting countries in East Asia on which data are available (Indonesia, the Philippines, and Vietnam). These costs are also far lower in Eastern Europe and Central Asia, in upper-middle-income countries in Sub-Saharan Africa, and in Latin America and the Caribbean.[20] Corruption (1.6 percent of sales, on average) and power outages (4.8 percent of sales) are especially high in Africa.

Other evidence also suggests that indirect costs are high in Sub-Saharan Africa. As discussed below, transport costs other than breakage and theft are high. Similarly, data of the International Telecommunications Union suggest that broadband and telecommunications costs are high (Eifert, Gelb, and Ramachandran 2008).

High Tax Rates

As well as omitting indirect costs associated with the weak institutional environment and unreliable infrastructure, standard productivity measures do not consider taxes. If taxes are high, profitable firms can become unprofitable, especially if taxes are not levied directly on profits (for example, labor taxes or turnover taxes). If taxes are high, firms have to be productive to remain profitable and keep operating.

Because the Enterprise Surveys do not collect information on taxes, it is not possible to calculate after-tax measures of performance using data from these surveys. We therefore rely on other evidence. One useful and consistently calculated measure of the tax burden is the total tax rate in the World Bank's *Doing Business* report (2010a). The total tax rate is better than statutory corporate tax rates because it includes other taxes and weighs additional features of corporate taxes.

The total tax rate is high in Sub-Saharan Africa, averaging 68 percent of profits (table 3.7). In comparison, the average rate is about 40 percent in Eastern Europe and Central Asia, 33 percent in the Middle East and Africa, and 35 percent in East Asia and Pacific. The total tax rate is almost twice as high as in East Asia and Pacific, where it is 20 percentage points higher than the rate in the region with the next highest total tax rate (Latin America).

The *Doing Business* report breaks the total tax rate into three parts: profit taxes, labor taxes, and other taxes. Although labor taxes are similar in Sub-Saharan Africa and other regions and lower than in several regions, including Eastern Europe and Central Asia and the economies of the Organisation for Economic Co-operation and Development (OECD), profit taxes and other taxes are higher. This suggests that the high productivity of African firms might be misleading. Even if before-tax profits are relatively high, taxes erode them. Furthermore, as noted above, high indirect costs suggest that before-tax profits may not be so high.

Weak Competition That Distorts Productivity and Wages

Although high taxes and other indirect costs might mean that surviving manufacturing firms have to be productive, they do not explain why

Table 3.7   Tax Rates in Sub-Saharan Africa and Other Regions
percent

Region	Profit tax	Labor tax	Other taxes	Total tax rate, % profit
East Asia and Pacific	18.3	10.3	6.8	35.4
Eastern Europe and Central Asia	9.8	22.9	8.5	41.2
Latin America and the Caribbean	20.9	14.7	12.4	48.0
Middle East and North Africa	12.0	16.8	4.1	32.8
OECD	16.8	23.3	3.0	43.0
South Asia	17.8	7.8	14.2	39.9
Sub-Saharan Africa	23.1	13.5	31.5	68.0

Source: World Bank 2010a.
Note: OECD = Organisation for Economic Co-operation and Development.

wages are high. If indirect costs and taxes make it difficult for firms to survive, we would expect to see the firms paying low wages. This section discusses characteristics that could explain both high wages and high productivity: the possibility that workers are particularly productive and the possibility that weak competition distorts productivity measurements.

Labor Costs and Informality

An important question in most African countries is how firms in the small formal sector coexist with informal firms paying subsistence wages.[21] In low-income countries in Africa, most people work for informal firms. In Zambia, for example, about 84 percent of workers do so (Clarke and others 2010). Informal firms usually pay their workers far less relative to formal firms. Workers in large firms and the public sector in Ghana and Tanzania earn over twice as much as self-employed people or similar workers in smaller firms (Falco and others 2010).[22]

A similar pattern can be seen in Zambia. The median unregistered micro, small, and medium enterprise (MSME) there has monthly labor costs of less than US$30 per worker.[23] In comparison, the median formal manufacturing firm reports monthly labor costs of about US$120 per worker. In part, the difference in wages between the formal and informal sectors arises because of location. Wages are low in areas and sectors in which informality is high. Monthly per worker labor costs in Zambia are about US$57 per month for urban MSMEs, compared with only US$19 per month for rural MSMEs (figure 3.7, table 3.8). A large gap remains in Zambia, however, between large formal enterprises, registered MSMEs in urban areas, and unregistered MSMEs in urban areas. Monthly labor costs were about US$120 per worker for the large, formal urban firms in the Zambia Enterprise Survey. For registered MSMEs in urban areas, the average was US$95 per month, and for unregistered MSMEs in urban areas, the average was US$43 per month.

One possible reason for the large difference between wages in the small formal and large informal sectors is that labor regulations make the informal sector the employer of last resort. Although some countries, such as Rwanda and Uganda, have flexible labor markets, most countries in the region do not (table 3.9). Rigid labor markets can lead to rationing in high-paying formal sector jobs, forcing unemployed workers into the informal sector as they try to find employment.

Another possibility is that poor-quality basic education has resulted in a skills mismatch. Workers with adequate education and skills might be scarce despite the many unskilled workers in the informal economy, that

Figure 3.7   Monthly Labor Costs for Registered and Unregistered MSMEs in Zambia

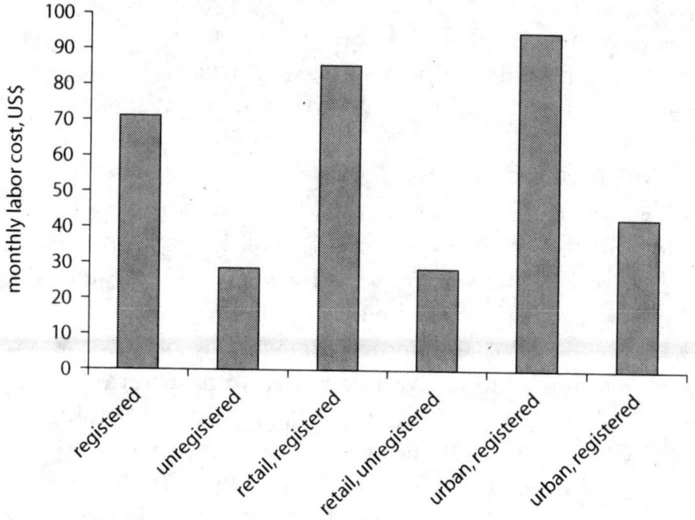

Source: Author calculations based on data of the 2008 Zambia Business Survey, which is described in Clarke and others 2010.
Note: See the note to table 3.8. MSME = micro, small, and medium enterprise.

Table 3.8   Average Monthly Labor Costs for MSMEs in Zambia, by Registration Status, Sector, and Location
U.S. dollars

Registration status, sector, or location	Average monthly labor cost
Registered	71
Unregistered	28
Urban	57
Rural	19
Manufacturing	71
Retail	28
Other services	43
Agriculture	20
Other	36
Retail, urban	57
Retail, rural	20
Retail, registered	85
Retail, unregistered	28
Urban, registered	95
Urban, unregistered	43

Source: Author calculations based on data of the 2008 Zambia Business Survey, which is described in Clarke and others 2010.
Note: Data are for firms with workers that are paid in cash. Workers paid in-kind are excluded, and in-kind payments are excluded. Firms with more than 50 employees are included. MSME = micro, small, and medium enterprise.

Table 3.9   Labor Regulations in Sub-Saharan Africa and Other Regions
index

Region	Difficulty of hiring	Rigidity of hours	Difficult of redundancy	Rigidity of employment
East Asia and Pacific	19.2	8.6	19.6	15.8
Eastern Europe and Central Asia	31.9	29.9	25.9	29.2
Latin America and the Caribbean	34.4	21.3	24.1	26.6
Middle East and North Africa	21.3	22.1	30.0	24.5
OECD	26.5	30.1	22.6	26.4
South Asia	27.8	10.0	41.3	26.3
Sub-Saharan Africa	37.3	29.3	39.8	35.5

Source: World Bank 2009a.
Note: Higher values mean more rigid regulations (on a 0–100 scale). OECD = Organisation for Economic Co-operation and Development.

is, poorly paid informal workers might not have the skills and education to compete in the modern formal economy.[24] Combined with the problems in the investment climate that drive productivity downward and the other rising costs associated with exporting, this might mean that formal firms cannot compete with exporters in regions such as East Asia.[25]

Labor market rigidities and shortages of skilled workers are not, however, the only possible reasons why informality might fail to drive formal wages downward. Another possibility is that formal sector jobs might be unattractive, that is, the informal sector might be large because people prefer working for informal firms. Maloney (1999, 2004) notes that this is the case in Latin America: many people say they would prefer to be self-employed in the informal sector rather than work for somebody else in a formal firm.

This could also be true in Africa. In Zambia, less than half of self-employed people said they would take a full-time job in the formal sector if offered one. Furthermore, many would prefer to work for the government (67 percent), a state-owned enterprise (4 percent), or a nongovernmental organization (17 percent). Only 10 percent of MSME owners said they would like to work for a formal private sector firm.

So, why do some people prefer to work for informal firms? Although informal firms pay low wages, Maloney (2004) notes that it is difficult to compare wages in the formal and informal sectors. For example, informal workers avoid taxes, meaning that before-tax wage comparisons are not useful. Moreover, some people like to work for themselves, and informal sector jobs can be more flexible. Informal enterprises also have lower indirect costs than formal enterprises: they avoid dealing with license fees and other regulations and might avoid much of the cost of corruption.[26]

Even for informal workers who are not the owners, there are benefits to working for informal firms. Many workers—if not most—are family members who receive in-kind payments.[27] Some characteristics, however, make formal employment preferable. Formal firms often pay benefits that informal firms do not pay, and employment is more secure. Maloney (2004) argues that these large positive and negative differences make wage comparisons between formal and informal jobs difficult.

Low Levels of Competition

The relationship between competition and measured productivity is complicated. For the most part, we would expect competition to increase productivity, that is, if unproductive firms in competitive markets fail to improve their performance to the levels of the market leaders, they will be forced out of business. In contrast, if firms have market power, they can earn excess profits, thereby allowing management to underperform. Hicks (1935, 8) argues that "[monopolists] are likely to exploit their advantage much more by not bothering to get very near the position of maximum profit, than by straining themselves to get very close to it. The best of all monopoly profits is a quiet life."

Although competition will tend to lead to higher productivity, productivity appears artificially high if competition is low. This is so because labor productivity is measured using revenue rather than physical measures of output.[28] If productivity is measured in monetary terms, firms with market power that can charge higher prices than they would be able to do in competitive markets will appear to be highly productive.[29]

Although it is difficult to measure competition, competition appears limited in most countries in Sub-Saharan Africa. One reason is that there are relatively few modern manufacturing firms in most low-income African countries, suggesting that most firms have few direct competitors. In Zambia in 2008, for example, there were only about 150 manufacturing firms with more than 50 employees.[30] Although most countries in the region have large and vibrant informal microenterprise sectors, microenterprises do not usually compete directly with large manufacturing firms.

Another reason competition is limited is that the cost of registering a business is high, making entry difficult (table 3.10). On average, it takes 45 days and costs an amount equal to 95 percent of per capita income to start a formal limited liability company in Sub-Saharan Africa. In comparison, it takes only 16 days and costs an amount equal to 8.5 percent of per capita income to start a business in the average country in Eastern Europe and Central Asia. The formal sector tends to be smaller and more

Table 3.10   Time and Cost to Start a Business in Africa and Other Regions

Region	Procedures, number	Time, days	Cost, % of income per capita	Paid-in minimum capital, % of income per capita
East Asia and Pacific	7.8	39.0	27.1	50.6
Eastern Europe and Central Asia	6.3	16.3	8.5	12.3
Latin America and the Caribbean	9.3	56.7	36.2	4.6
Middle East and North Africa	8.1	20.0	38.0	104.0
OECD	5.6	13.8	5.3	15.3
South Asia	7.1	24.6	24.5	24.1
Sub-Saharan Africa	8.9	45.2	95.4	145.7

Source: World Bank 2010a.
Note: OECD = Organisation for Economic Co-operation and Development.

concentrated in countries in which it takes a long time to start a business (Djankov and others 2002; World Bank 2003).

A final reason is that the competition from imports is also limited. Although tariffs have fallen and quotas have been reduced, some natural and policy barriers to trade remain.[31] As a result, it is expensive to import manufactured goods into most countries in the region.[32] The World Bank's *Doing Business* report notes that it takes an average of 38 days to complete all procedures to import manufactured goods into Africa. This is at least as long as in any other region (table 3.11). It is also expensive to import goods into Africa. It costs an average of about US$2,500 to import a standard container into Africa from overseas. This is far higher than in any other region: it costs less than US$1,000, on average, in East Asia.

The aggregate impact of competition on measured productivity will depend on which of the mechanisms is stronger. If lower levels of competition reduce productivity by allowing inefficient firms to stay in the market more than they increase measured productivity by raising prices, then measured productivity will be lower in countries with less competition. If the reverse is true, measured productivity will be higher in countries with less competition.

If we add a variable representing the cost of importing to the productivity regressions in the previous section, the coefficient of import costs is negative and statistically significant for the whole sample of countries (table 3.12). This suggests that the first mechanism dominates in the world as a whole.

But, if the sample is restricted to countries in Sub-Saharan Africa, labor productivity is higher in countries with high import costs. In part, this

Table 3.11   Cost of Importing and Exporting

days and US$

Region	Time to export, days	Cost to export, US$ per container	Time to import, days	Cost to import, US$ per container
East Asia and Pacific	22.7	889.8	24.1	934.7
Eastern Europe and Central Asia	26.7	1,651.7	28.1	1,845.4
Latin America and the Caribbean	18.0	1,228.3	20.1	1,487.9
Middle East and North Africa	20.4	1,048.9	24.2	1,229.3
OECD	10.9	1,058.7	11.4	1,106.3
South Asia	32.3	1,511.6	32.5	1,744.5
Sub-Saharan Africa	32.3	1,961.5	38.2	2,491.8

Source: World Bank 2010a.

Note: OECD = Organisation for Economic Co-operation and Development.

seems to be passed on to workers in the form of higher wages: workers in formal manufacturing firms in countries with high import costs appear to be paid more than workers at similar firms in countries with low import costs (table 3.13). The high productivity and high labor costs in low-income countries in Africa might therefore reflect limited competition rather than high productivity.

Conclusion

Few countries in Africa have successfully diversified into export-oriented manufacturing. Most have small, underdeveloped manufacturing sectors, and even successful countries such as Kenya mostly export to nearby countries rather than to developed economies. With a large pool of underemployed, low-skilled workers earning subsistence wages in the informal sector, this seems puzzling: many African countries should be able to enter labor-intensive export-oriented light manufacturing.

The failure to succeed in export-oriented manufacturing suggests that African firms are not competitive in international markets. This is not because productivity is low. In fact, labor productivity is higher, on average, in African countries than in other countries at similar levels of development. High productivity, however, is offset by relatively high wages. Moreover, at least relative to successful exporters in East Asia, high wages appear to more than offset the high productivity observed in the region.

The observation that wages and productivity are high leads to the two questions that are the focus of the chapter. Why do firms in Africa appear

Table 3.12 **Differences in the Median Values of Productivity Variables, by Region**

Indicator/region	Value added per worker, 2005 US$	Labor costs per worker, 2005 US$	Monthly wage, production workers, 2005 US$	Unit labor costs
Observations	26,340	29,112	27,431	27,497
Cost of importing (log, US$)	−0.310* (−1.76)	−0.206 (−1.40)	−0.320** (−2.55)	0.118 (1.26)
Per capita GDP (log)	0.776*** (7.84)	0.767*** (7.34)	0.567*** (6.57)	−0.020 (−0.30)
Region dummies[a]				
Asia and Pacific, manufacturing only	−0.430 (−1.04)	−1.082*** (−3.93)	−0.733*** (−2.75)	−0.673*** (−2.94)
Asia and Pacific, other	−0.546* (−1.79)	−0.565** (−2.12)	−0.790*** (−5.23)	−0.345*** (−2.68)
Eastern Europe and Central Asia	−0.556* (−1.79)	−0.553** (−2.12)	0.014 (0.05)	−0.087 (−0.54)
Latin America and the Caribbean	−0.191 (−0.69)	−0.251 (−1.11)	0.134 (0.58)	−0.089 (−0.63)
South Asia	−0.470*** (−2.89)	−0.190 (−1.50)	0.051 (0.36)	−0.166 (−0.73)
Africa, middle income	0.153 (0.41)	0.164 (0.39)	0.297 (1.02)	0.085 (0.40)
Constant	4.152*** (2.74)	2.628* (1.87)	2.486** (2.24)	−1.570 (−1.66)
R^2	0.27	0.35	0.52	0.15

Source: Author calculations based on Enterprise Surveys (database), World Bank, Washington, DC, http://www.enterprisesurveys.org/.

Note: See the note to table 3.4. The cost of importing is included. GDP = gross domestic product.

a. The omitted dummy is the dummy for Sub-Saharan Africa.

Significance level: * = 10 percent, ** = 5 percent, *** = 1 percent. *t*-statistics are in parentheses.

Table 3.13   Differences in the Median Values of Productivity Variables, Africa

Indicator	Value added per worker, 2005 US$	Labor costs per worker, 2005 US$	Monthly wage, production workers, 2005 US$	Unit labor costs
Observations	5,527	5,853	5,170	5,893
Cost of importing (log, US$)	0.494** (2.18)	0.502** (2.46)	0.494** (2.63)	0.006 (0.05)
Per capita GDP (log)	0.707*** (5.16)	0.739*** (4.68)	0.616*** (5.79)	0.042 (0.78)
Constant	−1.369 (−0.57)	−2.557 (−1.10)	−3.965* (−2.00)	−1.301 (−1.11)
R^2	0.34	0.40	0.46	0.03

Source: Author calculations based on data of Enterprise Surveys (database), World Bank, Washington, DC, http://www.enterprisesurveys.org/.
Note: See the note to table 3.4. The table only includes low-income and lower-middle-income countries in Sub-Saharan Africa. The cost of importing is included. GDP = gross domestic product.
Significance level: * = 10 percent, ** = 5 percent, *** = 1 percent. t-statistics are in parentheses.

productive relative to firms in other countries at similar levels of development? And, given that there are many informal firms paying subsistence wages, why are wages not forced downward, thereby allowing labor-intensive formal firms to be competitive in international markets?

One possibility is that African firms have to be productive to survive because the business environment in the region is so difficult. There are two possible reasons why this might be the case. First, taxes on formal firms are high. Because labor productivity does not take taxes into account, unproductive firms might find it harder to remain profitable in Sub-Saharan Africa than in other regions. Second, previous studies have found that other indirect costs are high (Eifert, Gelb, and Ramachandran 2005, 2008). Most productivity measures do not take the costs imposed by poor infrastructure (for example, transport and communication costs), poor governance (the bribe tax), or crime into account. These high indirect costs might make productive firms unprofitable. Both high taxes and high indirect costs might therefore force moderately productive firms out of business in Africa, making measured productivity high for the surviving firms.

Although high taxes and indirect costs might partly explain why firms are relatively productive, they do not explain why wages are high, that is, if indirect costs and taxes drive profits downward, they should also drive wages down to competitive levels.

It is plausible that other factors might also keep wages high. The high cost of food and other necessities in urban areas in Africa, in particular, might force wages upward for formal firms in the region, that is, if subsistence-level wages are higher in Africa, this might force formal firms to pay higher wages. Some of the characteristics that make indirect costs high (for example, high transportation costs, unreliable power, and limited competition) might also make food costly in Africa. Unfortunately, it is difficult to find consistent cross-country data on this issue. A detailed study that compares prices for food and other necessities across Africa, East Asia, and other regions would therefore be useful.

There is another explanation that could clarify both the high wages and the high productivity: weak competition makes profits artificially high, and firms share these high profits with workers. Although competition will improve firm performance (inefficient firms will be driven from the market), competition leads to lower prices. Because we measure productivity using revenue (price multiplied by physical output) rather than physical output, weak competition might increase rather than decrease measured productivity, that is, high measured productivity might reflect high prices rather than high physical output. This is relevant in Sub-Saharan Africa because most firms sell only in small domestic markets with weak competition. Although most countries have reduced tariffs, transportation costs and other barriers mean that firms in these markets are often well protected against international competitors.

Annex 3.1   Data Description

The Enterprise Survey data are carefully collected using a standard and rigorous approach across countries. The surveys provide representative samples of each country's private sector, collecting standard accounting measures of firm performance and information on each country's investment climate. (Table 3A.1 shows a list of countries with data.) Summaries of the broad survey results are included on the Enterprise Survey website (http://www.enterprisesurveys.org/). More detailed summaries of Enterprise Surveys have been completed for the World Bank's Investment Climate Assessment program.

The surveys have used almost identical questionnaires and identical sampling methodologies since 2006. They are conducted in two to five cities in each country and cover firms with more than five employees in the following industries (according to the International Standard Industrial Classification of All Economic Activities, revision 3.1): all manufacturing sectors (group D); construction (group F); retail and wholesale services (subgroups 52 and 51 of group G); hotels and restaurants (group H); transport, storage, and communications (group I); and computer and related activities (subgroup

Table 3A.1   List of Countries, Regions, and Number of Observations for Productivity Data

Country	Region	Observations	Country	Region	Observations
Afghanistan	SA	73	Kazakhstan	ECA	134
Albania	ECA	42	Kenya	AFR	395
Angola	AFR	215	Kosovo	ECA	84
Argentina	LAC	510	Kyrgyz Republic	ECA	73
Armenia	ECA	83	Lao PDR	EAP	143
Azerbaijan	ECA	101	Latvia	ECA	74
Belarus	ECA	62	Liberia	AFR	72
Benin	AFR	17	Lithuania	ECA	73
Bolivia	LAC	258	Macedonia, FYR	ECA	79
Bosnia and Herzegovina	ECA	84	Madagascar	AFR	148
			Malawi	AFR	55
Botswana	AFR-UMI	110	Malaysia	EAP-M	775
Brazil	LAC	992	Mali	AFR	301
Bulgaria	ECA	385	Mauritania	AFR	79
Burkina Faso	AFR	47	Mauritius	AFR-UMI	129
Burundi	AFR	102	Mexico	LAC	1,000
Cambodia	EAP	129	Micronesia, Fed. Sts.	EAP	9
Cameroon	AFR	89	Moldova	ECA	101
Cape Verde	AFR	45	Mongolia	ECA	128
Chad	AFR	21	Montenegro	ECA	22
Chile	LAC	528	Mozambique	AFR	341
China	EAP-M	10,697	Namibia	AFR-UMI	102
Colombia	LAC	582	Nepal	SA	124
Congo, Dem. Rep.	AFR	149	Nicaragua	LAC	314
Congo, Rep.	AFR	14	Niger	AFR	17
Côte d'Ivoire	AFR	137	Nigeria	AFR	2,008
Croatia	ECA	270	Panama	LAC	158
Czech Republic	ECA	60	Paraguay	LAC	198
Ecuador	LAC	286	Peru	LAC	303
El Salvador	LAC	410	Philippines	EAP-M	689
Eritrea	AFR	53	Poland	ECA	88
Estonia	ECA	80	Romania	ECA	91
Gabon	AFR-UMI	24	Russian Federation	ECA	391
Gambia, The	AFR	33	Rwanda	AFR	58
Georgia	ECA	76	Samoa	EAP	17
Ghana	AFR	292	Senegal	AFR	259
Guatemala	LAC	297	Serbia	ECA	126
Guinea	AFR	134	Sierra Leone	AFR	43
Guinea-Bissau	AFR	50	Slovak Republic	ECA	54
Honduras	LAC	233	Slovenia	ECA	85
Hungary	ECA	92	South Africa	AFR-UMI	678
Indonesia	EAP-M	857	Swaziland	AFR	68

(continued next page)

Table 3A.1   *(continued)*

Country	Region	Observations	Country	Region	Observations
Tajikistan	ECA	91	Ukraine	ECA	279
Tanzania	AFR	271	Uruguay	LAC	219
Thailand	EAP-M	1,385	Uzbekistan	ECA	118
Timor-Leste	EAP	38	Vanuatu	EAP	8
Togo	AFR	13	Venezuela, RB	LAC	0
Turkey	ECA	542	Vietnam	EAP-M	670
Uganda	AFR	307	Zambia	AFR	304

Source: Author calculations based on data of Enterprise Surveys (database), World Bank, Washington, DC, http://www.enterprisesurveys.org/.
Note: Number of observations are for labor productivity calculations. Other productivity measures may have slightly more or slightly fewer observations. AFR = Africa (low income and lower-middle income). AFR-UMI = Africa (upper-middle income). EAP = East Asia and Pacific (nonmanufacturing). EAP-M = East Asia and Pacific (manufacturing). ECA = (Eastern) Europe and Central Asia. LAC = Latin America and the Caribbean. SA = South Asia.

72 of group K). The surveys are delivered to the managing directors or their direct representatives. Accountants or human resource managers sometimes provide information on company accounts and labor practices.

The samples are stratified random samples: stratified by industry, location, and, if information is available, by firm size. Sample sizes are set within each stratum to allow certain variables to be calculated to specified levels of precision, and firms are randomly selected from each group. Weights are constructed to take account of the varying probabilities of selection between strata.

The sampling frames are constructed from lists of registered enterprises in each country. Lists of firms are obtained from government agencies in each country, usually the bureaus of statistics, business registrars, or ministries of trade and industry. These lists are then verified and updated to obtain complete and up-to-date sampling frames. The survey methodology is described in more detail and the survey data are available for download on the World Bank Enterprise Surveys website (http://www.enterprisesurveys.org/).

Although Enterprise Surveys were conducted before 2006, we restrict the analysis to data collected after 2006. We do this because there was considerable heterogeneity across countries and regions in terms of sectors covered, questionnaire format, coverage of microenterprises with fewer than five employees, and sampling methodology before 2006. Moreover, the Enterprise Surveys conducted before 2006 were not generally representative of the formal economies in this region, and weights are not available to allow for the computation of population averages.

The data have some limitations. One concern is that firm managers might not report accurate data to interviewers. One specific problem might be that firm managers underreport their sales because they are concerned about the tax authorities using the data to target them, that is, although managers are assured that the data are confidential, they might underreport because of a sense of concern (better safe than sorry). Meanwhile, other pressures might lead them to overreport performance: managers are often concerned about their competitors gaining information about their performance. Recent studies using Enterprise Survey data for Nigeria suggest that managers who appear deceptive appear to over report, not underreport, labor productivity.[33]

Annex 3.2   Measures of Firm Performance

The chapter focuses on several measures of firm productivity. These are calculated in a uniform way across all countries on which Enterprise Survey data are available for 2006–09. All values are converted into 2005 U.S. dollars. For firm surveys conducted in 2007 and 2008 (that is, with accounting data from 2006 and 2007), data are deflated to 2005 values in local currency using the GDP deflator. The values in 2005 local currency are then converted into U.S. dollars using the 2005 exchange rates.

The measures of firm performance are as follows:

Labor productivity. Value added per worker is the basic measure of labor productivity used in this chapter. It is the value of the goods and services that the firm produces, less the cost of the raw materials (such as iron or wood) and intermediate inputs (such as engine parts or textiles) used to produce the output, divided by the number of full-time workers in the firm.[34] Firms that produce more output with fewer raw materials and fewer workers have higher labor productivity.

Output is measured in dollars, not in physical units.

Differences in labor productivity can be the result of differences in technology, organizational structure, worker education or skills, management ability, or capital use. Because labor productivity does not take capital use (that is, machinery and equipment) into account, it will generally be higher in firms that use capital in place of labor (that is, firms that are capital intensive).

Labor costs per worker. The cost of labor is the cost of wages, salaries, bonuses, other benefits, and social payments for workers at the firm, divided by the number of workers. The data are taken from firm accounts. They include the wages and salaries paid to all workers and managers, not merely to production workers.

Average monthly wage for production workers. The average monthly wage for production workers generally does not come from company accounts. Instead, it reflects the wages the manager reports paying to a typical production worker. Although it should provide information similar to the labor costs per worker, it provides a useful robustness check because it does not come from the same source (that is, it is not from company accounts).

Unit labor costs. This measure represents labor costs as a percentage of value added. Although it is an approximation of true unit labor costs (that is, it measures output in dollars rather than as a physical measure of production), it can be calculated using information from the Enterprise Surveys. It is a better measure of labor costs than labor cost per worker in that it takes differences in productivity into account in assessing labor costs. Unit labor costs are higher if higher labor costs are not fully reflected in higher productivity. If unit labor costs are higher (that is, if labor costs are higher compared with productivity), all else being equal, firms will face more difficulties in competing on international markets than if these costs are lower. Although unit labor costs are not the only factor that affects competitiveness (for example, they do not take the cost of capital or capital intensity into account), they are a better measure of competitiveness than labor costs alone.

Notes

1. Although high on average, wages are low in some countries in the region. For example, in a selection of light manufacturing sectors, Dinh and others (2012, table 1.1) show that wages in Ethiopia were low in 2010 (US$34–US$53 per month). Although Ethiopia was not included in the most recent set of Enterprise Surveys, evidence from the 2002 Ethiopia survey suggests that wages were low at that time. Per worker labor costs were about US$489 per year, lower than in any of the 35 other African economies in the first round of surveys with the exception of Guinea. In comparison, Dinh and others (2012, table 1.1) show that wages for unskilled workers were US$197–US$278 per month in China, US$80–US$130 in Tanzania, US$78–US$131 in Vietnam, and US$157–US$208 in Zambia. It is important to note, however, that per capita income is considerably higher in China and Vietnam than in the three African countries. In purchasing power parity–adjusted terms, per capita GDP was about US$6,800 in China and US$2,900 in Vietnam compared with between US$900 and US$1,400 in the three African countries.

2. Clarke, Shah, and Pearson (2010) note that, of the 4,800 MSMEs in the Zambia business survey, only 15 exported, and only 2 exported outside the subregion. Even among formal manufacturing enterprises (that is, enterprises

larger than microenterprises), studies have found that large enterprises are more likely to export. Clerides, Lach, and Tybout (1998) find evidence consistent with this for Colombia, Mexico, and Morocco. Similarly, Grenier, McKay, and Morrissey (1999) find that, in Tanzania, large enterprises export more than smaller enterprises. Using data from several countries in Sub-Saharan Africa from the mid-1990s, Bigsten and others (2004) and Söderbom and Teal (2003) find similar results, and Clarke (2009) finds similar results using data from the earlier round of Enterprise Surveys for Ethiopia, Kenya, Mali, Mozambique, Senegal, Tanzania, Uganda, and Zambia.

3. Although Ethiopia appears to be an exception to this rule (Germany, Italy, and the United Kingdom are the three most important export destinations for Ethiopian enterprises), few Ethiopian enterprises export. Over half of Ethiopian exporters export to the country's main industrial market (Italy), but this represents less than 4 percent of Ethiopian enterprises. In contrast, although only about 8 percent of Kenyan exporters export to their main industrial market (the United Kingdom), this represents over 4 percent of Kenyan enterprises because 58 percent of Kenyan enterprises export. The poor performance of Ethiopian exporters in regional markets probably reflects regional difficulties that have prevented Ethiopian enterprises from developing export partnerships with firms in neighboring countries (for example, in Eritrea, Somalia, and Sudan).

4. All monetary values in this section are presented in 2005 U.S. dollars. See annex 3.2 for a description.

5. Annex 3.2 describes in greater detail the productivity measures discussed in this section.

6. Moreover, it is important to note that the two countries in which surveys have been conducted in South Asia (Afghanistan and Nepal) are not representative of the region.

7. The analysis focuses on median measures of firm performance because, relative to means, medians are less sensitive to outliers. For brevity, the term median firm is used to refer to the median firm on each measure of firm performance. For example, in this section, median firm refers to the median firm in the country in terms of labor productivity.

8. Previous studies using enterprise-level data on Sub-Saharan Africa have found that firms are better performing if managers are more highly educated (Biggs, Ramachandran, and Shah 1998).

9. See, for example, Eifert, Gelb, and Ramachandran (2008), who show that indirect costs related to infrastructure and services account for a relatively high share of firm costs in poor African countries and pose a competitive burden on African firms.

10. In 2012, the average country in Sub-Saharan Africa ranked 137th in the *Doing Business* rankings, worse than any other region (World Bank 2011).

11. See, for example, Acemoglu, Johnson, and Robinson (2001).

12. See, for example, Svensson (2005) on corruption. Many papers have shown the strong link between corruption and other measures of institutional quality. See, for instance, Langbein and Knack (2010).

13. These countries have been chosen because manufactured goods accounted there for over 20 percent of output between 2005 and 2009 (see table 3.1).

14. Our measures differ from standard measures of unit labor costs in that we use value added rather than measures of physical output.

15. Annex 3.2 describes the performance measures: labor productivity, per worker labor costs, average wages for production workers, and unit labor costs.

16. The coefficients on the region dummy variables can be transformed into percentages using the following formula: % Difference $= 100 \int (e^{\gamma^l} - 1)$; see Hardy (1993).

17. The null hypothesis that the coefficient is 1 cannot be rejected at conventional significance levels for labor productivity ($p = .15$) and cannot be rejected at a 5 percent level for labor costs ($p = .08$). In contrast, the null hypothesis can be rejected for average monthly wages for production workers.

18. Labor productivity excludes the cost of capital. Other standard measures of productivity such as total factor productivity and technical efficiency take the cost of capital into account.

19. Clarke (2011a) shows that it is difficult to compare these costs with costs shown in company accounts because many managers overestimate these other costs.

20. Although costs are higher in South Asia, the countries on which data are available in that region (Afghanistan, Bangladesh, Bhutan, and Nepal) might not be representative.

21. Although it is difficult to compare the size of the informal sector across countries because of difficulties associated with both definitions and measurement, most evidence suggests that informality is greater in Africa than in other regions. Schneider (2005) and Schneider and Klinglmair (2004) estimate that the informal sector accounts for about 41 percent of GDP in the 24 African countries on which data were available. This is similar to Latin America, but higher than in most other regions. As in most regions, informality is higher in low-income countries. See, for example, World Bank (2010b), figure 1.5.

22. As discussed in de Mel, McKenzie, and Woodruff (2009), wages and productivity are likely to be understated in the informal sector for several reasons. Firms often do not keep detailed accounts and might underreport profits either intentionally, if they are concerned about the tax authorities getting access to the data, or unintentionally (that is, because of recall errors). In practice, however, taxes might affect self-reported data even for formal firms in the Enterprise

Surveys. As noted in Clarke (2011c), close to two-thirds of formal sector firms do not report productivity data directly from their written accounts.

23. This excludes workers who are not paid in cash and excludes in-kind payments. The exclusion of in-kind payments might partially explain the exceedingly low wages in the agricultural sector.

24. See, for example, Pritchett (2001) for a discussion of education.

25. Eifert, Gelb, and Ramachandran (2008) show that indirect costs such as those related to poor infrastructure, crime, and corruption are high in Sub-Saharan Africa.

26. Using data from informal enterprises in Zambia, Clarke (2011b) shows that formal microenterprises pay more in bribes than informal enterprises. The difference appears to arise, at least in part, because formal microenterprises demand more government services than informal enterprises.

27. See, for example, Conway and Shah (2010).

28. See, for example, Pakes (2008). A related concern is that exchange rates can also affect measured productivity. For cross-country comparisons, value added has to be denominated in a common currency (for example, U.S. dollars, as in this chapter). Because sales and intermediate inputs are denominated in local currency in the Enterprise Surveys, cross-country comparisons of productivity are vulnerable to exchange rate fluctuations. If the exchange rate is overvalued relative to the long-run equilibrium, then productivity might look artificially low.

29. See, for example, the discussion by Levinsohn (2008) on the Escribano–Guasch methodology (Escribano and Guasch 2005; Escribano and others 2005, 2008).

30. The 2009 Investment Climate Assessment was based on a survey of formal enterprises of five or more employees in Kitwe, Livingstone, Lusaka, and Ndola. The list of enterprises, which was provided by the Central Statistical Office, yielded a final list of only 3,336 enterprises in manufacturing and services with over five employees in these cities. Only 449 of these enterprises had over 50 employees. Most of these, however, were in retail trade and other services. Only about 156 of these 449 enterprises were in manufacturing. At the time of the last census (2000), these cities accounted for about 20 percent of the total national population and probably account for a greater share of the number of large enterprises in the country. (For more details, see World Bank 2009b, 2009c.)

31. Most countries in the region took steps toward liberalizing trade by reducing tariffs and quotas during the 1990s and 2000s. According to data of the World Bank, the average weighted tariff in the manufacturing sector fell from about 15–18 percent at the beginning of the 1990s to about 8 percent by 2008 (World Development Indicators [database], World Bank, Washington, DC [accessed 2010], http://data.worldbank.org/data-catalog/world-development-indicators).

32. Several studies have noted that high transportation costs discourage firms in Africa from exporting. Clarke (2009), Iwanow and Kirkpatrick (2009), and Yoshino (2008) show that problems with trade regulation and customs administration make exporting difficult for firms in Africa. Djankov, Freund, and Pham (2010) show that increasing the days required to export by one day has an impact on trade equivalent to an addition of 70 kilometers in distance in a gravity model of trade.

33. Azfar and Murrell (2009) develop a methodology using random response questions to identify reticent respondents who appear to be evasive or deceitful. They show that reticent respondents in Romania appear to underreport bribe transactions. Clausen, Kraay, and Murrell (2010) repeat this analysis for firms in Nigeria and show similar results with respect to direct questions on corruption. They also show that reticent managers appear to overreport that they are certified by the International Organization for Standardization. They suggest that this is because reticent managers appear to exaggerate their firm's performance. Using the same data as Clausen, Kraay, and Murrell (2010), Clarke (2011c) shows that reticent managers appear to overreport how productive and capital intensive their firms are.

34. The number of workers is the number of permanent and temporary full-time workers. Data on part-time workers are not collected in most countries outside Sub-Saharan Africa, and, so, these workers are omitted for reasons of comparability. In practice, for countries with data on part-time workers, including these workers does not have a large effect on relative rankings.

References

Acemoglu, Daron, Simon Johnson, and James A. Robinson. 2001. "The Colonial Origins of Comparative Development: An Empirical Investigation." *American Economic Review* 91 (5): 1369–401.

Azfar, Omar, and Peter Murrell. 2009. "Identifying Reticent Respondents: Assessing the Quality of Survey Data on Corruption and Values." *Economic Development and Cultural Change* 57 (2): 387–411.

Biggs, Tyler, Vijaya Ramachandran, and Manju Kedia Shah. 1998. "The Determinants of Enterprise Growth in Sub-Saharan Africa: Evidence from the Regional Program on Enterprise Development." Regional Program for Enterprise Development Discussion Paper 103, World Bank, Washington, DC.

Bigsten, Arne, Paul Collier, Stefan Dercon, Marcel Fafchamps, Bernard Gauthier, Jan Willem Gunning, Abena Oduro, Remco Oostendorp, Catherine Pattillo, Mans Söderbom, Francis Teal, and Albert Zeufeck. 2004. "Do African Manufacturing Firms Learn from Exporting?" *Journal of Development Studies* 40 (3): 115–41.

Clarke, George R. G. 2009. "Beyond Tariffs and Quotas: Why Do African Manufacturers Not Export More?" *Emerging Markets Finance and Trade* 45 (2): 44–64.

———. 2011a. "How Petty Is Petty Corruption? Evidence from Firm Surveys in Africa." *World Development* 39 (7): 1122–32.

———. 2011b. "Firm Registration and Bribes: Results from a Microenterprise Survey in Africa." MPRA Paper 31857, Munich Personal RePEc Archive, Munich. http://mpra.ub.uni-muenchen.de/31857/1/MPRA_paper_31857.pdf.

———. 2011c. "Lying about Firm Performance: Evidence from a Firm Survey in Nigeria." Texas A&M International University, Laredo, TX. http://papers.ssrn.com/sol3/papers.cfm?abstract_id=1971575; MPRA Paper 35382, Munich Personal RePEc Archive, Munich. http://mpra.ub.uni-muenchen.de/35382/1/MPRA_paper_35382.pdf.

Clarke, George R. G., Juliet Munro, Roland V. Pearson Jr., Manju Kedia Shah, and Marie Sheppard. 2010. *The Profile and Productivity of Zambian Businesses.* Lusaka, Zambia: World Bank.

Clarke, George R. G., Manju Kedia Shah, and Roland V. Pearson, Jr. 2010. *The Business Landscape for MSMEs and Large Enterprises in Zambia.* Washington, DC: World Bank.

Clausen, Bianca, Aart Kraay, and Peter Murrell. 2010. "Does Respondent Reticence Affect the Results of Corruption Surveys? Evidence from the World Bank Enterprise Survey for Nigeria." Policy Research Working Paper 5415, World Bank, Washington, DC. http://go.worldbank.org/J10YIDC0A0.

Clerides, Sofronis K., Saul Lach, and James R. Tybout. 1998. "Is Learning by Exporting Important? Micro-Dynamic Evidence from Colombia, Mexico, and Morocco." *Quarterly Journal of Economics* 113 (3): 903–47.

Collier, Paul. 1998. "Globalization: Implications for Africa." In *Trade Reform and Regional Integration in Africa*, ed. Zubair Iqbal and Moshin S. Khan, 147–81. Washington, DC: International Monetary Fund.

Conway, Patrick, and Manju Kedia Shah. 2010. *Who's Productive in Zambia's Private Sector.* Lusaka, Zambia: World Bank.

de Mel, Suresh, David J. McKenzie, and Christopher Woodruff. 2009. "Measuring Microenterprise Profits: Must We Ask How the Sausage Is Made?" *Journal of Development Economics* 88 (1): 19–31.

Dinh, Hinh T., Vincent Palmade, Vandana Chandra, and Frances Cossar. 2012. *Light Manufacturing in Africa: Targeted Policies to Enhance Private Investment and Create Jobs.* Washington, DC: World Bank. http://elibrary.worldbank.org/content/book/9780821389614.

Djankov, Simeon, Caroline Freund, and Cong S. Pham. 2010. "Trading on Time." *Review of Economics and Statistics* 92 (1): 166–73.

Djankov, Simeon, Rafael La Porta, Florencio López-de-Silanes, and Andrei Shleifer. 2002. "The Regulation of Entry." *Quarterly Journal of Economics* 117 (1): 1–37.

Eifert, Benn, Alan Gelb, and Vijaya Ramachandran. 2005. "Business Environment and Comparative Advantage in Africa: Evidence from the Investment Climate Data." CDG Working Paper 56, Center for Global Development, World Bank, Washington, DC.

————. 2008. "The Cost of Doing Business in Africa: Evidence From Enterprise Survey Data." *World Development* 36 (9): 1531–46.

Escribano, Alvaro, and J. Luis Guasch. 2005. "Assessing the Impact of the Investment Climate on Productivity Using Firm-Level Data: Methodology and the Cases of Guatemala, Honduras, and Nicaragua." Policy Research Working Paper 3621, World Bank, Washington, DC. http://go.worldbank.org/F4W5VBGDR0.

Escribano, Alvaro, J. Luis Guasch, Jorge Pena, and Manuel de Orte. 2005. *Investment Climate Assessment on Productivity and Wages: Analysis Based on Firm Level Data from Selected South East Asian Countries*. Washington, DC: World Bank. http://www.bnm.gov.my/microsites/rcicc/papers/s1.escribano.pdf.

————. 2008. *Investment Climate Assessment Based on Demean Olley and Pakes Decompositions: Methodology and Application to Turkey's Investment Climate Survey*. Madrid: Universidad Carlos III de Madrid.

Falco, Paolo, Andrew Kerr, Neil Rankin, Justin Sandefur, and Francis Teal. 2010. "The Returns to Formality and Informality in Urban Africa." CSAE Working Paper 2010–03, Centre for the Study of African Economies, Oxford University, Oxford.

Grenier, Louise, Andrew McKay, and Oliver Morrissey. 1999. "Exporting, Ownership, and Confidence in Tanzanian Enterprises." *World Economy* 22 (7): 995–1011.

Hardy, Melissa A. 1993. *Regression with Dummy Variables*. Newbury Park, CA: Sage Publishing.

Hicks, J. R. 1935. "Annual Survey of Economic Theory: The Theory of Monopoly." *Econometrica* 3 (1): 1–20.

Iwanow, Tomasz, and Colin Kirkpatrick. 2009. "Trade Facilitation and Manufactured Exports: Is Africa Different?" *World Development* 37 (6): 1039–50.

Langbein, Laura, and Stephen Knack. 2010. "The Worldwide Governance Indicators: Six, One, or None?" *Journal of Development Studies* 46 (2): 350–70.

Levinsohn, James. 2008. *Comments on Methodology Used by Escribano, Guasch, and Co-Authors in Analyzing World Bank Investment Climate Surveys*. Ann Arbor, MI: University of Michigan.

Maloney, William F. 1999. "Does Informality Imply Segmentation in Urban Labor Markets? Evidence from Sectoral Transitions in Mexico." *World Bank Economic Review* 13 (2): 275–302.

————. 2004. "Informality Revisited." *World Development* 32 (7): 1159–78.

Pakes, Ariel. 2008. "Theory and Empirical Work on Imperfectly Competitive Markets." NBER Working Paper 14117, National Bureau of Economic Research, Cambridge MA. http://www.nber.org/papers/w14117.

Pritchett, Lant. 2001. "Where Has All the Education Gone?" *World Bank Economic Review* 15 (3): 367–91.

Schneider, Friedrich. 2005. "Shadow Economies around the World: What Do We Really Know?" *European Journal of Political Economy* 21 (3): 598–642.

Schneider, Friedrich, and Robert Klinglmair. 2004. "Shadow Economies around the World: What Do We Know?" Discussion Paper 1043, Institute for the Study of Labor, Bonn.

Söderbom, Mans, and Francis Teal. 2003. "Are Manufacturing Exports the Key to Economic Success in Africa?" *Journal of African Economies* 12 (1): 1–29.

Svensson, Jakob. 2005. "Eight Questions about Corruption." *Journal of Economic Perspectives* 19 (3): 19–42.

World Bank. 2003. *Doing Business in 2004: Understanding Regulations.* Washington, DC: World Bank; New York: Oxford University Press. http://www.doingbusiness .org/reports/global-reports/doing-business-2004.

————. 2009a. *Doing Business 2010: Reforming through Difficult Times.* Washington, DC: World Bank; New York: Palgrave MacMillan. http://www.doingbusiness .org/reports/global-reports/doing-business-2010.

————. 2009b. "An Assessment of the Investment Climate in Zambia." Regional Program on Enterprise Development, Africa Private Sector Group, World Bank, Washington, DC.

————. 2009c. *Enterprise Survey (Productivity and Investment Climate Survey) in Zambia: Sample Survey Design.* Washington, DC: World Bank.

————. 2010a. *Doing Business 2011: Making a Difference for Entrepreneurs.* Washington, DC: World Bank. http://www.doingbusiness.org/reports/global-reports/doing-business-2011/.

————. 2010b. *Cape Verde: Initial Assessment of the Formal Labor Market.* Report 58551-CV, Washington, DC: World Bank. http://www-wds.worldbank.org/external/default/WDSContentServer/WDSP/IB/2011/05/12/000333037_2011 0512234257/Rendered/PDF/58551OESW0P11200Market0002010012017.pdf.

————. 2011. *Doing Business 2012: Doing Business in a More Transparent World.* Washington, DC: World Bank. http://www.doingbusiness.org/reports/global-reports/doing-business-2012.

Yoshino, Yutaka. 2008. "Domestic Constraints, Firm Characteristics, and Geographical Diversification of Firm-Level Manufacturing Exports in Africa." Policy Research Working Paper 4575, World Bank, Washington, DC.

CHAPTER 4

The Binding Constraint on the Growth of Firms in Developing Countries

Hinh T. Dinh, Dimitris A. Mavridis, and Hoa B. Nguyen

Introduction

Private sector growth remains one of the main challenges facing developing countries in their quest for development and poverty reduction. Extensive evidence shows that a favorable business environment helps promote the growth of firms. As shown in recent research, however, firms in developing countries, especially in Africa, face a tougher business environment than their counterparts in the developed world.

Our aim in this chapter is twofold. First, we seek to go beyond the traditional menu of constraints on firm growth to find out which of these constraints is the most binding. As the growth diagnostics approach points out, developing countries have scarce resources and therefore need to focus on removing the most binding constraint. Second, we examine the effects of the most binding constraint on firm growth not only across countries, but also according to firm characteristics.

We first explore the relationship between the business environment and firm growth as measured by employment growth. Among 15 components of the business environment, we identify the most binding constraint using both subjective and objective measures. Our focus is on the most binding constraints for existing firms and, more specifically, the binding constraint that matters the most for firm growth. The methodology follows two steps. The first is to find out which constraints are statistically significant among all regressions after we control for firm characteristics and country fixed effects. The second is to identify the most binding constraint. We find that, besides informal sector competition, access to finance is the obstacle that matters the most for growth. This result is robust for all regions and all sectors.

Our analysis contributes to the existing literature in several ways. First, using subjective measures and a large sample containing more than 39,000 firms across 98 countries, we identify the most binding constraint on firms, then evaluate the importance of this constraint to firm growth using objective measures and controlling for firm characteristics. The sample comes from World Bank Enterprise Surveys conducted in 2006–10 in mostly emerging and developing countries. The surveys provide both subjective data on perceived obstacles and objective measures of many constraints.

Second, we investigate the effect of financial access variables on firm growth by using firm-level regressions across countries while controlling for the effects of different firm sizes, firm ages, sectors, and regions. Our results show that access to finance in the form of a loan, sales credit, or external finance helps microfirms the most. This finding holds not only for the full sample, but also for different regions. Sales credit is important only to micro and small firms, probably because it substitutes for bank loans. Having a loan or overdraft facility and receiving external finance for investment help growth among firms of all sizes across regions.

Third, we find clear evidence that a low level of financial sector development affects the firm size distribution and therefore contributes to the phenomenon of the missing middle in developing countries. Firm size distribution is skewed toward small and medium firms and, more so in Africa, among firms that are credit constrained and among firms that perceive access to finance as an obstacle. Our analysis shows that firm size and age are significantly correlated with firm growth. Distinguishing across different types of ownership, we find that firms tend to enjoy greater growth if they are exporters, are part of entities with multiple establishments, are foreign owned, or are privately owned.

The chapter begins with the literature review, followed by an overview of the data and the sample. The section then examines the most binding constraint in the business environment, followed by a section on the effect of access to finance on employment growth in the full sample and by region. The ensuing sections look at determinants of access to finance and differences in the effect of financial access variables on employment growth. The penultimate section covers the relationship between firm size and financial constraints before the conclusions in the final section.

Literature Review

Since the World Bank Enterprise Surveys became available, there has been an explosion of studies on the effect of business environments on development at the firm level.[1] Under "business environment," the literature covers anything affecting a firm's daily operations, its decisions to invest, and the risks it faces. Xu (2011) notes that the business environment can be broadly divided into three categories: the macroeconomic framework (taxes, inflation, the exchange rate regime), the governance facing the firm (Are Institutions stable?, Is there corruption?, Are licenses and permits expensive to obtain?), and the infrastructure at a firm's disposal (How reliable and easy to use are the electricity, water, transportation, and telecommunications networks?).

Effect of the Business Environment on Firm Growth

Using the World Bank Enterprise Surveys, the studies we review below find that different components of the business environment matter for firm development. For example, the relative ease of access to finance, the importance of corruption, or the transparency in the enforcement of property rights have all been found to play a major role in facilitating firm growth (Ayyagari, Demirgüç-Kunt, and Maksimovic 2006; Batra, Kaufmann, and Stone 2003). Some papers have narrowed their focus to particular countries or to a small group of countries to try to avoid the multicollinearity present between different parts of the business environment and the country controls. For example, Dollar, Hallward-Driemeier, and Mengistae (2005) study firm growth in Bangladesh, China, India, and Pakistan; Bigsten and Söderbom (2006), in Africa. Individual country-level studies also abound.[2]

Several papers have emphasized that financing obstacles and failing financial markets are a main culprit in preventing firms from expanding. A corollary idea is that stable and trustworthy legal institutions might help in fostering the development of financial markets, thus supporting firms in their growth. Several papers have looked for a relationship among firm growth, access to finance, and the reliability of legal enforcement. Using firm-level subjective data on the ease of access to credit, Demirgüç-Kunt and Maksimovic (1998) provide evidence on the importance of the financial system and legal enforcement for firm growth. Similarly, Rajan and Zingales (1998) present supporting evidence on the role of external finance for more rapid growth in countries with more well developed financial systems. Galindo and Micco (2007) find that credit shrinks more severely in the face of external shocks in countries with weaker creditor protections. While these papers provide valuable insights on the effect of different dimensions of the business environment on firm growth, they do not look into how other constraints might also relate to the failure of financial markets, nor do they show that access to finance is the most binding constraint for firms.

Labor and entry regulations have also been extensively studied as a determinant of firm growth. By influencing the cost of hiring and firing, labor regulations affect the matching process between firms and employees and, as a corollary, reduce competition and make it more difficult for firms to expand.[3] Testing whether labor flexibility (the ease with which workers may be fired) correlates with firm performance, Hallward-Driemeier, Wallsten, and Xu (2006) find that, in Chinese cities and industries with more nonpermanent workers, firms report better performance. Other papers investigate the impact of employment regulations and business licensing on firm creation and growth. Klapper, Laeven, and Rajan (2004) find that the regulation of entry achieves its goal: it reduces entry, thus reducing firm creation. Djankov and others (2002) find that the regulation of entry pushes firms into the informal sector (where they cannot expand). It also reduces the quality of the goods produced and is associated with greater corruption.

The relationship between the business environment and firm growth has been studied not only across countries, but also across regions and according to firm characteristics within countries: by firm size, age, sector, and ownership type. In examining this relationship, the literature has focused largely on the effect of access to finance by firm type, particularly firm size. Generally, the finding is that smaller firms are more financially constrained and are the ones that would benefit most from improved access to finance. For example, Love and Mylenko (2003) and Borensztein, Levy Yeyati, and Panizza (2006) find that smaller firms would grow more quickly if they were not credit constrained. Using the World Business Environment Survey, Beck, Demirgüç-Kunt, and Maksimovic (2005) include measures of corruption and property rights and, based on firms' perceptions of potential constraints, find small firms benefiting the most from greater financial and institutional development.

Aterido and Hallward-Driemeier (2010) and Aterido, Hallward-Driemeier, and Pagés (2007, 2009) analyze the effect of several aspects of the business environment—access to finance, corruption, and regulations—on the growth of firms. Their findings show that the business environment affects small, medium, and large firms differently. The reason is that small firms and large firms are exposed to different sets of constraints. Access to electricity, for example, has heterogeneous effects: small and medium firms are often affected by power cuts, while large and microfirms tend not to be. The main reason is that microfirms use tools that are less energy intensive, while large firms are more likely to secure their own energy supplies (Gelb and others 2007). Thus, infrastructure, such as the electricity grid, affects the growth rate of small and medium firms directly, but has only an indirect effect on the growth rate of micro and large firms. Microfirms are much more credit constrained and must rely less on external funds to finance investment. Improving access to finance might boost the entry rate and the growth of small firms, perhaps at the expense of larger incumbents.

According to Dollar, Hallward-Driemeier, and Mengistae (2005), improving the business environment is an important complement to trade policies aimed at increasing international trade integration. Factors such as short customs clearance times, good infrastructure, and the availability of financial services have a significant impact on the probability of a firm's exporting and receiving foreign investment. Freund and Rocha (2010) provide more evidence of the link between the business environment and international trade. Using data from Africa, they find that, even though poor trade infrastructure is one of the main obstacles to trade, most of the burden is caused by red tape: bureaucratic customs practices that increase the time and cost of trade.

Gelb and others (2007) use subjective data on the business environment in 26 African countries to show that perceived constraints are not always independent of scale. Complaints about access to finance and land are more common among small firms, while complaints about infrastructure and corruption are more evenly distributed. They also find that a country's level of development strongly determines which constraints are present (country fixed effects are more important than within-country variations). This finding is shared by the World Economic Forum's *The Africa Competitiveness Report 2009*, which shows that, as a country's income rises, its set of constraints changes.

All these studies share a common result: business environment variables affect firm growth in the expected direction. The results are heterogeneous by firm size, and they are robust.

Financial Development and Firm Size Distribution

A common finding in the literature is that firm size distribution in developing countries is skewed toward small and medium firms. Small firms
are often credit constrained and cannot borrow to engage in productive
investments, which limits their growth and can prolong the skewness. If
lack of access to finance prevents small firms from growing, the allocation
of resources will be distorted. Capital and labor will not be able to flow
to where they are most productive, and growth will suffer.

Cooley and Quadrini (2001) and Cabral and Mata (2003) present different models of firm growth, showing that capital constraints can cause
a skewness in firm size distribution. Their prediction is verified empiri-
cally. Cabral and Mata (2003) find that the size distribution of firms is
skewed toward small firms and that the skewness decreases with firm age.
Many subsequent papers confirm the skewness of firm size distribution,
such as Angelini and Generale (2008), Beck, Demirgüç-Kunt, and
Maksimovic (2005), and Desai, Gompers, and Lerner (2003).

Desai, Gompers, and Lerner (2003) find that, in countries with less
well developed capital markets, firm size distribution is significantly more
skewed. They also find that a better legal environment favors entry (more
small firms will enter), while the growth of small firms reduces the skewness. Angelini and Generale (2008) and Beck, Demirgüç-Kunt, and
Maksimovic (2005) find that capital-constrained firms grow more slowly
than their counterparts.

The Growth Diagnostics Approach

The growth diagnostics approach proposed by Hausmann, Rodrik, and
Velasco (2005) (hereafter, the HRV approach) provides a theoretical
framework for identifying the most binding constraints on economic
growth in general. This methodology recognizes that constraints on the
growth of a developing economy are numerous and that previous
approaches to reforms and growth are either unrealistic (as with wholesale reform that attempts to eliminate all obstacles at the same time) or
wrong (by seeking to carry out as many reforms as possible, the current
prevailing approach goes against the principle of second best).

The HRV approach is based on the theory of second best (Lipsey and
Lancaster 1956). According to this theory, if there are many distortions in

an economy, fixing any one distortion would not necessarily lead to a better Pareto outcome. The HRV approach shows that, if there are many distortions, whether removing one growth constraint will have a positive effect on growth depends on the interaction effects and the coefficients of the other constraints. In the face of uncertainty about these effects, Hausmann, Rodrik, and Velasco (2005) recommend a practical approach based on removing the most binding constraint, which they define as the constraint with the largest effect in a context in which issues of second-best effects are likely to be minimal.

This Study's Contribution to the Literature

In this chapter, based on the HRV approach, we investigate the most binding constraint on the growth of firms, which we define as the constraint with the largest estimated coefficient across all models and across regions and sectors. Compared with studies using the World Business Environment Survey data set, our chapter uses a much larger sample. And, while other studies use subjective firm responses as measures of the business environment at the firm level, we also include objective measures, in part to deal with endogeneity and in part to avoid measurement errors of perception at the country level.

In exploring the relationship between the business environment and firm growth, we go beyond distinguishing effects by firm size. We look closely at the effect of financial access variables—loan, credit constraint, sales credit, and external investment finance—on firm growth by firm size and age in different sectors and regions. We combine multiple financial access variables in a single regression, in addition to evaluating the effect of each variable on employment growth controlled for firm size, age, and other characteristics. This allows an understanding of the impact of each dimension of finance on firm growth as firm characteristics change.

Moreover, our chapter emphasizes the element of the business environment that matters most for firms, especially small firms. And it analyzes the effect of different financial access variables on the firm size distribution across regions and sectors.

Data

In this chapter, we use a newly available firm-level data set from the World Bank Enterprise Surveys. The surveys cover more than 100,000 firms across more than 120 economies and six regions during 2006–10. We use a sample of 39,538 firms in 98 countries on which data are complete. The unit in the sample is the establishment; one firm may have more than one establishment. For simplicity, we use the term *firms* throughout the chapter, though the analysis is based on establishment data.

Our outcome variable of interest is employment growth, measured by the number of permanent employees. Our policy interest is in achieving an understanding of the determinants that are important to the long-term business operation and employment growth of firms.[4] Because there are no data on temporary employees collected three fiscal years before the survey fiscal year, we focus on permanent full-time employees rather than general full-time employees.

Firm growth rate is calculated as the log difference between the current number of employees and the number of employees three fiscal years before the survey fiscal year. The formula for employment growth is as follows:

$$EG_{it} = [(\ln S_{it} - \ln S_{i,t-3})/3] \qquad (4.1)$$

where S_{it} is firm size, and EG_{it} is employment growth for firm i at time t.[5] The description and summary statistics for the employment growth variable are reported in table 4.1.

World Bank Enterprise Surveys are conducted to provide information on different aspects of the business environment and the performance of firms. The core questionnaire, which contains survey questions answered by business owners and top managers around the world, provides both subjective and objective information on the business environment that firms confront. The questionnaire includes a section asking firms to rank 15 components of the business environment, indicating which represent the biggest obstacles, and to evaluate these 15 components on a scale of 0–4 (0 being no obstacle; 1, a minor obstacle; 2, a moderate obstacle; 3, a major obstacle; and 4, a severe obstacle). Summary statistics for the related variables are provided in table 4.1.

These subjective evaluations show the severity of obstacles across regions and countries. This makes it possible to identify the top obstacles and examine the obstacles firms consider the most important. But, because the data are subjective (reflecting the perceptions of entrepreneurs on the impact of the business environment on firm operation, whereby successful entrepreneurs may be likely to consider the business environment to be less restrictive), we need to control for firm characteristics in explaining firm growth. In addition, we need to include objective measures of business environment constraints.

Table 4.1 Variable Descriptions and Summary Statistics

Variable	Description	Mean	Standard deviation
Employment growth	Employment growth $[(\ln S_{it} - \ln S_{i,t-3})/3]$	0.052	0.127
Labor size	Number of permanent employees $[\ln S_{i,t-3}]$	3.112	1.350
Age	Years of firm's operation	2.602	0.741
Multi	Equal to 1 if firm is independent, single establishment; 0 otherwise	0.138	0.345
Manuf	Equal to 1 if firm is in manufacturing or construction sector; 0 otherwise	0.555	0.497
Exporter	Equal to 1 if direct exports account for more than 10 percent of firm's sales; 0 otherwise	0.130	0.336
Foreign	Equal to 1 if firm has 10 percent or more of foreign ownership; 0 otherwise	0.117	0.321
Govt	Equal to 1 if firm has 10 percent or more of government ownership; 0 otherwise	0.017	0.129
Loan	Equal to 1 if firm has loan, line of credit, or overdraft facility; 0 otherwise	0.573	0.495
Credit constraint	Equal to 1 if firm did not apply for loan for some reason; 0 otherwise	0.334	0.472
Sales credit	Equal to 1 if firm has positive sales paid for after delivery; 0 otherwise	0.702	0.458
External finance	Equal to 1 if firm has a positive amount of external funds; 0 otherwise	0.237	0.425
Access to finance	How much of an obstacle to firm's operation is access to finance?	1.725	1.564
Informal competition	How much of an obstacle to firm's operation are informal sector competitors?	1.627	1.453
Labor regulations	How much of an obstacle to firm's operation are labor regulations?	0.958	1.181
Inadequate education	How much of an obstacle to firm's operation is an inadequately educated workforce?	1.408	1.353
Electricity	How much of an obstacle to firm's operation is electricity?	1.843	1.526
Transport	How much of an obstacle to firm's operation is transport of goods, supplies, and inputs?	1.224	1.310
Customs and trade	How much of an obstacle to firm's operation are customs and trade regulations?	0.954	1.242
Access to land	How much of an obstacle to firm's operation is access to land?	1.031	1.334
Courts	How much of an obstacle to firm's operation are courts?	1.025	1.280
Crime	How much of an obstacle to firm's operation are crime, theft, and disorder?	1.423	1.382
Tax rates	How much of an obstacle to firm's operation are tax rates?	1.828	1.374
Tax administration	How much of an obstacle to firm's operation is tax administration?	1.439	1.319
Licensing and permits	How much of an obstacle to firm's operation are business licensing and permits?	1.095	1.238
Political instability	How much of an obstacle to firm's operation is political instability?	1.615	1.504
Corruption	How much of an obstacle to firm's operation is corruption?	1.780	1.530

Source: Data of Enterprise Surveys (database) (2006–10), World Bank, Washington, DC, http://www.enterprisesurveys.org/.

Note: Govt = government owned; manuf = manufacturing; multi = multiestablishment.

The World Bank Enterprise Surveys provide a large set of objective measures of business environment constraints. In addition to subjective information on access to finance as an obstacle, the questionnaire also collects objective information on aspects of financial access, allowing us to create several variables, as follows: *Loan* is a dummy variable indicating whether a firm has a loan or line of credit from a financial institution or an overdraft facility. *Credit constraint* is a dummy variable indicating whether a firm did not apply for loans or lines of credit for one or more of the following reasons: application procedures for loans or lines of credit are complex; interest rates are not favorable; collateral requirements are too high; the size and maturity of loans are insufficient; getting bank loans requires making informal payments; or the firm did not think its application would be approved.[6] *Sales credit* is a dummy variable indicating whether the firm uses positive purchasing for its material inputs or services paid for after delivery (about 70 percent of firms in the sample have sales credit). We also include a dummy variable indicating whether a firm has a positive share of investment financed through external funds (this applies to 24 percent of firms in the sample).

The World Bank Enterprise Surveys also provide important information on firm characteristics, including size, age, sector, export activity, and ownership, as well as whether a firm is an independent single establishment.[7] The sample used in this chapter is stratified by size, age, sector, region, and other firm characteristics. (Variable descriptions and distributions are reported in tables 4.1–4.3.) Firms are divided into four categories by size: *micro* (1–10 permanent employees), *small* (11–50), *medium* (51–200), and *large* (more than 200). The sample includes mostly micro-firms (39 percent of the total) and small firms (37 percent); only 16 percent are medium, and 7 percent are large. Firms are divided into three categories by age: *young* (1–5 years), *mature* (6–15), and *older* (more than 15).[8] Most are mature (47 percent) or older (41 percent); only 11 percent are young firms. Ownership is defined as *foreign* or *government* if 10 percent or more of the firm is foreign or government owned; 12 percent of the firms in the sample are foreign owned, and only 2 percent are government owned. *Exporter* is a dummy variable indicating that direct exports account for 10 percent or more of a firm's sales; 13 percent of the sample firms are exporters.

Whether a firm has a single establishment or multiple establishments matters for firm growth, especially in the manufacturing sector (see Dunne, Roberts, and Samuelson 1989). We therefore include a dummy variable indicating whether a firm is an independent single establishment.

Table 4.2   Firm Characteristics According to Different Groups of Controls

	Frequency	Percent	Cummulative percent
By size			
Micro	15,357	38.84	38.84
Small	14,791	37.41	76.25
Medium	6,499	16.44	92.69
Large	2,845	7.20	99.88
Unknown	46	0.12	100
By age			
Young	4,440	11.23	11.23
Mature	18,551	46.92	58.15
Older	16,146	40.84	98.99
Unknown	401	1.01	100
By type of establishment			
Multiestablishment	5,397	13.65	13.65
Single establishment	33,729	85.31	98.96
Unknown	412	1.04	100
By sector			
Manufacturing	24,168	61.13	61.13
Retail	5,460	13.81	74.94
Other services	8,901	22.51	97.45
Unknown	1,009	2.55	100
By trade orientation			
Nonexporter	34,405	87.02	87.02
Exporter	5,133	12.98	100
By foreign ownership			
Domestically owned	34,587	87.48	87.48
Foreign owned	4,579	11.58	99.06
Unknown	372	0.94	100
By government ownership			
Privately owned	37,858	95.75	95.75
Government owned	649	1.64	97.39
Unknown	1,031	2.61	100
Total establishments	39,538		

Source: Data of Enterprise Surveys (database) (2006–10), World Bank, Washington, DC, http://www.enterprisesurveys
.org/.

Most of the firms in the sample are single establishments (85 percent), while 14 percent are part of multiestablishment entities. Finally, we divide the firms into three sectors: *manufacturing* (61 percent), *sales* (14 percent are in the retail and wholesale sector), and *services* (23 percent). The sample includes firms in six regions: 31 percent in Sub-Saharan Africa, 20 percent in Latin America and the Caribbean, 27 percent in Eastern Europe and Central Asia, 11 percent in East Asia and Pacific, and only 3 percent in the Middle East and North Africa and in South Asia.

Table 4.3   Employment Growth, by Firm Characteristics and Region

Characteristic or region	Mean	Minimum	Maximum
By size (number of employees)			
Micro (1–10)	0.086	−0.536	0.866
Small (11–50)	0.035	−0.732	0.844
Medium (51–200)	0.025	−0.638	0.594
Large (201+)	0.007	−0.562	0.753
Unknown	0.606	0.231	0.880
By age (years of operation)			
Young (1–5)	0.100	−0.732	0.880
Mature (6–15)	0.061	−0.623	0.807
Older (16+)	0.029	−0.584	0.866
Unknown	0.022	−0.458	0.448
By establishment number			
Multiestablishment	0.051	−0.732	0.880
Single establishment	0.055	−0.452	0.866
By sector			
Manufacturing	0.049	−0.638	0.880
Sales	0.057	−0.525	0.855
Services	0.054	−0.732	0.799
By region			
Sub-Saharan Africa	0.066	−0.732	0.813
East Asia and Pacific	0.025	−0.638	0.880
Eastern Europe and Central Asia	0.043	−0.547	0.799
Latin America and the Caribbean	0.056	−0.510	0.697
Middle East and North Africa	0.043	−0.384	0.462
South Asia	0.076	−0.623	0.866

Source: Data of Enterprise Surveys (database) (2006–10), World Bank, Washington, DC, http://www.enterprisesurveys.org/.

Table 4.3 provides an overview of firm growth according to firm characteristics and region. Young, small firms experience rapid growth in their labor force. The mean growth rate among microfirms is twice the corresponding rate among small firms and three times the rate among medium firms. There appears to be little growth in employment among large firms, on average. The mean growth rate among young firms is nearly twice that among mature firms and more than three times that among older firms. On average, there is little difference in growth rate between independent single establishments and establishments that are part of multiestablishment entities or across the manufacturing, sales, and services sectors. Firms in Africa and Latin America grow more quickly than those in Eastern Europe and Central Asia and those in East Asia and Pacific.

The Most Binding Constraint in the Business Environment

Having the managers of firms rate constraints on the operations and growth of their firms is a useful start to identifying important obstacles in the business environment. We analyze these obstacles not only by using econometric tools, but also by examining the importance of these obstacles across regions and sectors.

Understanding Obstacles to Firm Operations

In the World Bank Enterprise Surveys, firms rate 15 obstacles in their business environment. These are access to finance, the practices of competitors in the informal sector, electricity, corruption, crime, an inadequately educated workforce, labor regulations, business licensing and permits, political instability, tax administration, tax rates, transport, customs and trade regulations, courts, and access to land.

A review of firm responses shows that the biggest reported obstacles differ across regions and countries (annex 4.1; see also annex 4.2). Using model 2 (as explained in greater detail in the next subsection), we find that different sectors must also confront different obstacles. For example, in the manufacturing sector, access to finance, informal sector competition, tax rates, and labor regulations matter the most, while in the sales and services sectors, only access to finance and informal sector competition are negatively and significantly correlated with firm growth (table 4.4). Estimation results for the same model show that each country faces its own set of significant obstacles.[9] So does each region (table 4.5).

Many of these obstacles are linked directly or indirectly to poor firm performance. In an ideal world, a country would address all these problems to improve firm performance. But governments in developing countries have limited financial and human resources and, as argued by the growth diagnostics approach, should therefore prioritize reform efforts to remove the most important constraints.

The top three obstacles to firm operations emerging from the survey data for our sample are electricity, access to finance, and tax rates (figure 4.1). But we do not know whether these are the top obstacles to employment growth. We therefore need to analyze which obstacles have a significant effect on employment growth.

Identifying the Most Binding Constraint on Firm Growth

With figure 4.1 as a starting point, we set up an econometric model to investigate which of the 15 constraints is the most binding. We define a

Table 4.4   The Effect of Business Environment Obstacles on Employment Growth, by Sector

| | Dependent variable: Employment growth | | |
| | Manufacturing | Sales | Services |
Variable	(1)	(2)	(3)
Labor size	−0.026*** (0.001)	−0.014*** (0.002)	−0.021*** (0.002)
Age	−0.024*** (0.002)	−0.025*** (0.002)	−0.018*** (0.003)
Multi	0.022*** (0.003)	0.014*** (0.004)	0.014*** (0.005)
Exporter	0.026*** (0.003)	0.017** (0.007)	0.010 (0.007)
Foreign	0.011*** (0.003)	0.009* (0.005)	0.012** (0.005)
Govt	−0.009 (0.007)	−0.036** (0.015)	−0.020* (0.011)
Access to finance	−0.004*** (0.001)	−0.002* (0.001)	−0.004*** (0.002)
Informal sector competition	−0.004*** (0.001)	−0.002* (0.001)	−0.004*** (0.001)
Inadequate education	0.008*** (0.001)	0.007*** (0.001)	0.003** (0.002)
Electricity	0.002*** (0.001)	0.001 (0.001)	−0.002 (0.001)
Customs and trade	0.004*** (0.001)	0.006*** (0.001)	0.007*** (0.002)
Access to land	0.003*** (0.001)	0.003*** (0.001)	0.001 (0.002)
Political instability	−0.002 (0.001)	−0.001 (0.001)	−0.002 (0.002)
Courts	−0.001 (0.001)	−0.001 (0.002)	−0.002 (0.002)
Crime	0.001 (0.001)	−0.001 (0.001)	0.001 (0.002)
Tax rates	−0.002** (0.001)	0.001 (0.002)	−0.001 (0.002)
Tax administration	0.001 (0.001)	−0.002 (0.002)	−0.001 (0.002)
Licensing and permits	0.000 (0.001)	0.000 (0.002)	0.002 (0.002)
Corruption	−0.001 (0.001)	−0.001 (0.001)	−0.001 (0.002)
Transport	0.000 (0.001)	0.001 (0.001)	−0.001 (0.002)
Labor regulations	−0.002* (0.001)	−0.003 (0.002)	0.004** (0.002)
Constant	0.191*** (0.005)	0.151*** (0.007)	0.167*** (0.009)
Adjusted R^2	0.146	0.118	0.114
Number of observations	15,322	6,014	5,237
Number of countries	95	95	95

Source: Author estimates based on data of Enterprise Surveys (database) (2006–10), World Bank, Washington, DC, http://www.enterprisesurveys.org/.

Note: Govt = government owned; multi = multiestablishment. Standard errors (in parentheses) are robust to heteroskedasticity and clustered on countries. Model: *EG* = *b*0 + *b*1All 15 Obstacles + *b*2Firm Characteristics + Region + Country Fixed Effects + *e.*
Significance level: * = 10 percent, ** = 5 percent, *** = 1 percent.

constraint as the most binding if it is statistically significant, has a large coefficient in all estimations (models), and has the right sign, that is, has a negative effect on employment growth. We design three models:

Model 1:

$$EG = b0 + b1\text{Individual Obstacle} + b2\text{Firm Characteristics} + \text{Country Fixed Effects} + e1 \qquad (4.2)$$

Model 2:

$$EG = b0 + b1\text{All 15 Obstacles} + b2\text{Firm Characteristics} + \text{Country Fixed Effects} + e2 \qquad (4.3)$$

Table 4.5 The Effect of Business Environment Obstacles on Employment Growth, by Region

	Dependent variable: Employment growth				
Variable	World (1)	AFR (2)	EAP (3)	ECA (4)	LAC (5)
Labor size	-0.022*** (0.001)	-0.026*** (0.001)	-0.029*** (0.002)	-0.018*** (0.001)	-0.019*** (0.001)
Age	-0.023*** (0.001)	-0.021*** (0.002)	-0.019*** (0.004)	-0.031*** (0.003)	-0.024*** (0.002)
Multi	0.018*** (0.002)	0.012*** (0.003)	0.010 (0.007)	0.020*** (0.006)	0.022*** (0.004)
Manuf	0.003 (0.002)	0.012*** (0.003)	0.012** (0.006)	-0.009** (0.004)	0.005 (0.003)
Exporter	0.020*** (0.002)	0.020*** (0.004)	0.018** (0.007)	0.020*** (0.004)	0.025*** (0.004)
Foreign	0.011*** (0.002)	0.008** (0.003)	0.009 (0.006)	0.021*** (0.006)	0.011** (0.005)
Govt	-0.017*** (0.005)	-0.013 (0.011)	0.017 (0.012)	-0.022** (0.008)	-0.020 (0.017)
Access to finance	-0.004*** (0.001)	-0.002* (0.001)	-0.008** (0.002)	-0.004*** (0.001)	-0.005*** (0.001)
Informal sector competition	-0.003*** (0.001)	-0.003*** (0.001)	-0.008*** (0.002)	-0.002* (0.001)	-0.003*** (0.001)
Inadequate education	0.007*** (0.001)	0.005*** (0.001)	0.008*** (0.002)	0.006*** (0.001)	0.010*** (0.001)
Electricity	0.001* (0.001)	-0.001 (0.001)	0.004** (0.002)	0.001 (0.001)	0.002** (0.001)
Customs and trade	0.005*** (0.001)	0.004*** (0.001)	0.006** (0.003)	0.006*** (0.002)	0.003* (0.001)
Access to land	0.003*** (0.001)	-0.000 (0.001)	0.004* (0.002)	0.004** (0.001)	0.005*** (0.001)
Political instability	-0.002* (0.001)	-0.001 (0.001)	-0.002 (0.003)	-0.001 (0.001)	-0.003** (0.002)
Courts	-0.001 (0.001)	-0.001 (0.001)	0.001 (0.003)	-0.004** (0.002)	0.000 (0.001)
Crime	0.000 (0.001)	0.001 (0.001)	0.002 (0.003)	-0.000 (0.001)	-0.001 (0.001)
Tax rates	-0.001* (0.001)	-0.002 (0.001)	-0.000 (0.003)	-0.000 (0.002)	-0.002 (0.002)
Tax administration	-0.000 (0.001)	0.002* (0.001)	-0.002 (0.003)	-0.002 (0.002)	-0.002 (0.002)
Licensing and permits	0.001 (0.001)	-0.001 (0.001)	0.003 (0.003)	0.002 (0.002)	0.002 (0.002)
Corruption	-0.001* (0.001)	-0.001 (0.001)	-0.002 (0.003)	0.000 (0.002)	-0.002 (0.001)
Transport	0.000 (0.001)	-0.002 (0.001)	0.002 (0.002)	0.001 (0.001)	0.001 (0.001)
Labor regulations	-0.001 (0.001)	-0.001 (0.001)	-0.001 (0.003)	-0.002 (0.002)	-0.001 (0.002)
Constant	0.176*** (0.004)	0.182*** (0.006)	0.156*** (0.011)	0.184*** (0.008)	0.174*** (0.008)
Adjusted R²	0.130	0.129	0.148	0.130	0.112
Number of observations	26,574	8,600	3,079	6,596	7,592
Number of countries	95	37	10	30	15

Source: Author estimates based on data of Enterprise Surveys (database) (2006–10), World Bank, Washington, DC, http://www.enterprisesurveys.org/.

Note: Standard errors (in parentheses) are robust to heteroskedasticity and clustered on countries. Regressions for the Middle East and North Africa and for South Asia are excluded because of insufficient data. Model: $EG = b0 + b1$ All 15 Obstacles $+ b2$ Firm Characteristics + Region + Country Fixed Effects + *e*. AFR = Africa; EAP = East Asia and Pacific; ECA = (Eastern) Europe and Central Asia; govt = government owned; LAC = Latin America and the Caribbean; manuf = manufacturing; multi = multiestablishment. Significance level: * = 10 percent, ** = 5 percent, *** = 1 percent.

Figure 4.1   Distribution of the Top Obstacle Cited by Enterprises, All Economies

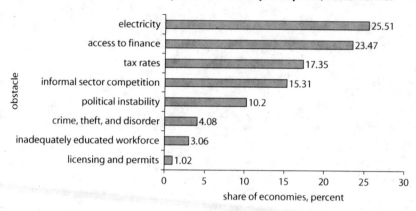

Source: Data of Enterprise Surveys (database) (2006–10), World Bank, Washington, DC, http://www.enterprisesurveys .org/.

Model 3:

$$EG = b0 + b1\text{Only Significant Obstacle (in model 2)}$$
$$+ b2\text{Firm Characteristics + Country Fixed Effects} + e3, \quad (4.4)$$

where EG refers to the employment growth of firm i at time t; *Individual Obstacle* is each obstacle among the 15 shown in the last 15 rows of table 4.1; *Firm Characteristics* include labor size (the number of permanent employees at the beginning of period t–3), labor size squared, age, age squared, and indicators of whether a firm is part of a multiestablishment entity (*multi*), is in manufacturing (*manuf*), is an exporter, is foreign owned (*foreign*), or is government owned (*govt*). Note that, by relating constraints to firm growth, we are assuming that these constraints do not change during the three-year period, which is a reasonable assumption because these constraints are not known to vary in developing countries from year to year.

The results suggest that access to finance and competition from the informal sector are the most binding constraints: the effects are statistically significant in all models. Columns 1–15 in table 4.6, presenting the estimation results for model 1 for each obstacle, show that only access to finance and competition from the informal sector have a significant negative effect on employment growth. Column 16 shows the estimation results for model 2 run for all 15 obstacles together, and column 17 presents the results for model 3, which includes all significant obstacles. Once again, we find that access to finance and competition from the informal

Table 4.6   The Effect of Business Environment Obstacles on Employment Growth

									Dependent variable: Employment growth								
	1	*2*	*3*	*4*	*5*	*6*	*7*	*8*	*9*	*10*	*11*	*12*	*13*	*14*	*15*	*16*	*17*
Access to finance	-0.002*** (0.000)															-0.004*** (0.001)	-0.003*** (0.000)
Competition		-0.003*** (0.000)														-0.003*** (0.001)	-0.004*** (0.001)
Inadequate education			0.005*** (0.001)													0.007*** (0.001)	0.006*** (0.001)
Electricity				0.002*** (0.000)												0.001* (0.001)	
Customs and trade					0.005*** (0.001)											0.005*** (0.001)	0.004*** (0.001)
Access to land						0.003*** (0.001)										0.003*** (0.001)	0.002*** (0.001)
Political instability							-0.001 (0.001)									-0.002** (0.001)	
Courts								-0.000 (0.001)								-0.001 (0.001)	
Crime									0.001** (0.001)							0.000 (0.001)	

(continued next page)

Table 4.6 *(continued)*

| | \multicolumn{17}{c}{Dependent variable: Employment growth} |
	1	2	3	4	5	6	7	8	9	10	11	12	13	14	15	16	17
Tax rates										−0.001* (0.001)						−0.001* (0.001)	
Tax administration											−0.000 (0.001)					−0.000 (0.001)	
Licensing and permits												0.001 (0.001)				0.001 (0.001)	
Corruption													−0.000 (0.000)			−0.001* (0.001)	
Transport														0.002*** (0.001)		0.000 (0.001)	
Labor regulations															0.002*** (0.001)	−0.001 (0.001)	
Adjusted R^2	0.143	0.143	0.144	0.141	0.146	0.142	0.142	0.137	0.141	0.142	0.142	0.142	0.142	0.142	0.141	0.151	0.155
Number of observations	35,837	35,466	36,216	36,554	32,967	35,399	35,814	32,794	36,278	36,287	36,154	35,350	35,435	36,222	36,297	26,574	30,206
Number of countries	96	96	96	96	96	96	96	95	96	96	96	96	96	96	96	95	96

Source: Author estimates based on data of Enterprise Surveys (database) (2006–10), World Bank, Washington, DC, http://www.enterprisesurveys.org/.

Note: Standard errors (in parentheses) are robust to heteroskedasticity and clustered on countries. Model 1 (columns 1–15): $EG = b0 + b1$Individual Obstacle + $b2$Firm Characteristics + Country Fixed Effects + $e1$. Model 2 (column 16): $EG = b0 + b1$All 15 Obstacles + $b2$Firm Characteristics + Country Fixed Effects + $e2$. The hypothesis that the coefficients for access to finance and informal sector competition differ is tested and rejected.

Significance level: * = 10 percent, ** = 5 percent, *** = 1 percent.

sector are the most binding constraints. We also examine the significance of the effects of these obstacles on firm growth across regions and sectors to check the robustness of the findings. Tables 4.4 and 4.5 confirm that access to finance and competition from the informal sector matter the most after we control for firm characteristics.

Robustness: For the robustness check, we investigate whether our results are invariant to firm characteristics. Some might expect that older firms, exporters, or government- or foreign-owned firms achieve higher growth rates and face a different set of binding constraints. First, we examine whether firm ownership affects our most binding constraints. The sample includes 34,587 domestic firms and 4,579 foreign firms. Excluding the foreign firms from our sample does not change our result. Our most binding constraints are still access to finance and competition from the informal sector. Second, if we exclude 649 government-owned firms from the sample and do the same analysis with our proposed models, access to finance and competition from the informal sector are still the most significant constraints with the same negative values. This result shows that firm ownership does not drive our result. Third, we run regressions without 5,133 exporters, and the result is exactly the same as in table 4.6.

We also exclude all firms younger than five years old. Besides the most binding constraints of access to finance and competition from the informal sector, we find that political instability and tax rates are statistically significant at 5 percent. But the individual effects of these on employment growth are only significant at 10 percent. This result nonetheless suggests that political stability and lower tax rates are important to ensure firm growth among young firms. In addition, age is sensitive to our result; so, we need to control for age as we do in tables 4.11 and 4.12 (see below).

We run another important robustness check to see if access to finance and competition from the informal sector are endogenous to employment growth.[10] A firm's low growth rate may be associated with the difficulty of gaining access to finance or of facing competition from the informal sector. To correct for this bias, we need to extract the exogenous component of these constraints. Even though firms may blame different constraints for their slow growth, it is less likely that all firms in a given country, region, and industry group will do the same. By replacing these obstacles with the average obstacle for each industry group in the country as the instrumental variable, we are able to isolate the exogenous part of the possibly endogenous obstacle the firm reports and, using that, predict growth. The country-region average in each industry also helps us deal with potential measurement errors that are largely idiosyncratic to the firm. Therefore, we use the average value of the obstacles for the industry groups in each country to instrument for the obstacles.

We find that, with the adjusted constraints in the models, including firm characteristics and country fixed effects as specified in models 1 and 2, access to finance and competition from the informal sector are still the most binding constraints. Therefore, our result is robust to bias correction (table 4.7).

To check whether our results are driven by specific outlier firms, we run our regressions again, but we redefine the outliers and exclude more. Our outliers are defined as firms with zero as the permanent number of employees in both years, firms with erroneous age (greater than 100 years, which accounts for 1.5 percent of the sample), and firms showing employment growth lying outside the range of three standard deviations from the mean of employment growth. Now, we have a sample with a positive permanent number of employees and the correct age. We find that access to finance remains the most binding constraint to firm growth in our reduced sample. This confirms that our result is not driven by the influential outliers. However, we also find that political instability is statistically significant both individually and collectively, as well as that it has a negative sign. We run the regressions again across regions and sectors; however, political instability does not show consistency. This implies that the impact of political instability on firm growth is less robust than that of access to finance or of competition from the informal sector. Moreover, political instability only occurs in some countries; so, it will not be significant in some regions or some sectors.[11]

Our results demonstrate that, both econometrically and economically, access to finance and competition from the informal sector matter the most for firm employment growth, findings that are in line with the starting point of the rankings of reported obstacles shown in annex 4.1. While, statistically, both constraints are equally binding, the meaning of the second constraint is ambiguous. The survey asks firms whether they see competition from the informal sector as an obstacle. To any individual firm, competition poses a threat to survival. Yet, at the level of the economy, it is competition that drives firms to improve productivity, and, therefore, it is competition that drives growth. So, it is not clear to us that competition from the informal sector should be considered an obstacle to firm operations. The finding that competition from the informal sector is the second most important binding constraint may indicate that the formal firms covered by the survey are not the appropriate firm organization form in developing countries. Moreover, this survey question is not followed by

Table 4.7 The Effect of Business Environment Obstacles on Employment Growth, Average Industry-Wide Obstacles

| | | | | | | | | | | | | | | | | | Dependent variable: Employment growth |
	1	2	3	4	5	6	7	8	9	10	11	12	13	14	15	16	17
Access to finance	-0.002*** (0.000)															-0.003*** (0.001)	-0.003*** (0.000)
Competition		-0.003*** (0.000)														-0.003*** (0.001)	-0.004*** (0.001)
Inadequate education			0.005*** (0.001)													0.007*** (0.001)	0.006*** (0.001)
Electricity				0.002*** (0.000)												0.001* (0.001)	0.001 (0.001)
Customs and trade					0.005*** (0.001)											0.005*** (0.001)	0.004*** (0.001)
Access to land						0.003*** (0.001)										0.003*** (0.001)	0.002*** (0.001)
Political instability							-0.001 (0.001)									-0.001** (0.001)	
Courts								-0.000 (0.001)								-0.001 (0.001)	
Crime									0.001** (0.001)							0.000 (0.001)	

(continued next page)

Table 4.7 (continued)

								Dependent variable: Employment growth									
	1	2	3	4	5	6	7	8	9	10	11	12	13	14	15	16	17
Tax rates										−0.001*						−0.001	
										(0.001)						(0.001)	
Tax administration											−0.000					−0.001	
											(0.001)					(0.001)	
Licensing and permits												0.000				0.001	
												(0.001)				(0.001)	
Corruption													−0.001			−0.001*	
													(0.000)			(0.001)	
Transport														0.002***		−0.000	
														(0.001)		(0.001)	
Labor regulations															0.002***	−0.001	−0.001
															(0.001)	(0.001)	(0.001)
Number of observations	35,837	35,466	36,216	36,554	32,967	35,399	35,814	32,794	36,278	36,287	36,154	35,350	35,435	36,222	36,297	26,574	30,206
Number of countries	96	96	96	96	96	96	96	95	96	96	96	96	96	96	96	95	96
Adjusted R²	0.143	0.143	0.144	0.141	0.146	0.142	0.142	0.137	0.141	0.142	0.142	0.142	0.142	0.142	0.141	0.151	0.155

Source: Author estimates based on data of Enterprise Surveys (database) (2006–10). World Bank, Washington, DC, http://www.enterprisesurveys.org/.

Note: Standard errors (in parentheses) are robust to heteroskedasticity and clustered on countries. Model 1 (columns 1–15): $EG = b0 + b1$Individual Obstacle $+ b2$Firm Characteristics + Country Fixed Effects + e1.

Significance level: * = 10 percent, ** = 5 percent, *** = 1 percent.

other questions on related aspects of competition, thus providing too little information to assess the importance of informal sector competition. Therefore, we do not further address this issue in the chapter.

While perception-based indicators such as those applied in the analysis discussed here are useful, quantitative indicators may give a more accurate picture of the business environment. Firm managers within a country may have different perceptions of the same obstacle, and firm managers in different countries and regions have different frames of reference. A problem perceived as a moderate obstacle by one firm may be perceived as a severe obstacle by another, even though the problem imposes a smaller cost on the second firm.

In the next three sections, we use objective measures to examine the importance of access to finance. We cannot analyze informal sector competition because of its ambiguity and because the data do not provide sufficient information (see above). We leave further analysis of this constraint for the future, when the data become available and when the work can be based on objective measures.

Impact of Financial Access Variables on Employment Growth

In this section, we examine the effect of financial access variables on firm employment growth, controlling for individual firm characteristics. The model is set up with the following specification:

$$EG = b0 + b1\text{Labor size} + b2\text{Age} + b3\text{Multi} + b4\text{Manuf}$$
$$+ b5\text{Exporter} + b6\text{Foreign} + b7\text{Govt} + b8FC(s)$$
$$+ \text{Country Fixed Effects} + e, \tag{4.5}$$

where EG refers to the employment growth of firm i at time t (the growth in the number of permanent employees between $t–3$ and t), and FC denotes each of the financial access variables: loan, credit constraint, sales credit, and external finance.

Our specification accounts for heteroskedasticity and country fixed effects. All outliers have been removed. (See the section below on the robustness check, for which we run regressions again with outliers.) We also emphasize the importance of ownership structure by varying the type of establishment: single or multiple, foreign or government owned, exporter or nonexporter. The negative relationship between firm growth and firm size shown in table 4.8—along with the supportive evidence in table 4.1 showing that smaller firms grow more quickly than larger firms—suggests that Gibrat's law does not hold in this sample of firms. This finding is true across regions and sectors. The negative and statistically significant coefficient on firm age tells us that there is an inverse relationship between firm growth and firm age, which is consistent with Jovanovic's model (1982) of disproportionate growth.

With other firm characteristics held constant, the rate of growth is significantly lower among independent, single-establishment firms and government-owned firms. Exporters and foreign-owned firms tend to exhibit greater employment growth. In Africa and in East Asia, firms in the manufacturing sector show higher employment growth than firms in the sales and services sectors.

On average, a 1 percent increase in beginning-of-period firm size is associated with a 0.93 percent increase in end-of-period size (after three years) if the beginning-of-period age is held constant (based on the results in table 4.8, column 1). Based on the analysis across regions, we obtain estimated elasticities of end-of-period size with respect to beginning-of-period size at approximately 0.9 for Africa, East Asia and Pacific, Eastern Europe and Central Asia, and Latin America and the Caribbean (table 4.8, columns 6–9, respectively). With beginning-of-period size held constant, a 1 percent increase in beginning-of-period firm age is associated with a 0.07 percent decrease in end-of-period size (table 4.8, column 1).

The results in table 4.8 show that financial access variables have a significant effect on firm growth. Columns 1–4, respectively, indicate that, if other factors are held constant, having a loan or overdraft facility increases the growth in the number of permanent employees at a firm by 3.1 percent; being credit constrained reduces a firm's employment growth by 1.9 percent; having sales credit increases a firm's growth by 2.6 percent; and having external investment funds increases growth by 4.2 percent. If we include all these significant financial access variables in one model after controlling for firm characteristics, they still have significant effects on employment growth, though the effects are of smaller magnitude. And, if we use the same model and run the regressions in different regions, the significance and signs of the effects remain the same across regions. These strong results show that access to finance does indeed matter for firm growth.

Robustness: In terms of objective constraints, we analyze the determinants of access to finance variables and their effects on employment growth with a reduced sample. For instance, without government-owned or foreign-owned firms, without exporters, for young firms less than 5 years old, the result still holds. All the access to finance variables are still statistically significant with the same magnitudes and signs across sectors and regions in the whole world.

Table 4.8 The Effect of Objective Financial Access Variables on Employment Growth

Variable	\ Dependent variable: Employment growth \ World (1)	World (2)	World (3)	World (4)	World (5)	AFR (6)	EAP (7)	ECA (8)	LAC (9)
Labor size	−0.024*** (0.001)	−0.023*** (0.001)	−0.022*** (0.001)	−0.024*** (0.001)	−0.026*** (0.001)	−0.029*** (0.001)	−0.032*** (0.002)	−0.022*** (0.001)	−0.023*** (0.001)
Age	−0.024*** (0.001)	−0.023*** (0.001)	−0.023*** (0.001)	−0.022*** (0.001)	−0.023*** (0.001)	−0.020*** (0.002)	−0.018*** (0.003)	−0.030*** (0.002)	−0.023*** (0.002)
Multi	0.019*** (0.002)	0.018*** (0.002)	0.019*** (0.002)	0.019*** (0.002)	0.019*** (0.002)	0.013*** (0.003)	0.017*** (0.006)	0.020*** (0.005)	0.022*** (0.004)
Manuf	0.0003 (0.001)	0.001 (0.001)	−0.000 (0.001)	−0.001 (0.001)	−0.000 (0.001)	0.010*** (0.002)	0.010** (0.005)	−0.010*** (0.003)	−0.002 (0.003)
Exporter	0.022*** (0.002)	0.024*** (0.002)	0.024*** (0.002)	0.023*** (0.002)	0.021*** (0.002)	0.022*** (0.004)	0.023*** (0.007)	0.015*** (0.004)	0.028*** (0.004)
Foreign	0.013*** (0.002)	0.012*** (0.002)	0.013*** (0.002)	0.014*** (0.002)	0.014*** (0.002)	0.008** (0.003)	0.019*** (0.006)	0.020*** (0.005)	0.016*** (0.005)
Govt	−0.009** (0.005)	−0.011** (0.005)	−0.011** (0.005)	−0.010** (0.005)	−0.008* (0.005)	−0.008 (0.010)	0.024** (0.011)	−0.015** (0.007)	−0.016 (0.020)
Loan	0.031*** (0.002)				0.020*** (0.002)	0.014*** (0.003)	0.018*** (0.004)	0.023*** (0.003)	0.026*** (0.003)
Credit constraint		−0.019*** (0.002)			−0.010*** (0.002)	−0.004* (0.002)	0.001 (0.004)	−0.024*** (0.003)	−0.012*** (0.003)
Sales credit			0.026*** (0.003)		0.009*** (0.002)	0.010*** (0.002)	0.006 (0.005)	0.012*** (0.003)	0.005 (0.003)
External finance				0.042*** (0.002)	0.036*** (0.002)	0.021*** (0.003)	0.041*** (0.005)	0.036*** (0.003)	0.041*** (0.003)
Constant	0.163*** (0.003)	0.182*** (0.003)		0.166*** (0.003)	0.162*** (0.003)	0.174*** (0.005)	0.144*** (0.009)	0.165*** (0.006)	0.153*** (0.006)
Number of observations	34,894	35,641	36,722	36,722	34,524	10,270	3,971	9,423	9,911
Adjusted R^2	0.131	0.125	0.123	0.138	0.146	0.144	0.155	0.154	0.128

Source: Author estimates based on data of Enterprise Surveys (database) (2006–10), World Bank, Washington, DC, http://www.enterprisesurveys.org/.

Note: Standard errors (in parentheses) are robust to heteroskedasticity and clustered on countries. Regressions for the Middle East and North Africa and for South Asia are excluded because of insufficient data. Model: $EG = b0 + b1 Labor\ size + b2 Age + b3 Multi + b4 Manuf + b5 Exporter + b6 Foreign + b7 Govt + b8 FC(s) + Country\ Fixed\ Effects + e$. AFR = Africa; EAP = East Asia and Pacific; ECA = (Eastern) Europe and Central Asia; govt = government owned; LAC = Latin America and the Caribbean; manuf = manufacturing; multi = multiestablishment.

Significance level: * = 10 percent, ** = 5 percent, *** = 1 percent.

We run these regressions again with outliers (which means using the sample with a positive permanent number of employees and age less than 350 years), and our result is still robust.

Determinants of Financial Access

In this section, we estimate the probability that a firm has access to finance based on its characteristics. We use the following model:

$$FC = b0 + b1\text{Small} + b2\text{Medium} + b3\text{Large}$$
$$+ b4\text{Mature} + b5\text{Older} + b6\text{Multi} + b7\text{Manuf}$$
$$+ b8\text{Exporter} + b9\text{Foreign} + b10\text{Govt} + e, \qquad (4.6)$$

where *FC* denotes each of the financial access variables: loan, credit constraint, sales credit, and external finance.

We estimate this model by probit. We focus on firms of different sizes (micro, small, medium, and large; micro is the base category that is omitted from the regression) and different ages (young, mature, and older; young is the base category that is omitted from the regression). The results show that a firm's size, age, and status as an exporter are strong determinants of the firm's access to finance (table 4.9).

There is a bigger difference in access to finance between micro and large firms than between small and large firms. The analysis involving controls for firm characteristics and using country fixed effects shows that microfirms are more likely to be credit constrained. Holding other factors constant, we find that large firms are 85 percent less likely than microfirms to be credit constrained. In addition, relative to microfirms, large firms are 97 percent more likely to have a loan or overdraft facility and 75 percent more likely to have a share of investment financed externally. Medium and large firms are, respectively, about 32 and 43 percent more likely than microfirms to have sales credit, while small firms are about 19 percent more likely than microfirms to offer sales credit.

Relative to young firms, older firms are 29 percent more likely to have a loan, 8 percent more likely to have sales credit, and 20 percent less likely to be credit constrained. If we hold other factors constant, we find that mature firms are only 6 percent less likely than young firms to be credit constrained and about 10 percent more likely to have a loan.

Other interesting results also emerge. Firms in the manufacturing sector are 20 percent more likely to be credit constrained. Holding other factors constant, we find that, relative to nonexporters, exporter firms are 41 percent more likely to have a loan, 26 percent less likely to be credit

Table 4.9   The Effect of Objective Financial Access Variables, by Firm Characteristics

Variable	Loan (1)	Credit constraint (2)	Sales credit (3)	External finance (4)
Small	0.467*** (0.041)	−0.412*** (0.043)	0.187*** (0.035)	0.338*** (0.030)
Medium	0.779*** (0.063)	−0.721*** (0.068)	0.320*** (0.049)	0.572*** (0.038)
Large	0.973*** (0.072)	−0.852*** (0.073)	0.427*** (0.078)	0.747*** (0.045)
Mature	0.097** (0.040)	−0.063* (0.035)	0.055 (0.055)	0.023 (0.037)
Older	0.287*** (0.066)	−0.200*** (0.057)	0.079 (0.063)	0.034 (0.048)
Multi	0.032 (0.051)	−0.128*** (0.036)	0.023 (0.047)	0.007 (0.048)
Manuf	−0.089 (0.062)	0.196*** (0.048)	−0.031 (0.058)	−0.015 (0.048)
Exporter	0.412*** (0.064)	−0.261*** (0.053)	0.084* (0.049)	0.204*** (0.044)
Foreign	−0.101 (0.070)	−0.024 (0.049)	−0.026 (0.050)	−0.157*** (0.043)
Govt	−0.361*** (0.119)	0.199** (0.082)	0.042 (0.099)	−0.118 (0.094)
Constant	−0.325*** (0.104)	−0.071 (0.091)	0.070 (0.063)	−1.039*** (0.070)
Number of observations	34,916	35,663	36,746	36,746

Source: Author estimates based on data of Enterprise Surveys (database) (2006–10), World Bank, Washington, DC, http://www.enterprisesurveys.org/.
Note: Standard errors (in parentheses) are robust to heteroskedasticity and clustered on countries. Model: $FC = b0 + b1Small + b2Medium + b3Large + b4Mature + b5Older + b6Multi + b7Manuf + b8Exporter + b9Foreign + b10Govt + e$. Govt = government owned; manuf = manufacturing; multi = multiestablishment. Significance level: * = 10 percent, ** = 5 percent, *** = 1 percent.

constrained, and 20 percent more likely to have external finance for investment.

The Effect of Financial Access on Employment Growth, by Firm Size and Age

In this section, we investigate the effect of financial access on employment growth by firm size and firm age for each of the financial access variables individually and, then, for all the variables combined.

The Effect of Individual Financial Access Variables

To examine the effect of the financial access variables individually, we use the following model:

$$EG = b0 + b1FC + b2Small^*FC + b3Medium^*FC$$
$$+ b4Large^*FC + b5Mature^*FC + b6Older^*FC$$
$$+ b7Multi + b8Manuf + b9Exporter + b10Foreign$$
$$+ b11Govt + \text{Country Fixed Effects} + e, \qquad (4.7)$$

where *EG* refers to the employment growth of firm i at time t (the growth in the number of permanent employees between $t-3$ and t), and *FC* denotes each of the financial access variables: loan, credit constraint, sales credit, and external finance.

Table 4.10 shows the effect of each of the financial access variables—loan, credit constraint, sales credit, and external finance—on employment growth in turn. Microfirms are, again, the base category that is omitted from the regression.

Among size categories, microfirms appear to benefit the most from having access to finance. Table 4.10, column 1 shows that having a loan increases employment growth by 9 percent in a microfirm, but by only 4 percent in a medium firm, and 2 percent in a large firm if we hold other factors constant. The results in columns 3 and 4 tell the same story. Micro and small firms gain the most from finance in forms ranging from the simple to the more sophisticated, from having a loan or overdraft facility to sales credit to external finance for investment. Column 2 supports the argument that micro and small firms benefit the most from access to finance. Being credit constrained will make larger firms suffer more than smaller firms.

With access to the same forms of finance, young firms expand more relative to older firms. Having a loan or overdraft facility increases employment growth by 9 percent in a young firm, but by 6 percent in a mature firm, and 3 percent in an older firm if we hold other factors constant. Similarly, having sales credit or external finance increases growth more among young firms than among mature and older firms. Being credit constrained reduces firm growth as firms age. This finding emphasizes the importance that firm age exercises with respect to firm growth. The effect of being credit constrained also varies by sector, appearing to be stronger in manufacturing than in the sales or services sector.

We also look at the effect of financial access on employment growth across regions. The estimation results by region are presented in table 4.11 for each financial access variable separately. The finding that having a loan, or sales credit, or a share of investment financed externally helps microfirms the most still holds. Indeed, this finding holds across all regions. The finding that young firms expand more than older firms through access to the same forms of finance also holds across regions.

The Effect of Combined Financial Access Variables

In this section, we look at the combined effect of all four financial access variables—firm size, age, sector, and region—on employment growth. We use the following model:

Table 4.10   Differences in the Effects of Objective Financial Access Variables on Employment Growth, by Firm Size and Age

	Dependent variable: Employment growth			
	Loan	Credit constraint	Sales credit	External finance
	(1)	(2)	(3)	(4)
Financial access variable (FC)	0.091*** (0.004)	0.053*** (0.004)	0.106*** (0.012)	0.105*** (0.006)
Small*FC	−0.040*** (0.002)	−0.057*** (0.002)	−0.043*** (0.007)	−0.039*** (0.004)
Medium*FC	−0.051*** (0.003)	−0.065*** (0.004)	−0.057*** (0.008)	−0.056*** (0.004)
Large*FC	−0.069*** (0.003)	−0.078*** (0.007)	−0.066*** (0.009)	−0.073*** (0.005)
Mature*FC	−0.035*** (0.004)	−0.026*** (0.004)	−0.042*** (0.012)	−0.030*** (0.006)
Older*FC	−0.061*** (0.004)	−0.044*** (0.004)	−0.062*** (0.012)	−0.051*** (0.006)
Multi	0.008*** (0.002)	0.006*** (0.002)	0.003 (0.002)	0.004** (0.002)
Manuf	−0.005*** (0.001)	−0.006*** (0.001)	−0.009*** (0.001)	−0.009*** (0.001)
Exporter	0.009*** (0.002)	0.003 (0.002)	0.001 (0.002)	0.004* (0.002)
Foreign	0.003 (0.002)	0.003 (0.002)	0.000 (0.002)	0.001 (0.002)
Govt	−0.035*** (0.005)	−0.041*** (0.005)	−0.046*** (0.005)	−0.042*** (0.005)
Constant	0.045*** (0.001)	0.055*** (0.001)	0.055*** (0.001)	0.048*** (0.001)
Adjusted R^2	0.090	0.065	0.095	0.078
Number of observations	34,894	35,641	36,722	36,722
Number of countries	95	96	96	96

Source: Author estimates based on data of Enterprise Surveys (database) (2006–10), World Bank, Washington, DC, http://www.enterprisesurveys.org/.

Note: Standard errors (in parentheses) are robust to heteroskedasticity and clustered on countries. Model: $EG = b0 + b1FC + b2Small*FC + b3Medium*FC + b4Large*FC + b5Mature*FC + b6Older*FC + b7Multi + b8Manuf + b9Exporter + b10Foreign + b11Govt + Country Fixed Effects + e$. Govt = government owned; manuf = manufacturing; multi = multiestablishment. Significance level: * = 10 percent, ** = 5 percent, *** = 1 percent.
* In stub (first column) = multiplication sign.

$$EG = b0 + b1\text{Small} + b2\text{Medium} + b3\text{Large} + b4\text{Mature} + b5\text{Older}$$
$$+ b6\text{Multi} + b7\text{Manuf} + b8\text{Exporter} + b9\text{Foreign} + b10\text{Govt}$$
$$+ b11\text{Loan} + b12\text{Credit Constraint} + b13\text{Sales Credit}$$
$$+ b14\text{ External Finance} + \text{Country Fixed Effects} + e, \qquad (4.8)$$

where EG refers to the employment growth of firm i at time t (the growth in the number of permanent employees between $t-3$ and t).

Table 4.12 shows the estimation results for equation 4.8. The effects of all the financial access variables are statistically significant and have the right signs. The results in column 1 indicate that firm growth slows both as a firm expands its labor force and as it ages if we control for other firm characteristics. Columns 2–5 suggest that having a loan and having external finance are important for firms of all sizes, though the effects

Table 4.11 Differences in the Effects of Objective Financial Access Variables on Employment Growth, by Firm Size and Age across Regions

	Loan				Credit constraint				Sales credit				External finance			
	AFR	EAP	ECA	LAC	AFR	EAP	ECA	LAC	AFR	EAP	ECA	LAC	AFR	EAP	ECA	LAC
Financial access (FC)	0.063***	0.061***	0.108***	0.123***	0.044***	0.090***	0.044***	0.071***	0.056***	0.077***	0.109***	0.140***	0.070***	0.089***	0.108***	0.136***
	(0.007)	(0.011)	(0.008)	(0.008)	(0.004)	(0.012)	(0.010)	(0.014)	(0.018)	(0.034)	(0.020)	(0.021)	(0.010)	(0.017)	(0.012)	(0.011)
Small*FC	−0.026***	−0.033***	−0.035***	−0.054***	−0.049***	0.076***	0.043***	0.066***	−0.019***	−0.051***	0.031***	0.069***	−0.027***	−0.018	0.033***	−0.057***
	(0.004)	(0.007)	(0.004)	(0.004)	(0.003)	(0.008)	(0.006)	(0.006)	(0.012)	(0.031)	(0.013)	(0.012)	(0.007)	(0.014)	(0.006)	(0.006)
Medium*FC	−0.036***	−0.045***	−0.057***	−0.057***	−0.049***	0.082***	0.067***	0.064***	−0.026***	−0.057***	0.051***	0.086***	−0.035***	0.039***	0.058***	−0.071***
	(0.005)	(0.008)	(0.005)	(0.005)	(0.006)	(0.011)	(0.008)	(0.010)	(0.014)	(0.037)	(0.014)	(0.015)	(0.007)	(0.014)	(0.007)	(0.007)
Large*FC	−0.047***	−0.069***	−0.084***	−0.069***	−0.051***	0.111***	0.070***	0.065***	−0.079***	−0.024**	0.067***	0.087***	−0.057***	0.061***	0.080***	−0.083***
	(0.008)	(0.009)	(0.006)	(0.006)	(0.021)	(0.014)	(0.011)	(0.016)	(0.023)	(0.046)	(0.015)	(0.016)	(0.011)	(0.017)	(0.008)	(0.008)
Mature*FC	−0.039***	−0.018	−0.035***	−0.043***	−0.018***	0.040***	0.037***	−0.035**	−0.033***	0.012**	0.043***	0.049***	−0.037***	−0.025	−0.024**	−0.038***
	(0.007)	(0.011)	(0.008)	(0.008)	(0.004)	(0.013)	(0.010)	(0.014)	(0.020)	(0.033)	(0.019)	(0.022)	(0.010)	(0.018)	(0.012)	(0.011)
Older*FC	−0.062***	−0.037***	−0.059***	−0.076***	−0.037***	0.052***	0.058***	0.063***	−0.036***	−0.036***	0.069***	0.073***	−0.048***	0.055***	0.049***	−0.063***
	(0.007)	(0.011)	(0.008)	(0.008)	(0.005)	(0.012)	(0.011)	(0.014)	(0.021)	(0.031)	(0.020)	(0.022)	(0.011)	(0.018)	(0.012)	(0.011)
Multi	0.001	0.001	0.014***	0.012***	0.002	−0.001	0.008*	0.006	−0.003	−0.006	0.008***	0.006***	−0.001	−0.005	0.010**	0.007*
	(0.003)	(0.006)	(0.005)	(0.004)	(0.005)	(0.012)	(0.005)	(0.004)	(0.003)	(0.006)	(0.004)	(0.004)	(0.003)	(0.006)	(0.004)	(0.004)
Manuf	0.00002	0.001	−0.014***	−0.002	0.001	−0.001	−0.015***	−0.006**	−0.003	−0.004	−0.017***	−0.007	−0.003	−0.004	0.017***	−0.006**
	(0.002)	(0.005)	(0.003)	(0.003)	(0.002)	(0.005)	(0.003)	(0.003)	(0.002)	(0.004)	(0.003)	(0.003)	(0.002)	(0.004)	(0.003)	(0.003)

Dependent variable: Employment growth

Exporter	0.004	0.011***	0.020***	−0.002	−0.008	0.003	0.012***	−0.005*	−0.014	0.004***	0.012***	−0.003	−0.011*	0.006	0.014***
	(0.004)	(0.004)	(0.004)	(0.004)	(0.006)	(0.004)	(0.004)	(0.004)	(0.006)	(0.004)	(0.004)	(0.004)	(0.006)	(0.004)	(0.004)
Foreign	−0.003	0.017***	0.004	−0.003	0.006	0.012**	0.004	−0.008	0.002	0.011***	0.004	−0.007**	0.002	0.013***	0.006
	(0.003)	(0.005)	(0.005)	(0.003)	(0.006)	(0.005)	(0.005)	(0.003)	(0.005)	(0.005)	(0.005)	(0.003)	(0.005)	(0.005)	(0.005)
Govt	−0.036***	−0.041***	−0.031	−0.041***	−0.017	0.048***	−0.036*	−0.048***	−0.026	0.051***	−0.036*	−0.044***	−0.019*	−0.047***	−0.032
	(0.010)	(0.006)	(0.005)	(0.009)	(0.011)	(0.006)	(0.021)	(0.009)	(0.011)	(0.006)	(0.020)	(0.009)	(0.011)	(0.006)	(0.020)
Constant	0.068***	0.028***	0.033***	0.063***	0.025***	0.056***	0.058***	0.070***	0.030***	0.049***	0.053***	0.068***	0.026***	0.038***	0.042***
	(0.002)	(0.003)	(0.004)	(0.002)	(0.004)	(0.002)	(0.003)	(0.002)	(0.003)	(0.002)	(0.002)	(0.002)	(0.003)	(0.002)	(0.003)
Adjusted R^2	0.069	0.099	0.097	0.062	0.062	0.070	0.045	0.083	0.086	0.090	0.092	0.055	0.056	0.082	0.079
Number of observations	10,358	9,527	9,949	10,636	4,076	9,907	10,067	10,878	4,431	10,237	10,203	10,878	4,431	10,237	10,203
Number of countries	37	30	15	38	10	30	15	38	10	30	15	38	10	30	15

Source: Author estimates based on data of Enterprise Surveys (database) (2006–10), World Bank, Washington, DC, http://www.enterprisesurveys.org/.

Note: Standard errors (in parentheses) are robust to heteroskedasticity and clustered on countries. Regressions for the Middle East and North Africa and for South Asia are excluded because of insufficient data. Model: $EG = b0 + b1FC + b2Small*FC + b3Medium*FC + b4Large*FC + b5Mature*FC + b6Older*FC + b7Multi + b8Manuf + b9Exporter + b10Foreign + b11Govt + Region + Country$ Fixed Effects + e. AFR = Africa; EAP = East Asia and Pacific; ECA = (Eastern) Europe and Central Asia; govt = government owned; LAC = Latin America and the Caribbean; manuf = manufacturing; multi = multiestablishment.

Significance level: * = 10 percent, ** = 5 percent, *** = 1 percent, * in stub (first) column = multiplication sign.

are largest among small firms. The effects among medium and large firms are similar in size. The effect of being credit constrained increases with firm size.

Columns 6–8 show that having a loan is important for firms of all ages and that the largest effect is on young firms. Being credit constrained has the largest effect on medium firms and then large firms. The effects of having external finance are statistically significant for firms of all ages. In short, trust and external finance matter to firms, regardless of their age.

Columns 9–11 show that most forms of financial access are important to firms, no matter the sector. Having a loan has the largest effect on employment growth among firms in the manufacturing sector. Being credit constrained has a negative effect on firms in all sectors, and the largest effect occurs in the manufacturing and sales sectors. Having external finance matters in all sectors, and the effects are of similar magnitude.

Columns 12–15 present the estimation results across regions. Having a loan and external finance matters to firms in different regions, with the largest effects in Latin America. Being credit constrained has a significant effect on firm employment growth only in Eastern Europe and Central Asia and in Latin America. From these results, together with the results in tables 4.10 and 4.11, we find that the interaction between financial access variables and firm size or age is significant in explaining firm employment growth.

Firm Size Distribution

Because a firm's size plays a significant part in determining the firm's employment growth, we also assess the relationship between firm size and financial constraints. The survey data allow the creation of a variable showing which firms are credit constrained and which, according to our analysis, have applied for a loan and have been rejected or have been discouraged from applying for a loan.[12] The data also include extensive information on the sources of firm investments in fixed assets. These sources may be external (formal or informal) or internal.[13]

Confirming the findings of Cabral and Mata (2003), figure 4.2 shows that the firm size distribution is skewed to the right and that the skewness tends to diminish with age. The size distribution of older firms is more symmetric than that of young firms.

As shown in figure 4.3, the firm size distribution is skewed more to the right in the manufacturing and services sectors, where micro and small

Table 4.12 The Effect of Combined Objective Financial Access Variables on Employment Growth, by Firm Characteristics and Region

	Dependent variable: Employment growth														
	By size					By age			By sector			By region			
Variable	World	Micro	Small	Medium	Large	Young	Mature	Older	Manufacturing	Sales	Services	AFR	EAP	ECA	LAC
	(1)	(2)	(3)	(4)	(5)	(6)	(7)	(8)	(9)	(10)	(11)	(12)	(13)	(14)	(15)
Small	-0.052***					-0.082***	-0.051***	-0.044***	-0.060***	-0.037***	-0.056***	-0.046***	-0.058***	-0.042***	-0.061***
	(0.002)					(0.006)	(0.002)	(0.002)	(0.002)	(0.003)	(0.004)	(0.002)	(0.005)	(0.003)	(0.003)
Medium	-0.067***					-0.113***	-0.071***	-0.054***	-0.080***	-0.041***	-0.065***	-0.056***	-0.080***	-0.065***	-0.067***
	(0.002)					(0.010)	(0.003)	(0.003)	(0.003)	(0.005)	(0.005)	(0.004)	(0.006)	(0.004)	(0.004)
Large	-0.091***					-0.137***	-0.089***	-0.080***	-0.110***	-0.032***	-0.082***	-0.078***	-0.107***	-0.093***	-0.085***
	(0.003)					(0.019)	(0.005)	(0.004)	(0.004)	(0.008)	(0.008)	(0.007)	(0.008)	(0.005)	(0.006)
Mature	-0.030***	-0.036***	-0.016***	-0.014	-0.017				-0.038***	-0.025***	-0.019***	-0.024***	-0.021***	-0.041***	-0.037***
	(0.003)	(0.003)	(0.005)	(0.009)	(0.018)				(0.004)	(0.004)	(0.005)	(0.003)	(0.007)	(0.006)	(0.006)
Older	-0.053***	-0.064***	-0.038***	-0.032***	-0.043**				-0.060***	-0.047***	-0.040***	-0.046***	-0.036***	-0.065***	-0.065***
	(0.003)	(0.003)	(0.005)	(0.009)	(0.018)				(0.004)	(0.005)	(0.006)	(0.004)	(0.007)	(0.006)	(0.006)
Multi	0.014***	0.013***	0.017***	0.012***	0.010*	0.009	0.015***	0.014***	0.015***	0.012***	0.014***	0.008***	0.009	0.018***	0.015***
	(0.002)	(0.004)	(0.003)	(0.004)	(0.006)	(0.008)	(0.003)	(0.003)	(0.003)	(0.004)	(0.005)	(0.003)	(0.006)	(0.005)	(0.004)
Manuf	-0.001	0.011***	-0.002	-0.018***	0.032***	0.022***	-0.001	-0.007***				0.007***	0.009*	-0.011***	-0.001
	(0.001)	(0.002)	(0.002)	(0.004)	(0.006)	(0.005)	(0.002)	(0.002)				(0.002)	(0.005)	(0.003)	(0.003)
Exporter	0.014***	0.028***	0.024***	0.009**	-0.001	0.035***	0.011***	0.015***	0.020***	0.017**	0.007	0.011**	0.009	0.013***	0.022***
	(0.002)	(0.006)	(0.004)	(0.004)	(0.006)	(0.011)	(0.003)	(0.002)	(0.002)	(0.007)	(0.006)	(0.004)	(0.006)	(0.004)	(0.004)
Foreign	0.009***	0.006	0.013***	0.008*	0.009	0.019**	0.014***	0.001	0.010***	0.008*	0.011**	0.002	0.012**	0.020***	0.010**
	(0.002)	(0.005)	(0.004)	(0.004)	(0.006)	(0.008)	(0.003)	(0.003)	(0.003)	(0.005)	(0.005)	(0.003)	(0.006)	(0.005)	(0.005)
Govt	-0.023***	-0.031*	-0.007	-0.020***	0.028***	-0.030*	-0.019***	-0.022***	-0.015**	-0.032***	-0.032***	-0.024**	0.002	-0.028***	-0.024
	(0.005)	(0.018)	(0.010)	(0.007)	(0.009)	(0.017)	(0.008)	(0.006)	(0.006)	(0.012)	(0.008)	(0.010)	(0.010)	(0.006)	(0.022)
Loan	0.019***	0.014***	0.023***	0.017***	0.015**	0.027***	0.018***	0.017***	0.022***	0.015***	0.017***	0.011***	0.016***	0.023***	0.026***
	(0.002)	(0.003)	(0.003)	(0.004)	(0.007)	(0.006)	(0.002)	(0.002)	(0.002)	(0.003)	(0.004)	(0.003)	(0.004)	(0.003)	(0.003)

(continued next page)

Table 4.12 (continued)

		By size				By age			By sector			By region			
	Dependent variable: Employment growth														
Variable	World	Micro	Small	Medium	Large	Young	Mature	Older	Manufacturing	Sales	Services	AFR	EAP	ECA	LAC
	(1)	(2)	(3)	(4)	(5)	(6)	(7)	(8)	(9)	(10)	(11)	(12)	(13)	(14)	(15)
Credit constraint	-0.009***	-0.003	-0.014***	-0.017***	-0.018**	-0.005	-0.010***	-0.008***	-0.009*** (0.002)	-0.010***	-0.007*	-0.002	0.003	-0.023***	-0.010***
	(0.002)	(0.002)	(0.003)	(0.005)	(0.008)	(0.006)	(0.002)	(0.002)		(0.003)	(0.004)	(0.002)	(0.004)	(0.003)	(0.003)
Sales credit	-0.004	0.001	-0.008	-0.013**	0.004	0.011	-0.007	-0.006	-0.004 (0.004)	-0.007	-0.003	-0.002	0.006	-0.006	-0.003
	(0.003)	(0.007)	(0.005)	(0.006)	(0.008)	(0.014)	(0.005)	(0.004)		(0.006)	(0.007)	(0.006)	(0.012)	(0.005)	(0.005)
External finance	0.036***	0.034***	0.042***	0.030***	0.025***	0.032***	0.035***	0.037***	0.036*** (0.002)	0.036***	0.036***	0.019***	0.036***	0.038***	0.041***
	(0.002)	(0.004)	(0.003)	(0.004)	(0.006)	(0.008)	(0.003)	(0.003)		(0.004)	(0.004)	(0.004)	(0.006)	(0.005)	(0.005)
Constant	0.105***	0.106***	0.035***	0.036***	0.041**	0.102***	0.077***	0.048***	0.112*** (0.004)	0.087***	0.091***	0.107***	0.073***	0.109***	0.112***
	(0.003)	(0.003)	(0.005)	(0.010)	(0.019)	(0.005)	(0.002)	(0.003)		(0.005)	(0.006)	(0.004)	(0.007)	(0.006)	(0.007)
Adjusted R^2	0.135	0.107	0.100	0.097	0.105	0.130	0.115	0.100	0.151	0.116	0.130	0.119	0.122	0.143	0.135
Number of observations	34,524	13,169	13,060	5,739	2,527	3,734	16,387	14,403	21,675	7,978	4,870	10,270	3,971	9,423	9,911
Number of countries	95	95	95	94	89	95	95	95	95	95	95	37	10	30	15

Source: Author estimates based on data of Enterprise Surveys (database) (2006–10), World Bank, Washington, DC, http://www.enterprisesurveys.org/.

Note: Standard errors (in parentheses) are robust to heteroskedasticity and clustered on countries. Regressions for the Middle East and North Africa and for South Asia are excluded because of insufficient data. Model: $EG = b0 + b1Small + b2Medium + b3Large + b4Mature + b5Older + b6Multi + b7Manuf + b8Exporter + b9Foreign + b10Govt + b11Loan + b12Credit Constraint + b13Sales Credit + b14 External Finance + Country Fixed Effects + e.$ AFR = Africa; EAP = East Asia and Pacific; ECA = (Eastern) Europe and Central Asia; govt = government owned; LAC = Latin America and the Caribbean; manuf = manufacturing; multi = multiestablishment.

Significance level: * = 10 percent; ** = 5 percent; *** = 1 percent.

firms make up about two-thirds of the sample. Figure 4.4 suggests that Africa has the largest share of micro and small firms, while other regions have more medium and large firms. This represents more evidence of the missing middle in Africa.

Using the credit constrained indicator created for this analysis, we split the sample into two groups: credit-constrained firms and non-credit-constrained firms. As figure 4.5 shows, the firm size distribution is skewed to the right among credit-constrained firms. This result is in line with the finding that being credit constrained has a negative effect on firm growth and, especially, that this effect is largest among small firms. Taking this analysis a step farther, we investigate firm size distribution using the survey data on firm perceptions of access to finance, splitting the sample between those firms perceiving this access as a major or severe obstacle and those firms viewing the access as a minor obstacle or no obstacle. Figure 4.6 shows that the size distribution of firms perceiving access to finance as a major or severe obstacle is skewed to the right. This result is confirmed by the data for our sample showing that most of the firms regarding access to finance as a major or severe obstacle are microfirms or small firms. The size distribution among firms perceiving access to finance as a minor obstacle or no obstacle is more symmetric.

Figure 4.2   Firm Size Distribution, by Age

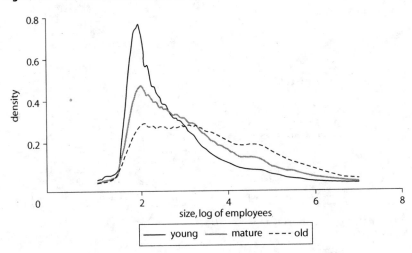

Source: Author estimates based on data of Enterprise Surveys (database) (2006–10), World Bank, Washington, DC, http://www.enterprisesurveys.org/.

Figure 4.3   Firm Size Distribution, by Sector

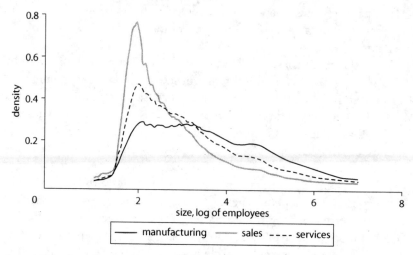

Source: Author estimates based on data of Enterprise Surveys (database) (2006–10), World Bank, Washington, DC, http://www.enterprisesurveys.org/.

Figure 4.4   Firm Size Distribution, All Sectors, by Region

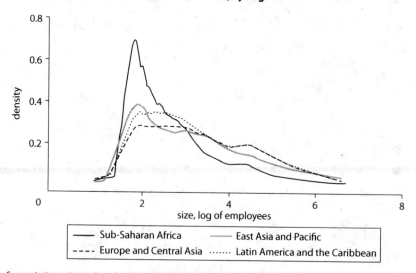

Source: Author estimates based on data of Enterprise Surveys (database) (2006–10), World Bank, Washington, DC, http://www.enterprisesurveys.org/.

Figure 4.5   Size Distribution: Credit-Constrained and Non-Credit-Constrained Firms

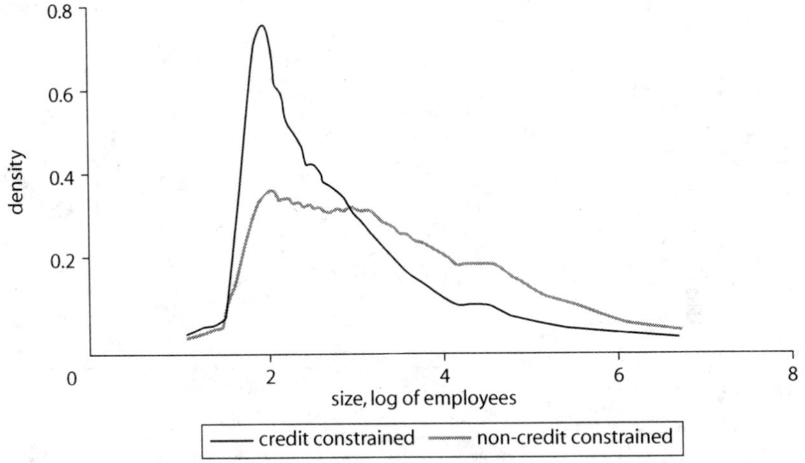

Source: Author estimates based on data of Enterprise Surveys (database) (2006–10), World Bank, Washington, DC, http://www.enterprisesurveys.org/.

The findings in this section and the previous sections suggest that a low level of financial development results in a skewed firm size distribution, with a larger relative share of small firms. Policies favoring the development of the financial sector should therefore have an effect on the firm size distribution and, ultimately, favor the adoption of different technologies and an improved allocation of resources if the industry in question benefits from the country's comparative advantages (Lin 2010).

Conclusion

Using a newly available data set from the World Bank Enterprise Surveys (2006–10) for 39,538 firms across 98 countries, we investigate the binding constraints on firm employment growth. Using an econometric model and subjective measures, we find that access to finance and informal sector competition are the most binding constraints both globally and in each region. Using objective measures and controlling for firm characteristics, we evaluate the importance of access to finance for firm employment growth. We find that access to different forms of finance matters. These results from our cross-country firm-level analysis suggest that governments

Figure 4.6   Size Distribution by the Perception of Access to Finance as an Obstacle

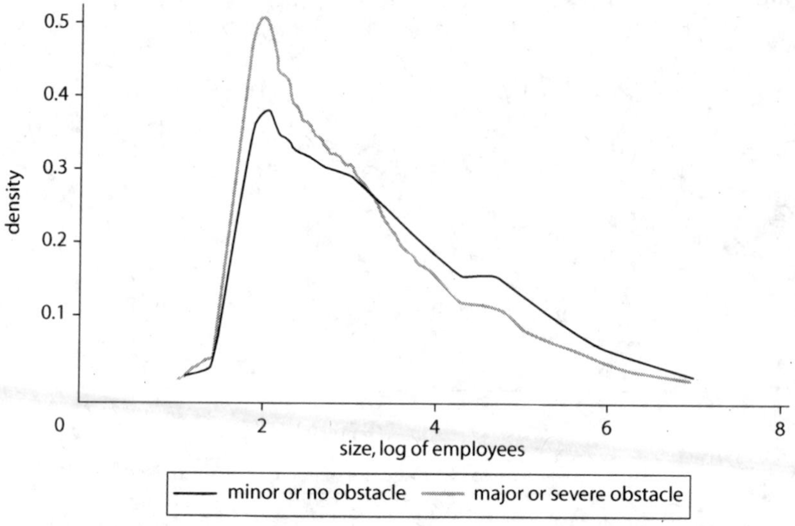

Source: Author estimates based on data of Enterprise Surveys (database) (2006–10), World Bank, Washington, DC, http://www.enterprisesurveys.org/.

seeking to improve the business environment and promote firm growth should make financial sector reforms a priority.

Objective business conditions vary systematically across firms of different sizes and ages, and good business conditions favor smaller firms, especially microfirms. Microfirms and small firms gain the most from access to finance in forms ranging from the simple to the more sophisticated, from a loan or overdraft facility to sales credit to external finance for investment. This finding holds not only globally, but also across different regions. While sales credit is important only for microfirms and small firms, having a loan or overdraft facility and receiving external finance for investment promote employment growth among firms of all sizes across regions. And sales credit and external finance matter for firms of all ages.

The firm size distribution is skewed toward smaller firms. The skewness declines with firm age and is more present in Africa, among firms that are credit constrained, and among firms that perceive access to finance as a serious obstacle. These findings call for policies favoring the development of the financial sector, which can help small firms grow into medium and large firms.

The findings have several implications for developing countries. First, because the constraints faced by firms differ across countries and, within countries, across sectors, policies to promote firm growth need to be tailored to each country and sector. Second, finance appears to be the most binding constraint across sectors and countries, suggesting that reforms in this sector could yield broad benefits, including by helping address the problem of the missing middle in developing countries. Third, while access to finance is a binding constraint on firm growth in all developing countries, the fact that industrial development in some countries took off more quickly and earlier than in others indicates that there are other constraints not captured by the Enterprise Surveys. Finally, reforms in finance take time, and a more rapid development strategy might involve identifying the binding constraints in a specific subsector and trying to address them through direct policy measures.

Annex 4.1   The Biggest Reported Obstacles

Figure 4A.1   The Biggest Reported Obstacles, by Region

a. Eastern Europe and Central Asia

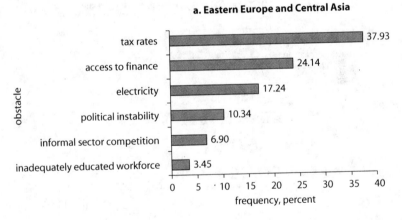

(continued next page)

Figure 4A.1   *(continued)*

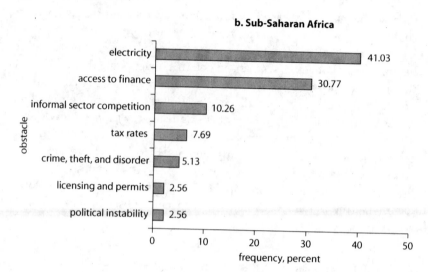

b. Sub-Saharan Africa

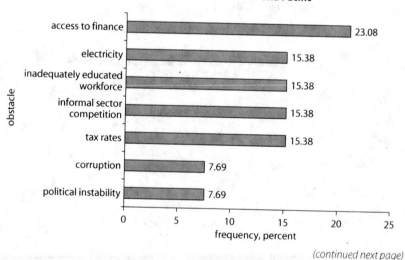

c. East Asia and Pacific

(continued next page)

Figure 4A.1 *(continued)*

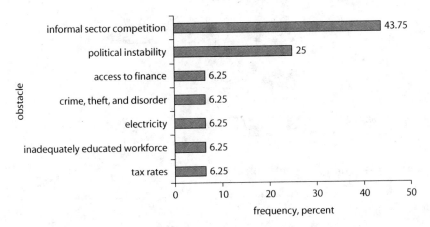

d. Latin America and the Caribbean

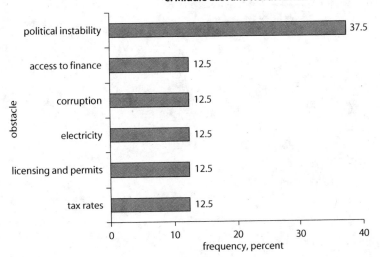

e. Middle East and North Africa

(continued next page)

Figure 4A.1   *(continued)*

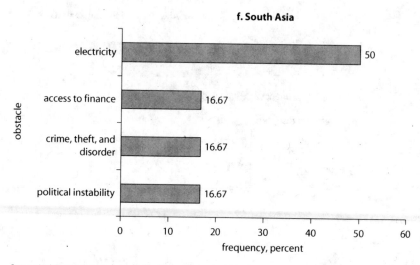

f. South Asia

Source: Author estimates based on data of Enterprise Surveys (database) (2006–10), World Bank, Washington, DC, http://www.enterprisesurveys.org/.

Annex 4.2 The Top Constraints Cited by Firms

Table 4A.1 Top Constraints Cited by Firms, by Country and Region

Country and survey year	Frequency, %	Most cited constraint	Frequency, %	Second most cited constraint	Frequency, %	Third most cited constraint
a. Sub-Saharan Africa						
Angola, 2006	36.8	Electricity	12.5	Corruption	11.6	Access to finance
Benin, 2009	18.2	Access to finance	15.0	Electricity	14.6	Practices, informal sector
Botswana, 2006	24.6	Access to finance	11.8	Practices, informal sector	11.0	Crime, theft, and disorder
Burkina Faso, 2009	35.5	Access to finance	17.7	Tax rates	10.8	Practices, informal sector
Burundi, 2006	41.3	Electricity	16.0	Access to finance	14.3	Political instability
Cameroon, 2009	24.9	Practices, informal sector	19.4	Tax administration	16.6	Access to finance
Cape Verde, 2009	17.1	Practices, informal sector	13.1	Access to finance	11.0	Electricity
Chad, 2009	29.5	Political instability	23.8	Electricity	13.5	Corruption
Congo, Dem. Rep., 2006	46.5	Electricity	14.9	Access to finance	9.6	Tax rates
Congo, Rep., 2009	31.9	Electricity	15.6	Access to finance	15.5	Political instability
Côte d'Ivoire, 2009	45.2	Access to finance	28.0	Political instability	7.5	Corruption
Eritrea, 2009	28.7	Licensing and permits	24.1	Political instability	17.0	Access to land
Gabon, 2009	23.4	Electricity	14.6	Transportation	10.3	Corruption
Gambia, The, 2006	54.5	Electricity	11.7	Access to finance	6.5	Tax rates
Ghana, 2007	48.8	Electricity	33.1	Access to finance	6.3	Tax rates
Guinea, 2006	64.3	Electricity	10.3	Transportation	8.3	Access to finance
Guinea-Bissau, 2006	47.1	Electricity	20.1	Access to finance	7.7	Political instability
Kenya, 2007	21.7	Tax rates	13.5	Access to finance	12.0	Practices, informal sector

(continued next page)

Table 4A.1 (continued)

Country and survey year	Frequency, %	Most cited constraint	Frequency, %	Second most cited constraint	Frequency, %	Third most cited constraint
Lesotho, 2009	15.9	Access to finance	14.7	Corruption	11.2	Tax rates
Liberia, 2009	39.8	Access to finance	17.4	Crime, theft, & disorder	13.3	Electricity
Madagascar, 2009	18.6	Electricity	15.4	Practices, informal sector	13.9	Crime, theft and disorder
Malawi, 2009	45.7	Access to finance	11.4	Transportation	8.9	Practices, informal sector
Mali, 2007	28.9	Electricity	23.5	Access to finance	15.1	Tax rates
Mauritania, 2006	21.6	Access to finance	14.4	Practices, informal sector	13.8	Electricity
Mauritius, 2009	30.2	Access to finance	18.0	Practices, informal sector	11.3	Electricity
Mozambique, 2007	23.2	Access to finance	21.4	Practices, informal sector	9.1	Electricity
Namibia, 2006	21.7	Crime, theft and disorder	17.6	Tax rates	12.1	Access to finance
Niger, 2009	21.2	Practices, informal sector	20.3	Access to finance	15.6	Political instability
Nigeria, 2007	63.6	Electricity	15.5	Access to finance	7.5	Transportation
Rwanda, 2006	32.9	Electricity	27.4	Tax rates	13.6	Access to finance
Senegal, 2007	41.2	Electricity	12.2	Access to finance	11.0	Access to land
Sierra Leone, 2009	17.1	Tax rates	14.8	Access to finance	14.3	Electricity
South Africa, 2007	40.4	Crime, theft, & disorder	14.7	Electricity	7.5	Access to finance
Swaziland, 2006	25.4	Practices, informal sector	18.5	Crime, theft and disorder	15.4	Tax rates
Tanzania, 2006	73.4	Electricity	9.8	Access to finance	4.0	Tax rates
Togo, 2009	23.7	Access to finance	23.3	Political instability	11.2	Practices, informal sector
Uganda, 2006	63.6	Electricity	11.3	Tax rates	8.5	Practices, informal sector
Zambia, 2007	18.6	Tax rates	15.3	Practice, informal sector	14.3	Access to finance

b. East Asia and Pacific

Country						
Fiji, 2009	44.4	Political instability	8.8	Labor regulations	8.6	Crime, theft and disorder
Indonesia, 2009	47.9	Access to finance	13.7	Practices, informal sector	6.9	Political instability
Lao PDR, 2009	36.8	Tax rates	21.2	Access to finance	16.5	Education of workforce
Micronesia, Fed. Sts., 2009	25.2	Education of workforce	15.8	Electricity	12.6	Transportation
Mongolia, 2009	30.3	Access to finance	16.0	Tax rates	10.2	Education of workforce
Philippines, 2009	26.4	Practices, informal sector	14.8	Access to finance	13.0	Tax rates
Samoa, 2009	16.9	Tax rates	13.8	Crime, theft, and disorder	13.8	Crime, theft, and disorder
Timor-Leste, 2009	36.3	Electricity	12.7	Crime, theft, and disorder	12.1	Access to finance
Tonga, 2009	20.1	Practices, informal sector	17.0	Corruption	15.6	Tax rates
Vanuatu, 2009	15.7	Electricity	14.8	Access to finance	14.3	Crime, theft, and disorder
Vietnam, 2009	24.7	Access to finance	19.3	Practices, informal sector	13.3	Transportation

c. (Eastern) Europe and Central Asia

Country						
Albania, 2007	27.7	Electricity	17.6	Practices, informal sector	11.0	Corruption
Armenia, 2009	21.8	Practices, informal sector	16.0	Tax rates	15.9	Political instability
Azerbaijan, 2009	23.1	Access to finance	22.2	Tax rates	18.2	Corruption
Belarus, 2008	25.9	Tax rates	14.6	Licenseing and permits	14.1	Education of workforce
Bosnia and Herzegovina, 2009	25.1	Political instability	18.7	Tax rates	11.4	Practices, informal sector
Bulgaria, 2009	17.2	Access to finance	15.2	Practices, informal sector	13.3	Political instability
Croatia, 2007	18.3	Access to finance	17.0	Education of workforce	15.8	Tax rates
Czech Republic, 2009	20.0	Access to finance	14.2	Tax rates	11.8	Education of workforce
Estonia, 2009	28.8	Education of workforce	15.9	Political instability	14.7	Practices, informal sector
Georgia, 2008	18.0	Access to finance	17.4	Political instability	16.4	Electricity
Hungary, 2009	38.4	Tax rates	24.2	Political instability	14.2	Tax administration
Kazakhstan, 2009	26.6	Tax rates	15.2	Corruption	13.2	Access to finance
Kosovo, 2009	33.5	Electricity	20.6	Corruption	12.8	Practices, informal sector

(continued next page)

131

Table 4A.1 (continued)

Country and survey year	Frequency, %	Most cited constraint	Frequency, %	Second most cited constraint	Frequency, %	Third most cited constraint
Kyrgyz Republic, 2009	24.5	Electricity	19.9	Access to finance	11.0	Practices, informal sector
Latvia, 2009	19.1	Tax rates	16.7	Political instability	11.3	Tax administration
Lithuania, 2009	35.2	Tax rates	12.0	Practices, informal sector	11.4	Access to finance
Macedonia, FYR, 2009	31.3	Practices informal sector	26.9	Access to finance	6.8	Political instability
Moldova, 2009	19.5	Access to finance	15.7	Education of workforce	10.4	Access to land
Montenegro, 2009	18.7	Electricity	17.9	Access to finance	12.7	Practices, informal sector
Poland, 2009	22.0	Tax rates	15.6	Education of workforce	13.8	Practices, informal sector
Romania, 2009	27.7	Tax rates	20.7	Education of workforce	19.9	Access to finance
Russian Federation, 2009	17.2	Tax rates	16.9	Access to finance	15.4	Education of workforce
Serbia, 2009	20.7	Political instability	19.9	Practices, informal sector	17.8	Access to finance
Slovak Republic, 2009	16.2	Tax rates	13.3	Informal sector competition	12.8	Informal sector competition
Slovenia, 2009	20.0	Tax rates	19.2	Access to finance	17.4	Practices, informal sector
Tajikistan, 2008	24.8	Electricity	22.5	Tax rates	17.5	Access to finance
Turkey, 2008	25.9	Access to finance	18.2	Tax rates	17.5	Political instability
Ukraine, 2008	23.2	Political instability	17.5	Tax rates	10.6	Corruption
Uzbekistan, 2008	23.6	Tax rates	17.9	Access to finance	9.2	Education of workforce
d. Latin America and the Caribbean						
Argentina, 2006	16.5	Political instability	15.7	Access to finance	15.4	Labor regulations
Bolivia, 2006	30.3	Political instability	28.1	Practices, informal sector	8.0	Corruption
Brazil, 2009	32.8	Tax rates	13.2	Tax administration	12.7	Access to finance

132

Country	Value 1	Constraint 1	Value 2	Constraint 2	Value 3	Constraint 3
Chile, 2006	18.5	Practices, informal sector	15.3	Electricity	14.3	Crime, theft, and disorder
Colombia, 2006	34.6	Practices, informal sector	12.9	Crime, theft, and disorder	12.5	Tax rates
Ecuador, 2006	28.4	Political instability	18.3	Corruption	14.2	Access to finance
El Salvador, 2006	31.3	Crime, theft, and disorder	15.3	Practices, informal sector	13.3	Corruption
Guatemala, 2006	21.0	Practices, informal sector	20.0	Crime, theft, and disorder	10.1	Political instability
Honduras, 2006	19.2	Access to finance	19.2	Corruption	15.6	Crime, theft, and disorder
Mexico, 2006	19.0	Practices, informal sector	17.9	Corruption	10.6	Tax rates
Nicaragua, 2006	26.0	Political instability	17.3	Access to finance	16.6	Electricity
Panama, 2006	30.6	Electricity	14.6	Tax rates	10.8	Corruption
Paraguay, 2006	25.8	Practices, informal sector	21.0	Access to finance	14.9	Corruption
Peru, 2006	22.1	Practices, informal sector	17.9	Tax administration	17.0	Political instability
Uruguay, 2006	32.4	Practices, informal sector	20.5	Tax rates	12.0	Access to finance
Venezuela, RB, 2006	29.2	Education of workforce	27.9	Crime, theft, and disorder	10.0	Corruption
e. South Asia						
Yemen, Rep., 2010	32.1	Electricity	26.6	Corruption	7.7	Political instability
Afghanistan, 2008	20.0	Crime, theft, and disorder	17.9	Electricity	16.8	Access to finance
Bhutan, 2009	21.7	Access to finance	12.5	Tax rates	10.5	Education of workforce
Nepal, 2009	62.1	Political instability	26.5	Electricity	2.6	Labor regulations

Source: Author estimates based on data of Enterprise Surveys (database) (2006–10), World Bank, Washington, DC, http://www.enterprisesurveys.org/.

Note: "Education of workforce" refers to inadequately educated workforce.

Notes

We are grateful for the valuable comments and help from Alvaro Gonzalez, Anders Isaksson, Justin Yifu Lin, Minh C. Nguyen, Vincent Palmade, and L. Colin Xu.

1. See Xu (2011). Earlier empirical studies of firm growth focused mainly on large manufacturing firms. For example, see Evans (1987a, 1987b); Hall (1987); Dunne, Roberts, and Samuelson (1989). These authors find that firm age and size are important in the analysis of firm growth because larger and older firms tend to grow proportionally more slowly than smaller firms. As a proxy for business environment, Knack and Keefer (1995) use a cross-country index of potential expropriation risk provided by a private country risk evaluator for potential foreign investors. For details on the Enterprise Surveys, see http://www.enterprisesurveys.org/.

2. Analyzing the growth of firms in Uganda, Fisman and Svensson (2007) find that both the rate of taxation and the rate of bribery are negatively correlated with firm growth. Reinikka and Svensson (2002), who also study firms in Uganda, find that poor infrastructure and deficient public services reduce the amount firms invest, a hint that some public investment is complementary to private investment.

3. Labor regulations include not only employment protection, such as the cost of firing an employee or the length of the prior notice of dismissal, but also the amount of severance payments or the bargaining power of unions.

4. Like other researchers, for several reasons, we use employment growth rather than sales growth. Sales growth is more volatile and is also more prone to reporting and measurement biases, especially if survey respondents are reporting sales realized three years previously. Moreover, for tax reasons, firms may not choose to report actual sales.

5. $\ln(1 + X)$ is considered approximately equal to $\ln(X)$. We therefore use $\ln(1 + X)$ to compute the log of the number of employees because some firms have zero employees in a specific year, but not in both years.

6. Because this information is available for only 14 percent of firms in the sample, no dummy variable is included for firms the applications of which for new loans or lines of credit were rejected.

7. The questionnaire provides information on industry, and we use this information to establish the sector variable.

8. Firms in operation for less than one year are classified as young firms.

9. The estimation results are available from the authors on request.

10. See Aterido, Hallward-Driemeier, and Pagés (2009) on this point.

11. The results are available from the authors on request.

12. Our measure of credit-constrained firms comprises those that have applied for a loan and have been rejected and those that have not applied for a loan

for one or more of the following reasons: fear of rejection, high collateral requirements, unfavorable interest rates, or a belief that the application would not be approved.

13. Formal sources are private or public banks, nonbank financial institutions, issues of new debt, and supplier credit. Informal sources are friends and moneylenders. Internal sources consist of issuances of new shares and own funds.

References

Angelini, Paolo, and Andrea Generale. 2008. "On the Evolution of Firm Size Distributions." *American Economic Review* 98 (1): 426–38.

Aterido, Reyes, and Mary Hallward-Driemeier. 2010. "The Impact of the Investment Climate on Employment Growth: Does Sub-Saharan Africa Mirror Other Low-Income Regions?" Policy Research Working Paper 5218, World Bank, Washington, DC.

Aterido, Reyes, Mary Hallward-Driemeier, and Carmen Pagés. 2007. "Investment Climate and Employment Growth: The Impact of Access to Finance, Corruption and Regulations across Firms." RES Working Paper 4559, Research Department, Inter-American Development Bank, Washington, DC.

———. 2009. "Big Constraints to Small Firms' Growth? Business Environment and Employment Growth across Firms." Policy Research Working Paper 5032, World Bank, Washington, DC.

Ayyagari, Meghana, Asli Demirgüç-Kunt, and Vojislav Maksimovic. 2006. "How Important Are Financing Constraints? The Role of Finance in the Business Environment." Policy Research Working Paper 3820, World Bank, Washington, DC.

Batra, Geeta, Daniel Kaufmann, and Andrew H. W. Stone. 2003. *Investment Climate around the World: Voices of the Firms from the World Business Environment Survey*. Washington, DC: World Bank.

Beck, Thorsten, Asli Demirgüç-Kunt, and Vojislav Maksimovic. 2005. "Financial and Legal Constraints to Growth: Does Firm Size Matter?" *Journal of Finance* 60 (1): 131–77.

Bigsten, Arne, and Mans Söderbom. 2006. "What Have We Learned from a Decade of Manufacturing Enterprise Surveys in Africa?" *World Bank Research Observer* 21 (2): 241–65.

Borensztein, Eduardo, Eduardo Levy Yeyati, and Ugo Panizza, eds. 2006. *Living with Debt: How to Limit the Risks of Sovereign Finance, 2007 Report*. Economic and Social Progress in Latin America Series. Cambridge, MA: David Rockefeller Center for Latin American Studies, Harvard University; Washington, DC: Inter-American Development Bank.

Cabral, Luis M. B., and Jose Mata. 2003. "On the Evolution of the Firm Size Distribution: Facts and Theory." *American Economic Review* 93 (4): 1075–90.

Cooley, Thomas F., and Vincenzo Quadrini. 2001. "Financial Markets and Firm Dynamics." *American Economic Review* 91 (5): 1286–310.

Demirgüç-Kunt, Asli, and Vojislav Maksimovic. 1998. "Law, Finance, and Firm Growth." *Journal of Finance* 53 (6): 2107–37.

Desai, Mihir, Paul Gompers, and Josh Lerner. 2003. "Institutions, Capital Constraints and Entrepreneurial Firm Dynamics: Evidence from Europe." NBER Working Paper 10165, National Bureau of Economic Research, Cambridge, MA.

Djankov, Simeon, Rafael La Porta, Florencio López-de-Silanes, and Andrei Shleifer. 2002. "The Regulation of Entry." *Quarterly Journal of Economics* 117 (1): 1–37.

Dollar, David, Mary Hallward-Driemeier, and Taye Mengistae. 2005. "Investment Climate and Firm Performance in Developing Countries." *Economic Development and Cultural Change* 54 (1): 1–31.

Dunne, Timothy, Mark J. Roberts, and Larry Samuelson. 1989. "The Growth and Failure of U.S. Manufacturing Plants." *Quarterly Journal of Economics* 104 (4): 671–98.

Evans, David S. 1987a. "The Relationship between Firm Growth, Size, and Age: Estimates for 100 Manufacturing Industries." *Journal of Industrial Economics* 35 (4): 567–81.

———. 1987b. "Tests of Alternative Theories of Firm Growth." *Journal of Political Economy* 95 (4): 657–74.

Fisman, Raymond, and Jakob Svensson. 2007. "Are Corruption and Taxation Really Harmful to Growth? Firm-Level Evidence." *Journal of Development Economics* 83 (1): 63–75.

Freund, Caroline, and Nadia Rocha. 2010. "What Constrains Africa's Exports?" Policy Research Working Paper 5184, World Bank, Washington, DC.

Galindo, Arturo José, and Alejandro Micco. 2007. "Creditor Protection and Credit Response to Shocks." *World Bank Economic Review* 21 (3): 413–38.

Gelb, Alan, Vijaya Ramachandran, Manju Kedia Shah, and Ginger Turner. 2007. "What Matters to African Firms? The Relevance of Perceptions Data." Policy Research Working Paper 4446, World Bank, Washington, DC.

Hall, Bronwyn H. 1987. "The Relationship between Firm Size and Firm Growth in the U.S. Manufacturing Sector." *Journal of Industrial Economics* 35 (4): 583–606.

Hallward-Driemeier, Mary, Scott Wallsten, and Lixin Colin Xu. 2006. "Ownership, Investment Climate and Firm Performance: Evidence from Chinese Firms." *Economics of Transition* 14 (4): 629–47.

Hausmann, Ricardo, Dani Rodrik, and Andrés Velasco. 2005. *Growth Diagnostics.* Cambridge, MA: John F. Kennedy School of Government, Harvard University.

Jovanovic, Boyan. 1982. "Selection and Evolution of Industry." *Econometrica* 50 (3): 649–70.

Klapper, Leora, Luc Laeven, and Raghuram Rajan. 2004. "Business Environment and Firm Entry: Evidence from International Data." NBER Working Paper 10380, National Bureau of Economic Research, Cambridge, MA.

Knack, Stephen, and Philip Keefer. 1995. "Institutions and Economic Performance: Cross-Country Tests Using Alternative Institutional Measures." *Economics and Politics* 7 (3): 207–27.

Lin, Justin Yifu. 2010. "New Structural Economics: A Framework for Rethinking Development." Policy Research Working Paper 5197, World Bank, Washington, DC.

Lipsey, R. G., and Kelvin Lancaster. 1956. "The General Theory of Second Best." *Review of Economic Studies* 24 (1): 11–32.

Love, Inessa, and Nataliya Mylenko. 2003. "Credit Reporting and Financing Constraints." Policy Research Working Paper 3142, World Bank, Washington, DC.

Rajan, Raghuram, and Luigi Zingales. 1998. "Financial Dependence and Growth." *American Economic Review* 88 (3): 559–86.

Reinikka, Ritva, and Jakob Svensson. 2002. "Coping with Poor Public Capital." *Journal of Development Economics* 69 (1): 51–69.

World Economic Forum. 2009. *The Africa Competitiveness Report 2009.* Geneva: World Economic Forum.

Xu, Lixin Colin. 2011. "The Effects of Business Environments on Development: A Survey of New Firm-Level Evidence." *World Bank Research Observer* 26 (2): 310–40.

CHAPTER 5

Results of Sample Surveys of Firms

Marcel Fafchamps and Simon Quinn

Introduction

This chapter presents the results of sample surveys among firms in three African countries (Ethiopia, Tanzania, and Zambia) and two East Asian countries (China and Vietnam). It focuses on small and medium manufacturing firms in five light manufacturing sectors.[1] The survey questionnaire is in annex 5.1.

China's success in manufacturing growth and exports has struck many people's imagination, especially compared with what is often perceived as dismal manufacturing performance in Africa. However, the picture that the data paint is quite different: the African firms in the sample show healthy growth rates. Ultimately, the main difference between China and the other countries is that the average firm size in China is much larger and manufacturing represents a sizable proportion of GDP. Hence, a 14.8 percent growth rate in sales has a large effect on aggregate growth. This is not true in the other countries, particularly in the three African countries in our sample, where firms are smaller and manufacturing only represents a minute portion of domestic GDP.

Why is the manufacturing sector larger in China? The survey results presented here suggest that, whatever the reason for China's success relative to Africa, such success is unlikely to have arisen because of easier regulation. If anything, China seems to have more stringent registration requirements and labor laws. It is unlikely to be corruption, which seems to generate more anxiety among respondents in China than respondents in the other countries: indeed, the more rapidly growing firms in the sample are more likely to report that they must pay government officials if they wish to operate properly. It also cannot be due to lower labor or land costs, which, in fact, appear to be higher in China. It cannot be social networks: Chinese firms report that they have fewer links with banks and politicians and fewer business friends. It is unlikely to be entrepreneurial experience: Chinese entrepreneurs have traveled less, have fewer friends abroad, and are more likely to come from a family background based on agriculture. There also are no strong differences across countries in the rate at which individual firms innovate and invest.

The dimensions along which Chinese firms appear at an advantage are few. The first one is finance: many Chinese firms seem to have access to bank finance at favorable conditions, including low interest rates and low collateral requirements. The second one is information about innovations: Chinese firms are much more likely to rely on external experts than African firms at start-up, as well as subsequently, when they introduce new products, change their technologies, or modify their distribution systems. The third one is competition: firms in China and Vietnam face less competition from imports, which suggests some form of direct or indirect trade protection. In contrast, manufacturing firms in Africa face stiff competition from imports, primarily from China. The fourth one is education: Asian workers and entrepreneurs in general have more schooling. Education, however, does not predict how quickly production workers are fully operational; so, it is unclear how much of an advantage schooling is for production workers.

It is impossible from a simple cross-sectional survey to ascertain which one of the above factors has had a positive causal effect on China's manufacturing success. But the results presented here, even though they can only document correlations and patterns, may nonetheless force us to reconsider some of our preconceptions.

The Quantitative Firm Surveys

The objective of the firm survey project was to obtain a randomly selected representative sample of firms of a given size range in five target light manufacturing sectors: food processing, garments, leather, metal products, and wood products. Given that the focus of the study is on small and medium manufacturing firms, but not on microenterprises, samples were drawn from firms in the main urban centers. In each of the three African countries in the study, we focus on the largest city, where the overwhelming majority of small and medium manufacturing is found.

The surveys were conducted through face-to-face interviews with representatives of the firms. (See annex 5.1 for a sample survey questionnaire.) Except in China, 70 to 80 percent of the interviews were held directly with the top managers of the firms, who, in many cases, were also the firm owners. In China, this share drops to 59 percent, probably reflecting the larger size of the survey firms there. Wherever the respondents are not the top managers, they tend to be deputy managers or branch managers. Most respondents were men.

In each of the five countries, the study aimed to cover 250 randomly sampled manufacturing firms, equally divided across five broadly defined sectors of activity. Table 5.1 presents the breakdown of firms according to sector. An attempt was made in all countries to achieve an equal breakdown of the sample over the five sectors. Unfortunately, in some countries, it proved difficult, if not impossible, to identify a large enough sample of firms of the intended size in certain sectors, for example, leather in China and food processing in Tanzania.

The sample is intended to cover small and medium firms with 2–40 paid permanent employees, excluding household members. To the extent possible, the initial intent was to divide the sample of interviewed firms more or less equally, within each sector, between small (2–20 permanent employers) and medium (21–40 employees) firms. In Tanzania and Zambia, it proved difficult to identify a sufficient number of firms in each of the five sectors. Consequently, the lower employment limit was lowered to 1, and the upper limit was raised to 100 in an effort to meet sample size targets. In China, the survey team met

Table 5.1   Breakdown of the Country Samples, by Sector
number (and percentage) of firms

Sector	China	Vietnam	Ethiopia	Tanzania	Zambia
Food processing and beverages	47 (15.5%)	62 (20.7%)	53 (21.2%)	21 (8.0%)	38 (14.4%)
Garments	71 (23.4%)	62 (20.7%)	48 (19.2%)	58 (22.1%)	65 (24.7%)
Leather products	26 (8.6%)	52 (17.3%)	49 (19.6%)	37 (14.1%)	42 (16.0%)
Metal products	85 (28.1%)	62 (20.7%)	46 (18.4%)	50 (19.1%)	61 (23.2%)
Wood products	74 (24.4%)	62 (20.7%)	54 (21.6%)	96 (36.6%)	57 (21.7%)
Total	303	300	250	262	263

Source: Compilation of the authors based on the Quantitative Entrepreneur Survey.

considerable difficulties finding a large enough number of small firms in the sectors of study.

The distribution of (the logarithm of) the regular workforce in the three countries is depicted in figure 5.1. We see that there are large differences in firm size across the five country samples. The Vietnamese sample follows the intended firm size distribution the most closely. For China, the entire distribution of the firm workforce is shifted to the right, but with a sizable overlap with Vietnam. In contrast, the firm size distribution is shifted to the left in the three African samples, with some differences among them as well: the Ethiopian and Tanzanian samples are fairly tightly distributed, while the Zambian sample is more diffuse, with more medium firms, as well as more small firms, than either the Ethiopia or the Tanzania samples.

Firm size varies dramatically across the countries in our sample. This makes direct comparison across countries perilous because many of the practices and outcomes we wish to study are known to vary systematically with firm size, although not always in a proportional or even monotonic manner. To correct for this, we conduct most of our analysis using nonparametric regression to net out the effect of firm size from comparisons between countries.

Figure 5.1   The Distribution of the Regular Workforce, by Country

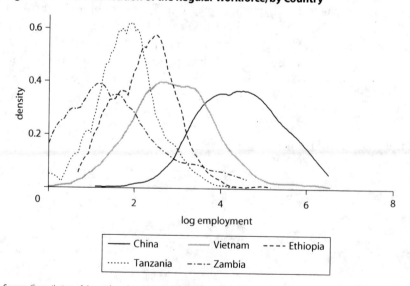

Source: Compilation of the authors based on the Quantitative Entrepreneur Survey.

Firm Characteristics

The overwhelming majority of the survey firms are stand-alone operations: only 8 percent of the survey firms are part of larger enterprises, and there is no strong difference across country samples. In the China and Vietnam samples, the median firm is 6 years old. Similar values are observed in the African sample, with slightly younger firms in Ethiopia (the median is 4 years old) and slightly older firms in Zambia (the median is 10 years old).

The legal status of the sample firms is summarized in table 5.2. Only a handful of firms in our samples are government owned, which is to be expected because we focus on relatively small firms. In Vietnam, a small proportion are cooperatives. The rest fall into two broad categories: with or without limited liability. In China, Ethiopia, and Vietnam, the majority of firms benefit from a limited liability status. Few of them, however, are publicly traded on a stock exchange. In contrast, most sample firms in Tanzania and Zambia are either held in sole proprietorship or in partnership and do not, as a result, enjoy the protection of limited liability. The proportion of limited liability firms is particularly small in Tanzania, but perhaps this is because of the small size of the sample firms in that country.

In terms of ownership, most sampled firms are privately and domestically owned. In the China sample, 7 percent of the survey firms are listed as fully foreign owned, and another 6 percent as partially foreign owned. For most foreign-owned firms, however, the nationality of the owner is listed as mainland Chinese (57 percent) or Taiwan Chinese (32 percent). In the other survey countries, the proportion of foreign ownership is negligible.

Table 5.2   Legal Status
number (and percentage) of firms

Status	China	Vietnam	Ethiopia	Tanzania	Zambia
Sole proprietorship	105 (35.5%)	95 (31.7%)	66 (26.4%)	187 (72.2%)	162 (63.8%)
Partnership	7 (2.4%)	0 (0%)	6 (2.4%)	64 (24.7%)	34 (13.4%)
Limited liability company	173 (58.4%)	187 (62.3%)	178 (71.2%)	7 (2.7%)	48 (18.9%)
Publicly traded company	10 (3.4%)	5 (1.7%)	0 (0%)	1 (0.4%)	8 (3.1%)
Cooperative	0 (0%)	12 (4.0%)	0 (0%)	0 (0%)	0 (0%)
Government owned	1 (0.3%)	1 (0.3%)	0 (0%)	0 (0%)	2 (0.8%)
Total observations	296	300	250	259	254

Source: Compilation of the authors based on the Quantitative Entrepreneur Survey.

The ownership structure of survey firms is fairly concentrated, as might be expected given the relatively small firm size. In the five study countries, except Ethiopia, the majority of survey firms have a single owner. If we add multiple-owner firms in which one owner has at least a 50 percent share of the business, we end up with 80 to 90 percent of the survey firms. Ethiopia stands out as an exception: only a third of the survey firms there have a single or majority owner. Furthermore, in Ethiopia, there are typically several owners who are rarely from the same family.

In the China sample, the main owner of the firm, that is, the person owning the largest share of the firm, is a woman 9 percent of the time. In the other countries, the percentages are higher: 28 percent (Vietnam), 25 percent (Ethiopia), 11 percent (Tanzania), and 14 percent (Zambia). The owners in China and Vietnam are 44 years old, on average. Those in the study countries in Africa are slightly younger: 37, on average, in Ethiopia; 39 in Tanzania; and 42 in Zambia. The owners of survey firms in China and Vietnam have the highest level of owner educational attainment: nearly 90 percent of owners have attained more than partial secondary education. Tanzania has by far the lowest rate: 80 percent of owners have, at most, some secondary education. Ethiopia and Zambia occupy an intermediate position: 50 percent of owners have educational levels similar to their Chinese counterparts.

Many entrepreneurs come from families of entrepreneurs. Most owners have parents who were self-employed either in farming (70 percent in China; 32 to 45 percent in the other countries) or in business (23 percent in China; 33 to 51 percent in the other countries). Few have fathers who were working for wages in government or the private sector: 8 percent in the China sample; 17 to 24 percent in the other countries. The entrepreneurs also have significant personal experience in the firm or in other businesses. The median owner has been running the firm since its inception. Over the entire sample, 12 percent of owners own other businesses.

Firm owners also have varied life experiences. This is particularly true in the African sample, where, in each of the three countries, the majority of firm owners have, at some point, resided in another part of the country. In Tanzania, this is true of 87 percent of the sample. In contrast, only 30 percent of Vietnamese owners and 9 percent of Chinese owners have ever resided in another part of their countries. A minority of owners have resided abroad at some point in their lives: 3 to 4 percent in China, Vietnam, and Ethiopia, but 9 percent in Tanzania, and 17 percent in

Zambia. The proportion of foreign nationals is, however, small among firm owners in our sample, less than 3 percent in the sample as a whole.

The Origins and Development of Entrepreneurial Capabilities

Given their relatively small size, the study firms tend to be entrepreneurial in nature, and, hence, the current owners have had a significant involvement in the creation of the firms. In all five countries, more than 86 percent of the principal owners contributed ideas for the creation of the firms; more than 83 percent participated in financing the creation of the firms; and more than 79 percent contributed technical expertise at firm creation. Where the country samples differ is in the involvement of people other than the owner in helping set the firms up. Table 5.3 presents the answers of respondents to questions about the people who contributed to the creation of the firms.

Table 5.3   Who Contributed to the Creation of the Firm?

Respondents who listed each distinct source, %

Contributor	China	Vietnam	Ethiopia	Tanzania	Zambia
Contributed ideas					
Family members and relatives	58.2	75.7	29.6	39.7	33.8
Business friends and acquaintances	56.5	9.7	30.4	15.3	17.7
Clients	25.0	4.3	1.6	6.9	1.2
Employees	29.5	2.0	1.2	1.1	4.6
Shareholder	—	0.7	14.0	—	—
Expert/consultant	21.6	3.0	2.8	2.7	3.1
Equipment suppliers	12.0	2.0	0.4	0	1.2
School teacher/professor	4.1	0	0	1.9	1.5
Other	1.0	0	4.4	5.7	6.2
No one else	4.8	17.3	32.4	37.0	38.8
Number of observations	292	300	250	262	260
Contributed technical expertise					
Family members and relatives	43.8	69.0	14.0	22.1	24.3
Business friends and acquaintances	37.9	11.3	24.0	18.3	13.1
Employees	41.0	3.3	11.2	2.3	6.6
Expert/consultant	21.4	3.7	1.2	4.6	9.3
Clients	12.8	4.7	0.4	7.6	0.4
School teacher/professor	3.1	0.3	1.2	16.0	4.2

(continued next page)

Table 5.3   *(continued)*

Contributor	China	Vietnam	Ethiopia	Tanzania	Zambia
Equipment suppliers	15.9	4.7	0.8	0.4	1.5
Other	1.0	1.7	9.6	4.6	4.7
No one else	9.7	18.3	47.6	33.2	42.9
Number of observations	290	300	250	262	259
Participated in financing					
Family members and relatives	54.5	62.3	22.8	21.0	23.9
Business friends and acquaintances	24.7	10.7	19.2	3.8	6.9
A nonbank financial institution	2.5	1.0	16.4	0.8	0.8
A bank	4.3	1.0	2.0	0.8	0.8
Equipment suppliers	4.7	0.3	0.4	0	0.4
Other	0.4	1.7	5.6	4.2	2.3
No one else	32.6	30.3	43.6	68.7	64.9
Number of observations	279	300	250	262	259

Source: Compilation of the authors based on the Quantitative Entrepreneur Survey.
Note: — = not available.

In the two Asian countries, a majority of respondents list family members and relatives as contributors in terms of ideas, technical expertise, and financing. The proportions are much smaller in Africa, especially for technical expertise and financing. Respondents in the three African study countries are much more likely than those in the two Asian countries to report that no one else other than themselves contributed to the creation of the firm. Respondents in the Asian firms are also more likely to list other sources of help. This is particularly true among the Chinese respondents, who are much more likely to list business acquaintances, experts and consultants, clients, employees, and equipment suppliers as sources of assistance at start-up.

Using regression analysis to investigate whether the kind of assistance entrepreneurs received at the start of business has an effect on firm performance, we see that receiving help from family and relatives is associated with a smaller start-up size, while receiving help from experts or finance from financial institutions is associated with a larger start-up size. It would be perilous to interpret this relationship as causal: entrepreneurs who seek advice from experts and who manage to secure start-up funding from financial institutions may simply be better managers than the average. The relationship nonetheless suggests that obtaining advice and finance at start-up may be an important channel by which good entrepreneurship comes to fruition. Further analysis indicates that assistance at start-up remains a strong predictor of future firm performance. In particular, we note, firms that received expert advice at start-up grow, on average, significantly more quickly than other firms, by 3 percentage points per year. Again, these relationships should not necessarily be interpreted as causal: help at start-up is likely to be correlated with entrepreneurial acumen. Still, they suggest that advice at start-up may be an important channel of firm performance. We also note that the country where expert advice is reported by the largest proportion of respondents, China, is also the country with the highest manufacturing growth rate.

The Regulatory Environment

Table 5.4 presents summary information about business registration and licenses. In all countries except Tanzania, the majority of sample firms have some form of business registration. In China and Vietnam, the majority of sample firms are also registered for the value added tax, implying that their manufacturing output is part of the country's tax base. This is not true in Ethiopia and Tanzania, where only a small proportion of the survey firms report being registered for this tax. In Zambia, the proportion is larger, but still less than half the firms.

Table 5.4   The Regulatory Environment

	China		Vietnam		Ethiopia		Tanzania		Zambia	
Indicator	Obs	Mean	Obs	Mean	Obs	Mean	Obs	Mean	Obs	Mean
Business registration	301	99.7%	300	93.3%	250	71.2%	262	40.3%	259	56.9%
Registration, value added tax	221	91.0%	300	82.0%	250	5.2%	262	6.5%	260	30.4%
Licenses before start-up, number	205	4.1	300	1.4	250	1.2	261	0.6	237	1.2
Licenses renewed the previous year, number	188	3.0	300	0.3	248	0.8	261	0.3	252	1.1
Penalty for nonregistration or lack of license	256	1.2%	300	2.0%	249	2.4%	259	9.7%	259	3.1%
Incidence of corruption	n.a.	—	300	26.0%	248	19.8%	260	13.1%	246	13.0%

Source: Compilation of the authors based on the Quantitative Entrepreneur Survey.
Note: Obs = number of observations. n.a. = not applicable, — = not available.

The number of licenses and permits required to start or operate a business is often seen as a disincentive to entrepreneurship not only because of the associated fees, but also because it takes up some of the entrepreneur's time, and this time is particularly precious in small and medium firms, where there is less delegation of these tasks to clerical staff. The number of licenses is much higher in China than in the other four survey countries. Tanzania is the sample country with the smallest number of licenses, but also with the least dynamic manufacturing sector and the smallest average firm size.

Respondents were asked whether, in the last year, they had paid a penalty for operating without registration or license. Except in Tanzania, the number of respondents who answered positively to the question is small, even in countries such as Ethiopia and Zambia, where the proportion of unregistered firms is well below 100 percent. Even in Tanzania, where the proportion of positive responses nears 10 percent, the share of penalized firms is well below the proportion of unregistered businesses among sample firms. This suggests that the enforcement of registration and license requirements is present in the three African countries in our sample, but not so strongly as to prevent informal business operations.

Respondents were asked whether firms have to give presents to government officials to operate properly. This question was not asked in China because it was deemed too sensitive (which, by itself, suggests that the incidence of this behavior is high). Corruption appears to be more prevalent in Vietnam than in the African sample. Of course, this may be because high growth implies a higher opportunity cost associated with a slowdown in operations and thus a greater willingness among firms to pay to speed up the administrative process. This is indeed what is suggested by regression analysis: when we regress the incidence of corruption on a firm's growth rate, controlling for country fixed effects, firm size, and a business registration dummy, we find that more rapidly growing firms are more likely to report that they have to pay government officials to operate properly. Note that this result is not driven by China because the incidence of corruption was not reported by Chinese respondents.

The country comparison in table 5.4 may be misleading, however, if the regulatory environment of firms varies systematically by firm size because we know that the countries in the study have different average firm sizes. To investigate this possibility, we regressed business registration nonparametrically on firm size for each country separately and found that firms above a certain size tend to be registered. There is, however, considerable heterogeneity in registration rates across countries among smaller firms and, in particular, a systematically lower registration probability in Africa than in Asia.

Most sampled firms use electricity for production, although, in Tanzania, this proportion drops to two-thirds of the survey firms. Perhaps surprisingly, the proportion of firms that have an account with an electricity provider is sizably less than the proportion of firms using electricity for production. What accounts for the difference is unclear, but it may, in part, be caused by illegal connections to the grid or to the provision of free electricity to some users. Except in China, the majority of the study firms experience power outages on a regular basis. The incidence of outages appears particularly high in Ethiopia, Tanzania, and Vietnam. If outages occur, they tend to be more frequent in the African countries in our sample. The severity of each incident, measured by the average duration of the outage, seems fairly comparable across the five countries, however. If some users do indeed secure electrical power illegally, it may explain why there are outages in the first place.

Competition

Respondent firms were asked to evaluate subjectively whether the market for their products is competitive. We see few differences across countries, with around half the firms responding that their markets are moderately competitive, and the rest that the markets are very competitive. Zambia is the only outlier: 71 percent of the respondents there qualify their markets as very competitive.

To measure geographical clustering, firms were asked how many businesses operate in the same sector within a 15-minute walk. The average number is smallest in China (fewer than 6) and largest in Ethiopia (more than 28). The other three countries occupy an intermediate position, with 10–15 firms in the same sector within a 15-minute walking distance. The reason why geographical clustering may appear most extensive in Ethiopia and least extensive in China may be because firms are larger in China and thus cannot be physically located so closely together.

Respondents were asked to evaluate the number of their competitors that are enterprises with 10 workers or more. We find few differences across countries. Chinese respondents list a smaller number of competitors. The same is true of Tanzanian respondents, but probably for a different reason, namely, the dearth of medium to large manufacturers in the country.

The countries do, however, differ markedly in terms of competition from foreign firms. Respondents were asked to evaluate the number of their foreign competitors. Their answers, which are depicted in figure 5.2 in the form of a cumulative distribution, indicate that Chinese firms face the lowest level of foreign competition, while African firms face the highest level. The proportion of Chinese firms that state they face no foreign competition is 94 percent. For Ethiopia and Zambia, the corresponding shares are 60 and 53 percent, respectively. In Tanzania, only 18 percent of respondents declare they face no competition from imports. Vietnam occupies an intermediate position between China and Zambia.

The contrast between the three African countries may be partly attributed to geography: while Dar es Salaam, where the Tanzania survey took place, is a port, both Addis Ababa (Ethiopia) and Lusaka (Zambia) are located within the continent in landlocked countries. The contrast between Africa and Asia, however, cannot be explained in the same way. Vietnam is a coastal country, and the two major cities are close to the

Figure 5.2   Number of Foreign Competitors

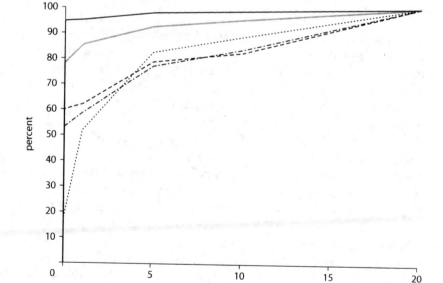

Source: Compilation of the authors based on the Quantitative Entrepreneur Survey.

sea. Similarly, much of China's manufacturing growth is located on the eastern seaboard. Yet, in both cases, competition from imports is perceived to be low by the respondent firms. Why this is the case is unclear. The reason may be because the two Asian countries in our sample have trade protection, either direct or indirect (for example, through exchange rate policy).

Alternatively, it is possible that Chinese (and Vietnamese) firms are more competitive, so that foreign firms do not seek to commercialize their products in the country. There is some evidence of this in the data in the sense that most African respondents list China as the major source of competing imports. The proportions of respondents who cite China as a source of foreign competition is large: 93 percent in Ethiopia, 84 percent in Tanzania, and 89 percent in Vietnam. The only exception is Zambia, where China is mentioned by "only" 56 percent of respondents. South Africa is a major source of competing imports in Zambia, mentioned by 57 percent of respondents. There is a direct rail link between the two countries, and many manufacturing imports into Zambia come through South African ports. South Africa is also mentioned by 6 percent of Tanzanian respondents. In contrast, no African country is mentioned as a source of competing imports by Chinese and Vietnamese respondents, who only mention other East Asian countries, Europe, or the United States.

Respondents who face foreign competition were asked to compare these imports to their own products in terms of price, quality, and adaptation to local taste. There were too few responses in China, so we ignore them here. In the other countries, 47–59 percent of respondents find competitive imports more expensive than their products, but only 17–26 percent find imports to be of better quality. In Tanzania, Vietnam, and Zambia, around 44–47 percent of the respondents find imported products to be better adapted to local tastes and fashion. This proportion rises to 85 percent in Ethiopia. This suggests that domestic producers seek to compete with imports primarily on quality and less on price and design. This, in turn, suggests that the manufacturing imports with which they compete are poorer-quality, lower-cost mass-produced items that suit well the limited budgets of local consumers.

Social Capital

Membership in associations differs markedly between firms in China and firms in the other four study countries. In China, 55 percent of the respondents do not belong to any business association. This share rises to over 80 percent in the other four countries, and there is little difference among them. Part of the variation in the propensity to join a business association arises because of the differences in firm size. Except for China, where there is no systematic relationship between association membership and size, we observe a positive relation between the two. We also note that, once we control for size, there is a difference between Ethiopia and Vietnam, as well as between the other three countries: after we control for size, firms in Ethiopia and Vietnam are less likely to belong to a business association.

If associations cannot serve their purpose, social networks offer a partial alternative. Respondents were first asked whether they have friends working as bank officials, as political figures, or in government. While nearly all respondents in the other four countries answered these questions, Chinese respondents were considerably more reluctant, and a third of these refused to respond. Chinese data on social networks should therefore be treated with caution because they are likely to be affected by selection bias, that is, those most reluctant to respond to the questions are those most keen to hide their privileged contacts in banks or government. Excepting China because of this caveat, we conclude that most respondents have friends or relatives in banks, government, or politics. Proportions are highest in the three African countries, where two-thirds to four-fifths of the respondents answered "yes" to at least one of the three questions. For comparison, the proportion is 52 percent in Vietnam. In China, two-thirds of those who responded answered "no" to all three questions. If we assume that all those who refused to answer would have answered "yes," this implies that, at most, 54 percent of the respondents know someone in banks, government, or politics, a figure that is not too different from the result in Vietnam. We can therefore conclude with confidence that owners and managers of the African small and medium firms in our study are significantly more likely than their East Asian counterparts to know someone in banks, government, or politics.

One possibility is that people with connections in banks or government can hope to benefit from these connections and are therefore more likely to start a business. This is the crony capitalism hypothesis. Another possibility is that entrepreneurs may not have started with connections, but, to succeed in business, they have to mingle with financial and political elites to secure advantage through the exchange of favors. This is the corruption hypothesis. Yet another possibility is that entrepreneurs belong to the burgeoning middle class and, as such, mingle socially with financial and political elites without necessarily seeking to obtain undue advantage from these acquaintances. This is the social class hypothesis. However, we are unable to disentangle these hypotheses using the data at hand.

Respondents were also asked about the contacts they have with other businesses. It is often believed that social contacts help disseminate business-relevant information and practices. If this is true, more well connected firms should be at an advantage and thus should grow more quickly and become more profitable. We therefore expect a positive correlation between business contacts and firm performance. From the survey data, we construct three summary variables: the number of business contacts respondents declare, the number of contacts from whom respondents have received assistance in the past, and the number of contacts to whom assistance has been provided by the respondents. Many different forms of assistance are considered, including identifying new markets or sources of raw materials, securing external finance, recruiting workers, exchanging technological information, and obtaining and repairing machinery.

The answers are tabulated in table 5.5. We first note that China stands out because of a much smaller number of declared business links relative to all the other countries. This finding should be regarded with some suspicion, however. First, Chinese respondents were more reluctant to answer the questions: the nonresponse rate is higher there than in the other countries. Second, those who responded were also much more likely to answer "no" to all questions. We therefore consider the Chinese data on business contacts to be subject to serious response bias. The data from the other four countries are, in contrast, consistent. Firms typically have many contacts with other firms, and these contacts are used for various business-related purposes involving either receiving help from others or providing help. The average firm

Table 5.5   Business Contacts

Indicator	China		Vietnam		Ethiopia		Tanzania		Zambia	
	Obs	Mean	Obs	Mean	Obs	Mean	Obs	Mean	Obs	Mean
Number of business contacts	245	1.9	300	12.9	250	9.2	257	11.2	226	7.6
Received help	174	0.7	282	5.1	250	2.7	260	3.1	258	3.4
Provided help	175	0.7	290	4.6	250	3.0	260	3.2	258	3.2

Source: Compilation of the authors based on the Quantitative Entrepreneur Survey.
Note: Obs = number of observations.

in the sample receives slightly more help than it gives, but the difference is small.

What kind of help are respondent firms most likely to give and receive? We present, in table 5.6, the share of respondents who report the kinds of assistance they have received or given. The reader will immediately notice that the data for China and Vietnam appear doubtful. In China, the proportion of missing information is large, and the answers that were given appear low and correlated, as if the respondents were giving the same answer to all questions. This is also the pattern we observe in Vietnam, where the answers are nearly all the same. We therefore focus our analysis on the three African countries in the study, on which there is a bit more variety. We note that business contacts are used to identify sources of raw materials, but the emphasis is more on foreign sourcing in Tanzania, where the survey took place in the port city of Dar es Salaam, than in Ethiopia and Zambia, which are landlocked countries. On the receiving side, other answers are fairly similar, though we should note that business contacts are slightly less likely to be used for securing external finance. The giving side largely mirrors the receiving side, with more emphasis on sourcing raw materials and less on external finance.

The above analysis does not tell us whether social networks play a causal role, that is, helping firms overcome barriers to trade and information asymmetries, or whether contact with others is simply one possible channel through which the relevant information, good, or service is obtained. If social networks play either a causal or a channel role, we should observe that firms with more contacts perform more effectively and thus achieve a larger size.

Although there is some evidence of a positive relationship between the number of contacts and firm size, this relationship is weak and limited to some countries only. (China is omitted because the data contain too many missing observations.) This could be because business contacts do not, ultimately, play an important role in firm performance. Alternatively, it could be that business contacts matter, but only for those firms that do not have alternative access to information. If sufficiently large firms obtain the necessary information in other ways, for example, by hiring consultants or specialized employees, then they have less need for business contacts. More work is needed to ascertain the exact role played by social networks in business performance. We anticipate that the social networks experiment will provide important new insights on this issue in due course.

Table 5.6 Giving Assistance to and Receiving Assistance from Business Contacts

Indicator	China Obs	China Mean (%)	Vietnam Obs	Vietnam Mean (%)	Ethiopia Obs	Ethiopia Mean (%)	Tanzania Obs	Tanzania Mean (%)	Zambia Obs	Zambia Mean (%)
Assistance received										
Identify local sources of inputs	170	7	261	80	250	57	257	26	257	53
Identify foreign sources of inputs	171	8	183	72	250	8	259	49	257	32
Identify new markets	173	9	239	78	250	48	259	40	254	49
Secure external finance	173	9	226	75	249	29	259	46	255	40
Recruit qualified workers	172	9	243	80	249	31	258	48	254	39
Provide technological information	173	10	245	77	249	38	260	53	256	44
Obtain secondhand equipment	174	10	238	79	249	25	259	47	255	44
Repair machinery	173	10	244	73	249	35	n.a.	—	256	41
Assistance given										
Identify local sources of inputs	257	32	250	77	250	60	258	65	252	57
Identify foreign sources of inputs	254	19	178	74	250	9	257	16	254	25
Identify new markets	253	29	234	76	250	53	258	47	256	48
Secure external finance	250	18	206	75	250	31	258	27	256	30
Recruit qualified workers	251	33	228	76	250	36	260	39	256	36
Provide technological information	255	35	223	76	250	42	259	47	257	45
Obtain secondhand equipment	246	29	221	77	249	27	260	47	256	38
Repair machinery	251	32	225	77	250	45	259	37	257	40

Source: Compilation of the authors based on the Quantitative Entrepreneur Survey.
Note: Obs = number of observations, n.a. = not applicable, — = not available.

Innovation

The questionnaire elicited detailed information on the innovation activities of the survey firms. This information is summarized in table 5.7. The first three rows refer to the introduction of new products, new production processes, or new product delivery systems since 2008. The next four rows cover less frequent innovation events, but refer to the lifetime of the firm. The bottom row combines all forms of innovation into a single index.

The most striking finding that emerges is how similar four of the countries are. Tanzania is the outlier, with a much lower innovation rate in the first three rows and across the board (see table 5.7). Tanzania is also the study country with the smallest average firm size, the highest share of informal firms, and the least well educated entrepreneurs. Apart from Tanzania, the other countries are similar. In particular, there is no essential difference between China and the other three countries in terms of product introduction and changes in delivery system, though the innovation index at the bottom of the table is slightly lower for China than for Ethiopia, Vietnam, and Zambia. The only form of innovation in which China shows more activity is production processes, in which firms in China are more likely to report that they have made changes in the recent past. The difference with the other three countries, however, is not large.

These results are surprising because, given China's rapid growth in manufacturing output, one would have expected the innovation rate to be higher. This is not the case. Chinese firms in the sample are also larger, and one would expect larger firms to innovate more. To investigate this idea further, we regress nonparametrically the innovation rate on firm

Table 5.7   Innovation
percent

Indicator	China	Vietnam	Ethiopia	Tanzania	Zambia
Introduced new products	44	43	46	24	44
Changed production processes	42	34	36	15	28
Changed delivery systems	20	19	22	5	25
Introduced new product in country	10	2	9	9	21
Exported new product from country	2	2	1	3	5
Imported new raw material in country	1	1	1	0	3
Introduced new machinery in country	7	1	6	1	5
Any of the above	57	58	60	34	61

Source: Compilation of the authors based on the Quantitative Entrepreneur Survey.

size. We find a positive relationship between innovation and firm size, as expected, although this relationship is stronger in some countries than in others. The most striking result from table 5.7 is that, after controlling for size, we see that Chinese firms innovate less, not more than firms in the other four countries, including Tanzania. This indicates that, contrary to common belief, African firms are no less open to innovation than their Asian counterparts, including China.

A possible explanation for these puzzling results is that we have measured a kind of innovation that is not associated with firm growth. To test this idea, we regressed firm growth (measured as the annual rate of growth in total firm employment since start-up) on innovation, and we found a positive correlation between the two, especially with the introduction of new products and new customer delivery systems. This confirms that, even in our sample, innovation is associated with better firm performance. Yet, average firm growth in China is greater: 14.6 percent annual employment growth since start-up, compared with 4.9 percent in Ethiopia, 7.4 percent in Tanzania, 7.7 percent in Vietnam, and 10.6 percent in Zambia. This may be because the effect of innovation on firm growth is more significant in China. To test this hypothesis, we regress firm growth on innovation and an interaction term between innovation and a China dummy, controlling for country fixed effects. If the effect of innovation on firm growth is stronger in China, the coefficient of the interaction term should be positive and significant. The results, however, do not suggest that the association between innovation and firm growth is stronger in China than in the other study countries.

Another issue we investigate is whether innovation in the African study countries is of the wrong kind and arises from the wrong source. To this effect, we examine what prompted innovation and what was the source of advice on innovation. In all countries, the most common answer is that the firm responded to customer demand. The next most common answer is that the firm noticed a gap in the market. One could argue that this answer indicates more initiative on the part of the firm: it did not wait for customers to suggest new products. This answer was given more often by Chinese and Ethiopian respondents, but the difference could simply be caused by differences in translation. In contrast, we find rather more difference between China and the other four countries in imitation: in China, imitating other producers, whether local or foreign, is seldom given as a reason for introducing new products; in the other four countries, it is a reason given by a small, but not negligible minority of firms.

This suggests that imitation is a more powerful driver of product innovation in these four countries than in China.

Survey participants were asked who helped them find customers for their newly introduced products. In all countries, the dominant answer is no one, that is, the firm relied on its own management and employees. Some 9 to 17 percent of the respondents mentioned friends and relatives as a source of help in finding new customers, except in Vietnam, where 40 percent of the respondents gave that answer. Other sources of help are generally unimportant, with some—possibly random—variation across countries. There is no evidence that, for the firms in this study, government agencies, research institutions, and foreign joint ventures play a bigger role in China than in the other study countries in terms of finding new customers.

This is not the case with respect to technical expertise. In table 5.8, we present the answers of respondents to a question about who provided them with the technical expertise needed to develop new products. The most common answers are no one and friends and relatives. There are sizable differences across countries, but these do not appear systematic. Customers tend to be cited as a source of technical expertise more often in China and Vietnam than in the three African countries covered by the study. Even sharper differences emerge regarding experts and consultants, who are cited by 27.7 percent of Chinese respondents, but only by a few respondents in the other countries. A similar pattern is observed for research institutions, which are cited by 10.8 percent of Chinese respondents, but hardly anyone in the other four countries. Finally, suppliers of equipment and raw materials are cited in China and Vietnam, but not in Africa. In contrast, competitors are cited by a number of African firms, but much less so in China and Vietnam.

The picture that emerges is that firms in the two Asian study countries, particularly those in China, have access to a much wider range of sources of information on the technical expertise needed to develop new products. Why this is the case is not entirely clear, however. It could be that wider access is what caused Asian and, especially, Chinese firms to grow more rapidly. Alternatively, because the manufacturing sector has grown dramatically in China, more institutions have been created that meet the need of entrepreneurs for technical advice. For instance, suppliers of equipment and raw material may find that providing advice is a useful marketing tool and gives them a competitive edge. Smaller markets for raw materials and equipment in Africa mean less entry and less competition, and this may account for our finding. More research is needed on this issue.

Table 5.8 Who Provided the Technical Expertise to Develop New Products?

Indicator	China		Vietnam		Ethiopia		Tanzania		Zambia	
	Obs	Mean (%)	Obs	Mean (%)	Obs	Mean (%)	Obs	Mean (%)	Obs	Mean (%)
No one	130	35.4	129	54.3	114	67.5	62	33.9	112	31.3
Friends and relatives	130	13.1	129	36.4	114	17.5	62	22.6	112	20.5
Customers	130	32.3	129	24.0	114	7.0	62	19.4	112	7.1
Other	124	0	129	9.3	114	7.0	62	0	112	25.9
Experts and consultants	130	27.7	129	0.8	114	1.8	62	1.6	112	8.9
Competitors	130	3.8	129	5.4	114	7.0	62	17.7	112	1.8
Raw material supplier	130	11.5	129	9.3	114	0	62	3.2	112	0.9
Research institution	130	10.8	129	1.6	114	0	62	6.5	112	1.8
Equipment supplier	130	6.2	129	10.1	114	0.9	62	0	112	0.9
Domestic joint venture	130	6.9	129	0	114	0	62	9.7	112	0
Government agencies	130	0	129	2.3	114	6.1	62	1.6	112	0.9
Foreign joint venture	130	3.1	129	1.6	114	0	62	1.6	112	0

Source: Compilation of the authors based on the Quantitative Entrepreneur Survey.
Note: Obs = number of observations.

In table 5.9, we report similar figures, but this time for changes in production processes or delivery systems. The pattern is similar to that in table 5.8. Many respondents state that they received help from no one. Customers and friends and relatives are commonly mentioned as sources of information. That customers are listed is not surprising given that the question partly refers to changes in delivery systems. Competitors are cited heavily in Tanzania. If firms are competing through innovation, this is not what we would expect. But technological upgrading among other firms in the neighborhood may generate agglomeration externalities if it helps attract customers. Such an externality is most likely to arise if similar firms cluster around each other to form a magnet for customers, as in a specialized retail district. Experts and consultants are cited heavily in China, while suppliers of equipment and, to a lesser extent, raw material tend to be cited more often in Asia more generally. In all countries, government agencies and joint ventures with foreign firms play a minor role, at least in terms of the number of affected firms. Of course, joint ventures may introduce new techniques of production and marketing that may subsequently spread locally, for example, through friends and relatives, customers, and the like.

Next, we examine whether there are differences in the way innovation adoption is financed by firms. Firms that introduced new products, production processes, or delivery systems were asked whether these changes required additional finance. The majority of respondents stated that they did, except in China, where a sizable minority (39–44 percent) said the changes called for additional finance. The corresponding numbers for Ethiopia, Vietnam, and Zambia are all above 63 percent. Tanzania stands between, with slightly over half of the firms requiring additional funding, but on a much smaller sample because the proportion of innovation adopters is much smaller in Tanzania.

Table 5.10 summarizes the answers of firms on how changes were financed. Most firms list retained earnings as the source of financing. Friends and relatives are cited by Asian respondents twice as often as African respondents. Banks are cited by a minority of respondents, but much more frequently in Asia than in Africa. New capital from existing owners is also cited, on average, more often by Asian respondents. In addition, Chinese respondents mention advances from customers and credit from financial institutions as significant sources of funding, while these sources are largely omitted by other respondents. Other possible sources are marginal.

Table 5.9 Who Provided the Technical Expertise to Change the Production Process or Delivery System?

Indicator	China Obs	China Mean (%)	Vietnam Obs	Vietnam Mean (%)	Ethiopia Obs	Ethiopia Mean (%)	Tanzania Obs	Tanzania Mean (%)	Zambia Obs	Zambia Mean (%)
No one	121	29.8	103	44.7	89	62.9	38	34.2	71	29.6
Friends and relatives	121	14.0	103	44.7	89	12.4	38	13.2	71	18.3
Customers	121	23.1	103	20.4	89	10.1	38	15.8	71	12.7
Competitors	121	10.7	103	5.8	89	15.7	38	34.2	71	4.2
Experts and consultants	121	24.0	103	0	89	2.2	38	13.2	71	8.5
Equipment supplier	121	13.2	103	14.6	89	2.2	38	5.3	71	0
Other	121	0	103	9.7	89	0	38	0	71	21.1
Domestic joint venture	121	19.0	103	0	89	0	38	0	71	0
Raw material supplier	121	6.6	103	4.9	89	0	38	2.6	71	2.8
Government agencies	121	2.5	103	0	89	4.5	38	2.6	71	1.4
Research institution	121	5.8	103	1.0	89	0	38	2.6	71	1.4
Foreign joint venture	121	2.5	103	1.0	89	0	38	2.6	71	0

Source: Compilation of the authors based on the Quantitative Entrepreneur Survey.
Note: Obs = number of observations.

Table 5.10   The Source of Funding for the Adoption of Innovations
percent

Source	China	Vietnam	Ethiopia	Tanzania	Zambia
Retention of earnings	55	87	88	47	79
Friends and relatives	16	16	6	8	8
Bank	19	16	4	11	1
New capital from owners	12	9	9	2	5
Customers	14	4	9	6	3
Financial institution	23	1	7	0	2
Raw material supplier	4	8	2	0	0
New owners	4	1	0	0	0
Domestic joint venture	3	0	0	0	0
Equipment supplier	3	0	0	0	0
Government agency	1	0	0	0	0
Foreign joint venture	0	1	0	0	0
Development agency	0	0	0	0	0
Other	0	0	2	0	5
Number of observations	73	121	113	66	99

Source: Compilation of the authors based on the Quantitative Entrepreneur Survey.

It is difficult to interpret these findings. The firms that responded to the finance questions are self-selected: they are the firms that succeeded in finding the necessary funding to innovate. By itself, this does not tell us anything about firms that did not innovate: we do not know whether the latter could have secured the funding but chose not to innovate or whether they did not innovate because they did not find the funding. The fact that the adoption of most innovations is funded out of retained earnings, however, suggests that firms may find innovation difficult if they do not make sufficient profits. If the failure to innovate makes a firm less productive and, hence, less profitable, the firm may not be generating the retained earnings needed to innovate: this is a vicious circle. We also note that Asian, particularly Chinese, firms seem to have access to a larger variety of funding sources. This, in turn, may facilitate innovation by firms. Finally, we should note that aggregate productivity is sometimes best served by letting inefficient firms disappear and fostering the entry of innovative firms. Given that the surveys deal with existing firms, answers to innovation questions tell us little about how the innovation environment affects the selection of entering firms.

Inputs

Ready access to inputs is important for the performance of manufacturing firms. The survey therefore includes several questions about suppliers.

Figure 5.3 summarizes the number of regular suppliers of material inputs for firms against firm size, using the same nonparametric regression method of the previous analyses. As the figure shows, it is primarily differences in firm size, not differences across countries, that explains the variation in the number of suppliers. The only visible difference is between large firms in China and Vietnam: large Vietnamese firms appear to have fewer suppliers than Chinese firms of similar size. This difference, however, is not statistically significant. What is clear is that Chinese and Vietnamese manufacturers do not combine inputs from a larger number of suppliers than African firms of the same size.

Even though the number of regular suppliers does not show markedly different trends across countries, there are some differences in the sources of inputs. In three of the study countries, China, Vietnam, and Zambia, government agencies represent a negligible source of manufacturing inputs. However, in Ethiopia and Tanzania, they account for 5.2 and 10.3 percent of inputs, respectively. Of the 27 Tanzanian firms reporting input purchases from government agencies, 15 indicate that all their inputs come from such agencies.

Imported material inputs are important for manufacturing in the study countries. The only exception is China, where imports represent a smaller proportion of all inputs and where we see no positive correlation between imports and firm size. This may be because China is such a large player

Figure 5.3   Firm Size and the Number of Regular Suppliers

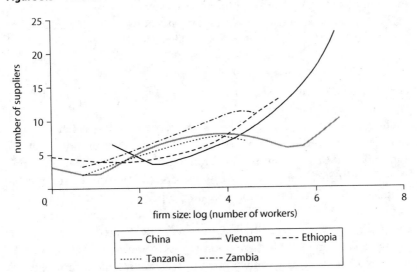

Source: Compilation of the authors based on the Quantitative Entrepreneur Survey.

in world manufacturing. We also note that small African firms are more likely to rely on imported inputs than Asian firms of equivalent size, possibly for similar reasons. Few manufacturers import inputs directly, however: the vast majority of imported inputs used by sample firms come from local importers. This is particularly true in Africa. Almost none of the African firms list a foreign country as the country of any of their three main suppliers.

This raises the issue of the ease with which the survey firms obtain material inputs. The questionnaire elicited information on the number of alternative suppliers from which firms could source "similar raw materials."[2] One would expect Chinese and, perhaps, Vietnamese manufacturers to have more viable alternative suppliers than firms in Africa, given the larger size of the manufacturing sector in the two former economics. This does not appear to be the case, however: indeed, firms in Ethiopia and Tanzania report a larger number of alternative suppliers.

One possible explanation is that Chinese and Vietnamese firms engage in more specialized manufacturing activities and, for this reason, rely on more specialized production inputs (for example, custom-made inputs), and, so, they have fewer alternative suppliers. We return to this possibility in considering firm outputs below. Alternatively, it may be that African manufacturing firms face greater demand fluctuations and, so, are more familiar with available alternative suppliers than are their Asian counterparts. Given that most African respondents source imported inputs locally, we also cannot rule out the possibility that multiple local importers ultimately rely on the same foreign supplier.

The questionnaires also asked respondents how many of their alternative suppliers they know personally. The responses show a gradual increase with firm size, but no systematic differences across countries. Yet, we find substantial heterogeneity across countries regarding supplier credit in each of the two regional samples. Firms in China and Vietnam are much more likely to purchase inputs on credit than their African counterparts. This is particularly true among small firms, which are typically most in need of external finance. We do, however, note that, in Tanzania and Zambia (but not in Ethiopia), there is a tendency for supplier credit to increase with firm size. The apparent lack of trust between supplier and client in Africa is puzzling, especially because there is no difference between countries in the number of alternative suppliers respondents know personally. This has been highlighted elsewhere (for example, Fafchamps 2004). We do not, however, observe significant differences across countries in the extent to which respondent firms extend credit to their own customers. This puts African manufacturers at a disadvantage: they do not receive credit from their suppliers, but they extend credit to their own clients.

Outputs

The survey reveals substantial heterogeneity across countries with regard to outputs. The main contrast is between China and the other survey countries. We find that larger firms are less likely to sell their output locally and more likely to sell their output in other parts of the country. Chinese firms ship a substantially smaller proportion of sales to customers in the same city or district relative to firms in the other study countries. This holds even after we control for firm size. Conversely, Chinese firms ship a larger proportion of domestic sales to customers in other cities or districts.

Why this is the case is not entirely clear, but a likely explanation is that the Chinese economy is geographically much more diversified, with many large cities and broadly distributed demand for manufactured products. In contrast, African economies are much smaller, and the demand for manufactures in Africa is concentrated in fewer cities with sufficient consumer purchasing power.

We also observe substantial country differences in the type of customers to whom firms sell. Relative to firms in the other study countries, Chinese firms sell a much greater proportion to other manufacturing firms. This relationship holds after we control for firm size. On average, Chinese respondents sell 29 percent of their output to other manufacturing firms. In Vietnam, the corresponding average is 10 percent, while it is only around 1 percent in each of the African countries surveyed. These results indicate that there is much less vertical specialization within the light manufacturing sector in Africa and, to a lesser extent, in Vietnam than in China. Thus, African firms produce light manufactures in a vertically integrated manner, with hardly any sales to downstream manufacturers. This means that gains from specialization are not captured. Such a feature is typically associated with less well developed economies in which the size of the market is insufficient to allow the emergence of producers who specialize in a specific part of the value chain. Other sales go to final consumers, wholesalers, traders, or export agencies. After controlling for firm size, we find no substantial differences across countries.

We note above that Chinese and Vietnamese firms have fewer alternative suppliers than African firms. We suggest that this may reflect the use of more specialized and, possibly, individually tailored industrial inputs. We now consider this issue from the perspective of firm output. Figure 5.4 shows the average proportion of output that each study firm sells to its main customer. It is striking that, even after we control for firm size, the Asian firms sell a substantially higher proportion of their production to their main customers. Similarly, a separate question indicates that the Asian firms do not have a larger number of alternative customers to whom they could sell.

Taken together, these results are consistent with the observation that the Chinese and Vietnamese manufacturing sectors involve a higher degree of vertical specialization, here reflected in specific firm-to-firm corporate relationships. This observation runs contrary to many standard models of manufacturing behavior whereby firms produce for a large market of anonymous customers. But it is consistent with industrial organization models of relational contracting and vertical integration through long-term buyer-seller relationships. It adds more weight to the idea that the network structure of a country's manufacturing sector may be an important determinant of sectoral performance.

Next, we examine whether Asian firms engage in less advertising, which should be the case if their output is more likely destined to another manufacturer with whom they have a long-term relationship.

Figure 5.4   Firm Size and Sales to Main Customers

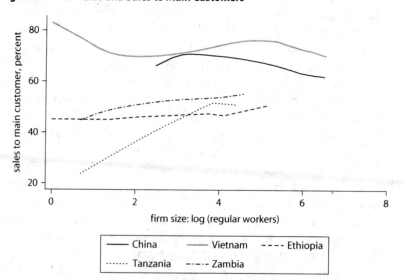

Source: Compilation of the authors based on the Quantitative Entrepreneur Survey.

Once we control for size, Asian firms appear, on average, less likely than African firms to engage in advertising. This is consistent with a number of potential explanations, but it is not inconsistent with the idea that African firms are more dependent on demand from a large open market, whereas Asian firms are more reliant on particular bilateral arrangements.

Finally, we consider the issue of exports. Figure 5.5 shows the proportion of exporting firms across the different countries. Almost 40 percent of the Chinese firms in our sample export part of their output. The corresponding figure for Vietnam is 17 percent. In contrast, manufacturers in our three African study countries are much less likely to export. The differences are statistically significant, including the difference between Vietnam and Tanzania. A similar finding obtains after we control for firm size. We also note that, of the five countries in our study, the two that are landlocked—Ethiopia and Zambia—tend to export fewer manufactures. This is hardly surprising given that the additional cost required to ship goods abroad reduces the competitiveness of exports from such countries.

Chinese and Vietnamese exporters have also been exporting longer, on average: the median year of the first exports by the firms in China and Vietnam is 2005 and 2004, respectively, while in Ethiopia, Tanzania, and Zambia, it is 2008, 2007, and 2008, respectively. The destination of

Figure 5.5   Exports

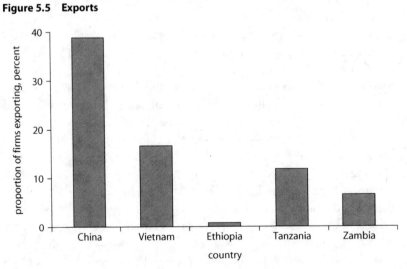

Source: Compilation of the authors based on the Quantitative Entrepreneur Survey.

African exports is also different. Asked about the main countries of destination of their exports, African firms cite other African countries primarily. In contrast, the Asian respondents cite both other Asian countries and a variety of large Western economies.

How representative these results are is unclear. African countries that have been more successful in exporting manufactures, such as Kenya (neighboring Ethiopia and Tanzania) and South Africa (an important commercial partner of Zambia), are not included in the study. But there is no denying that Africa has not been as successful as China in exporting manufactures outside the local region.

Labor

Table 5.11 shows the share of workers in four broad occupational categories during the year of the survey and the previous year. Skilled and unskilled production workers are workers who physically produce output. A firm, however, cannot operate efficiently without management and clerical workers. Management is in charge of making strategic choices, but also of organizing and monitoring production workers. Clerical workers help firms keep accounts and records and are essential in large hierarchical organizations because of their role in processing and channeling information essential to the organization of production.

Given that the firms we study are all in manufacturing, labor productivity would be theoretically maximized if the number of management and clerical workers is kept to a minimum. The extent to which firms can minimize their management and clerical workforce, however, depends on how easy it is to organize and monitor production workers. This, in turn, depends on the educational attainment of the workforce (for example, whether workers can read written instructions) and on social norms regarding discipline and effort. The less disciplined and less well educated the workforce is, the larger the need for monitoring and information processing workers and, thus, the larger the share of management and clerical workers in the total workforce.

The share of production workers in total employment is largest in Vietnam and smallest in Zambia. Vietnam also has the largest share of skilled production workers. In contrast, Zambia has the smallest share of production workers and the largest share of managers, suggesting that labor management is more problematic there. The other three countries—China, Ethiopia, and Tanzania—show a relatively similar breakdown between production and nonproduction workers. There is some variation

Table 5.11 Breakdown of Labor by Occupational Categories

percent

Occupational category	China		Vietnam		Ethiopia		Tanzania		Zambia	
	Now	*1 year ago*	*Now*	*1 year ago*	*Now*	*1 year ago*	*Now*	*1 year ago*	*Now*	*1 year ago*
Total production workers	73	75	81	81	73	73	75	74	66	66
Skilled	46	47	62	61	58	58	50	49	49	51
Unskilled	27	28	19	19	15	15	25	25	17	15
Management	16	14	4	3	23	23	15	16	27	27
Clerical and other	10	10	16	16	4	3	8	8	6	6
Number of observations	255	226	299	296	249	205	261	248	262	254

Source: Compilation of the authors based on the Quantitative Entrepreneur Survey.

between workers reported as clerical or management, but this variation is difficult to interpret because it may be affected by differences in translation and local legal definitions.

Next, we examine the breakdown of the workforce between permanent and casual workers. In the absence of legal restrictions, such a breakdown is expected to depend on the amount of fluctuation in demand: the more variable and unpredictable the demand over time, the larger the share of casual workers. Legal restrictions also affect the propensity of firms to hire permanent workers. In particular, restrictions on firing are thought to discourage firms from hiring permanent workers. The proportion of permanent workers is high in Ethiopia, Vietnam, and Zambia. It is slightly lower in China, which may be caused by fluctuations in demand associated with rapid growth. Alternatively, it may be caused by differences in labor laws and regulations. Tanzania stands out as an outlier, with a much larger share of casual workers in the total workforce: in the average Tanzanian sample firm, casual workers represent two-thirds of the workforce. This may arise because of differences in firm size, however: across the sample as a whole, there is, indeed, a strong positive association between the share of permanent workers and firm size. To investigate this possibility, we estimate a nonparametric regression. We find that variation in firm size cannot explain the differences across the sample countries: China and Tanzania stand out because they have a significantly lower proportion of permanent workers at all firm sizes relative to the other three countries.

In all countries, recruitment at the firm gate, that is, workers present themselves spontaneously to a firm, is the dominant method for identifying workers.[3] Job postings are used by about a quarter of respondents in China and Vietnam, but by few firms in Ethiopia and Tanzania; Zambia occupies an intermediate position. Around 17 percent of Chinese respondents rely on a public or private placement agency. Proportions are much lower in the other four countries. Close to a third of respondents in the three African countries mention other recruitment methods, mostly word of mouth and friends or relatives. Recruitment through job postings, schools, or placement agencies can be regarded as more formal than reliance on friends and relatives or waiting for workers to show up at the firm gate. With this definition, we see that 48 and 37 percent of Chinese and Vietnamese firms, respectively, make use of formal methods to recruit workers. These percentages drop to 12, 3, and 18 percent in Ethiopia, Tanzania, and Zambia, respectively.

Respondent firms were also asked about the proportion of new employees who are recommended by friends or relatives of owners or managers. The average responses are not particularly different across countries, but the distribution of the responses is. In the three African study countries, the median firm stated that there had been no hiring through recommendations by friends or relatives. There is, however, a sizable proportion of firms that hire workers in this manner, and those that do so tend to hire a large proportion of their new employees through this method. In contrast, firms in China and Vietnam are more likely to state that they hire some workers in this manner, but the proportion of total employment hired in this way remains small, around 10 percent of new recruits, for example. The data also show that recruitment through friends or family is much more common among small firms. Firms were also asked whether they ever hire production workers without a recommendation or referral. The most common answer is that they do, and there is little variation across countries.

From this, we tentatively conclude that the three African countries in our study are less formal in the way they recruit workers. This is partly because of the smaller size of the sample firms in Africa. But it also suggests that the labor market operates less efficiently: if firms rely on spontaneous applications and friends or relatives only, they are less likely to identify the workers who are most well qualified for jobs.

Respondents were also asked about the proportion of migrants in the workforce who are from other regions or other countries. In Tanzania and Vietnam, the average response is half the firm's workforce, but the share is only 5 percent in Zambia. China (26 percent) and Ethiopia (19 percent) occupy an intermediate position.

To ascertain the extent to which labor regulations affect firm size, we asked respondents how many workers their firms would wish to hire or lay off if there were no legal or regulatory restrictions on hiring and firing. It is unclear how much confidence one should put in the answers of the respondents, who may overstate in an attempt to influence policy. Most firms claim that, without legal or regulatory restrictions, they would not lay off any workers: the median number of workers respondents would lay off is 0 in all five countries. Except in China, where the average number of workers is 9, the average is quite low: around 1 worker per firm.

Respondents consistently report that they would hire more workers if restrictions on hiring and firing were removed. The average response is particularly large in China: 33 additional workers, on average, with a median of 20. In the other four countries, the average is around 3 to 5 workers, with a median of 0, 1, or 2. From these answers, we tentatively conclude that labor regulations are most distorting in China.

There are big differences across study countries in the provision of in-kind benefits to workers. The provision of housing is common in China, but rare elsewhere. The provision of free or subsidized meals varies across countries, and there is no strong regional pattern. Toilets with running water are much more common in China and Vietnam than in the three African countries in our sample, largely reflecting different standards of sanitation and water distribution across countries. The only country where a sizable share of workers belongs to a union is China. In the other four countries, unions are largely absent in manufacturing.

To conclude this section, we examine the educational attainment and experience of entry-level production workers. In figure 5.6, we report the cumulative distribution of the average educational level of a new production worker in each of the five countries. The lower the curve, the higher

Figure 5.6   Years of Schooling among Production Workers

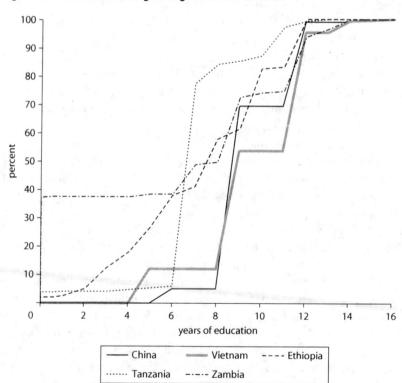

Source: Compilation of the authors based on the Quantitative Entrepreneur Survey.

the educational level of workers. We see that China and Vietnam have the lowest curve overall, indicating that their workforce is more well educated in general than production workers in the three African countries in this study. Among the African countries, Zambia has a large proportion of workers (37 percent) with no education at all. In contrast, only 5 percent of Tanzanian production workers have not completed primary school, but 77 percent have not gone beyond primary school. In China and Vietnam, only a small proportion of production workers have less than nine years of schooling. This probably reflects differences in past decades in legislation on compulsory schooling.

What is unclear is whether production workers with low educational levels require more training before they become fully productive on the factory floor. Respondents were asked how many weeks it takes to train a new production worker. We noticed strong differences across countries. In China and Ethiopia, 90 and 85 percent of respondents, respectively, report that it takes, at most, four weeks for new workers to be fully trained. Among Ethiopian respondents, 56 percent even state that new workers require no training at all. In contrast, in Tanzania and Zambia, only 58 and 48 percent of respondents, respectively, report that new workers are trained in four weeks or less. A sizable minority of respondents even report long training periods, in excess of six months. Vietnam occupies a somewhat intermediate position: new workers are seldom regarded as adequately trained when they begin work, but 87 percent of respondents estimate that, after four months, new workers are trained. Firms that report hiring more highly educated workers tend also to report shorter training periods, but the correlation is not particularly strong; so, it is unclear how much of a savings years of schooling represent for training in manufacturing firms.

Finance

Firm finance is an important aspect of firm performance. In all five countries, for example, at least half the firms surveyed reported that they had purchased or acquired machinery, equipment, or vehicles at some point in the previous three years. Table 5.12 summarizes the sources of finance that firms reported they had used for these acquisitions. The table shows that, for all countries, retained earnings are by far the most important source of finance. In all countries but Ethiopia, bank borrowing is the second most important; in Ethiopia, nonbank financial institutions appear to play a greater role than formal banks.

Table 5.12   Source of Finance for the Most Recent Purchase of Machinery, Equipment, or Vehicles

percent

Source	China	Vietnam	Ethiopia	Tanzania	Zambia
Internal funds and retained earnings	80	82	88	80	86
Borrowed from a bank	23	18	2	4	3
Borrowed from a nonbank financial institution	7	2	10	2	1
Borrowed from a government agency	0	0	0	0	0
Funds from family or friends	7	18	4	3	1
Hire-purchase, credit from the equipment supplier	5	1	0	0	0
Other	0	1	3	1	8
Number of observations	265	300	250	262	250

Source: Compilation of the authors based on the Quantitative Entrepreneur Survey.

This raises the question of the relationship that the study firms maintain with banks. Presumably, the first step before securing a loan from a bank is to have a current account. By observing the movements of funds on firm accounts, the banks can gain valuable information on the financial wherewithal of the firms. Not having this information should make banks more reluctant to lend. At the same time, if firms derive no benefit from banks in terms of loans or otherwise, there is little reason for them to maintain bank accounts. We therefore expect that fewer African firms have bank accounts, and this is, indeed, what we find, especially among smaller firms. Figure 5.7 shows the average probability that firms have bank current accounts after we control for firm size. We see that smaller Chinese firms are substantially more likely to have bank accounts than firms in the other four countries. In a probit regression with a size coefficient common across countries, we easily reject the hypothesis that African and Asian firms are equally likely to have bank accounts: Asian firms are, on average, 10 percentage points more likely to have accounts.

We also examine whether the possession of a bank account is associated with a higher probability that a firm can obtain the simplest form of bank finance, namely, an overdraft facility (for example, a line of credit). The results are stark: among firms with current accounts, only a small proportion have an overdraft facility. In Ethiopia and Vietnam, a handful of manufacturing firms (2 and 3 percent, respectively) have an overdraft facility. The proportions rise to 6 percent of firms with a bank account in

Figure 5.7   Firm Size and Firms with Bank Accounts

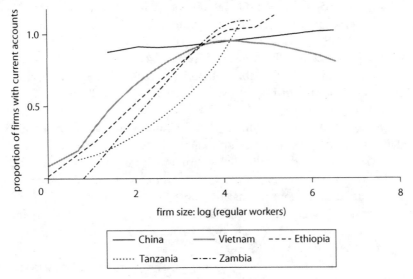

Source: Compilation of the authors based on the Quantitative Entrepreneur Survey.

Tanzania and 19 percent in Zambia, but, in these two countries, only a minority of firms have bank accounts. China stands out in sharp contrast to the other four countries: 63 percent of firms with bank accounts have an overdraft facility.

Overdraft facilities therefore appear to be an important mechanism by which Chinese manufacturing firms access short-term finance. Furthermore, the terms for the finance do not generally appear restrictive: to a series of follow-up questions, those Chinese firms with an overdraft facility reported a median annual interest rate on the overdraft of 7.5 percent, and only about 20 percent of the firms were required to provide collateral (where the median collateral value was 65 percent of the value of the overdraft facility).[4]

If firms cannot overdraw on their bank accounts to deal with emergencies or take advantage of passing investment opportunities, they need to accumulate positive balances to serve this purpose. Examining the proportion of firms having savings accounts, after we control for firm size, we find a substantial heterogeneity across countries. Contrary to expectations, it is not firms in countries other than China that accumulate balances as a substitute for bank credit; it is the Chinese firms. Why this is the case is unclear. One possibility is that returns on savings are higher than subsidized interest charges on overdraft facilities. We also note that Ethiopian firms make substantial use of savings accounts: across the entire sample, 56 percent of Ethiopian firms have savings accounts. This compares to 86 percent in the China sample, but only 22 percent in Vietnam, 5 percent in Tanzania, and 28 percent in Zambia.

We now turn to loans. Table 5.13 summarizes the responses to questions about whether firms borrowed money between 2006 and 2010 and, if so, about the source.

The table supports our finding that Chinese and Vietnamese firms make more extensive use of credit than do firms in Ethiopia, Tanzania, or Zambia. We also see that Ethiopian firms make substantial use of nonbank financial institutions, perhaps to compensate for limited access to bank finance. These conclusions are robust to our nonparametric controls for firm size. Furthermore, nonparametric regressions show that, as one might expect, finance from family or friends (or from moneylenders) is important only for smaller firms.

About a third of the survey firms in China, Ethiopia, and Vietnam currently owe money on loans. The proportions are much lower in Tanzania and Zambia: 11 and 6 percent, respectively. These findings are, by and large, in agreement with table 5.13 once we take into account the fact that loans from moneylenders or from family and friends are generally for a much shorter duration and are thus less likely to be observable at any given point in time.

Loan terms tend to differ across the study countries. Figure 5.8 shows the time for loan repayments after we control nonparametrically for firm size. The figure refers to the most recent loans from banks, nonbank financial institutions, or government agencies. We see that, except in

Table 5.13   Firms That Have Borrowed from Different Sources, 2006–10
percent

Source	China	Vietnam	Ethiopia	Tanzania	Zambia
Borrowed from a bank	33	36	4	3	3
Borrowed from a nonbank financial institution	15	4	32	2	4
Borrowed from a government agency	12	2	0	0	1
Funds from family or friends	15	19	18	2	3
Moneylender	0	5	0	0	1
Other	0	0	6	0	1
Number of observations	303	300	250	262	263

Source: Compilation of the authors based on the Quantitative Entrepreneur Survey.

Figure 5.8   Loan Duration

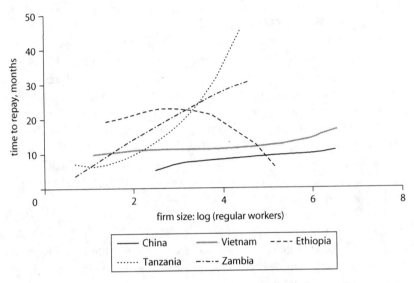

Source: Compilation of the authors based on the Quantitative Entrepreneur Survey.

Ethiopia, loan duration increases with firm size in Africa, while in Asia, there is no such association with firm size. Because there are more large firms in the China and Vietnam samples, it follows that, on average, loans to manufacturing firms in China and Vietnam are for shorter time periods than corresponding loans in Ethiopia, Tanzania, and Zambia.

Why loan duration increases rapidly with firm size in Africa is unclear. One possibility is that the transaction costs for borrowing are lower in China and Vietnam than in Ethiopia, Tanzania, or Zambia. If this is true, banks in China and Vietnam may be more willing to lend to manufacturing firms because the banks can profitably make many short-term loans.

To investigate this possibility, we examine the differences across countries with respect to collateral requirements and average interest rates. Even after we control for firm size, we find that Chinese firms face substantially lower average collateral requirements. Similarly, Chinese firms pay an average annual interest rate of about 4.7 percent, compared with average annual interest rates of about 10.0 percent in Ethiopia, 14.0 percent in Tanzania and Vietnam, and 21.0 percent in Zambia. These proportions change little across firms of varying sizes. These differences cannot be explained merely by differences in the information available to lenders: the proportion of firms that have their annual financial statements certified by external auditors increases systematically with firm size, but does not differ significantly across countries once we control for firm size.

Not having to incur the cost of securing collateral likely reduces total lending costs for lenders, and this may explain why Chinese banks are more likely to lend to manufacturers and charge smaller interest rates. Another possible explanation is that Chinese banks, many of which are still controlled by the government, have been instructed to lend to manufacturers at low interest rates and without insisting too much on collateral. As long as Chinese manufacturing output is increasing rapidly, the risk of default remains low. Should manufacturing growth fall for an extended time, however, these uncollateralized loans could lead to a crisis in the Chinese banking sector.

Actual loans may provide a misleading picture of firm access to credit if many firms that could obtain loans choose not to do so either because they prefer to self-finance, or because they have not identified suitable investment opportunities. To investigate this possibility, we asked firms whether they could borrow either to purchase equipment or to expand their working capital. In China and Vietnam, we find that the responses to the two questions largely mirror actual borrowing: a little over a third of the respondents (half on the issue of working capital in China) state that they could borrow from a bank, and 10 to 20 percent say they could borrow from family or friends. In Ethiopia, we find that 45 percent of the survey firms reckon that they could borrow from a nonbank financial institution. This compares with the 32 percent of respondents who had actually borrowed from such a source in the past. In contrast, a large proportion of the respondents in Tanzania and Zambia state that they could borrow from banks or financial institutions, which is far in excess of the negligible percentage of firms (that is, less than 5 percent) that had actually done so in the past.

The reason for the discrepancy is unclear. One possibility is that firms in Tanzania and Zambia could borrow if they wanted to, but choose not to either because they prefer to self-finance or because they prefer not to invest. Another possibility is that respondents have erroneous expectations. The latter explanation is a serious concern in the Tanzania sample, where most firms are quite small and unlikely to be appealing as borrowers from the average commercial bank.

We also asked firms about the maximum amount that a lender might allow the firm to borrow. Differences in the expected maximum loan amount are explained by differences in firm size, rather than by differences in country.

Productivity

We have considered measures of firm productivity and examined how different firms in the sample choose to organize their operations and how this relates to their output. Because productivity analysis requires balance sheet information, we asked respondent firms to provide basic accounting information. Unfortunately, the proportion of nonresponse is high. This is relatively common in surveys such as this because many firms are unable or unwilling to disclose information on their costs and profits. The results presented here are based on the available answers. In spite of this caveat, the information is useful in understanding differences in firm performance.

Even after we control for the number of regular workers, firms in China and Ethiopia earn higher profits than firms in Tanzania and Vietnam; Zambia occupies an intermediate position. However, our analysis of the relationship between reported annual profits and firm size is particularly affected by nonresponse: some 55 percent of Chinese firms and about 70 percent of firms in Tanzania and Zambia refused to answer this question. The nonresponse rates in Ethiopia and Vietnam were, fortunately, much lower, 15 and 4 percent, respectively. These general trends were confirmed when we examined the relationship between annual sales and firm size. This is important because response rates on the latter issue are higher and thus less subject to possible self-selection bias: nonresponse in China was about 29 percent, while it was about 70 and 45 percent in Tanzania and Zambia, respectively. Even after we control for firm size, Chinese firms sell significantly more than Vietnamese firms, which, over much of the firm size range, sell more than Ethiopian, Tanzanian, or Zambian firms.

This analysis implies that Chinese and Vietnamese manufacturing workers are, on average, more productive than manufacturing workers in Ethiopia, Tanzania, and Zambia. This finding prompts several questions. First, do Chinese and Vietnamese firms pay higher labor costs in return for having more productive workers? Second, to what extent can higher productivity be explained by the possession by Chinese and Vietnamese firms of more valuable capital in the form of machinery, equipment, vehicles, land, and buildings?

We begin with the question about labor costs. Figure 5.9 shows aggregate labor costs by firm size, including wages, salaries, bonuses, and social security. The graph shows that labor costs are higher in China than in Vietnam and Zambia, in which costs are higher than in Ethiopia and Tanzania. These results are in line with expectations: higher labor productivity translates into higher worker compensation.

How are Chinese and Vietnamese firms able to pay higher wages? One obvious possibility is that they have more machinery and equipment per worker. (Unfortunately, the analysis was hindered because firms in China refused to answer the survey questions.) We see that, over much of the firm size range, Vietnamese firms have more capital than their African counterparts. Large firms in Ethiopia and Tanzania, however, appear to have more capital invested relative to the case of large Vietnamese firms.

These results indicate that Chinese firms have larger profits and sales, but also larger labor costs. We suspect this is accounted for by a combination of larger capital investment, better infrastructure, and agglomeration effects, but, unfortunately, we have no information on capital among Chinese firms. Vietnamese firms occupy an intermediate position: small Vietnamese firms perform better than their African counterparts—that

Figure 5.9   Firm Size and Labor Costs

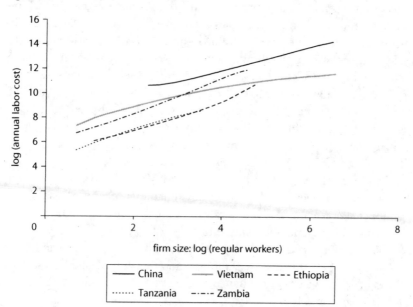

Source: Compilation of the authors based on the Quantitative Entrepreneur Survey.

is, they show higher profits and sales—and spend more on workers. But they do not perform significantly better than the larger African firms included in our study, which, by international standards, would be regarded as medium firms. Although it is perilous to extrapolate from this limited evidence, these results suggest that the aggregate productivity of African manufacturing ultimately depends on the presence of larger firms. Because research has already shown that small firms in Africa (and elsewhere) seldom if ever grow to be medium firms, what is needed is entry by entrepreneurs capable of operating medium manufacturing firms successfully.

This prompts consideration of the role of land and buildings. Like machinery, equipment, and vehicles, land is an important factor in firm production. Firms may face difficulties investing in land if land suitable for manufacturing development is scarce in urban centers. The questionnaires asked about (1) the resale value of land and buildings and (2) the purchase or other acquisition of land and buildings in 2010. Nonresponse was a particularly severe problem with the questions about land and buildings. We report data only on countries in which at least 20 firms responded. This excludes China and Ethiopia for the question on land value, and Ethiopia and Tanzania for the question on land acquisition.

Despite these limitations, the questions provide suggestive evidence on land availability. An analysis of the reported value of land and buildings, after we control for firm size, suggests that, for the sample of firms responding to the question, the value of land is higher in Tanzania and Vietnam than in Zambia. Even after we control for firm size, Chinese firms responding to the question about the acquisition of land and buildings in 2010 had spent significantly more on the acquisition of land and buildings than did firms in Vietnam, which, in turn, appear to have spent more than firms in Zambia (though the difference here is less significant).

There are two possible explanations for these differences. First, it may be that firms in some countries pay more for land and buildings because land is more productive, that is, is closer to higher-quality infrastructure. In effect, high prices may be driven by high firm demand. This is analogous to the discussion above about the high relative costs of labor in China: in the same way that high labor productivity may cause higher wages, high land productivity (for example, in terms of access to infrastructure) may drive high costs for land and buildings. Second, it may be that firms in some countries pay more because of limitations on the available land; in effect, high prices may be driven by limited land supply.

There are reasons to believe that both supply and demand factors are responsible for the answers given by survey respondents. Indeed, manufacturing firms in China and Vietnam are likely to exhibit a greater demand for land and buildings because of their relatively higher productivity, but they may also be more constrained in their access to suitable land if firms are competing for a limited supply of industrial land. Without exogenous variation in demand and supply, the questions in our survey do not allow us to separate out these effects. It remains an important area for further research.

Firm Growth

Finally, we consider firm growth. We measure firm growth as the average change in log sales between 2008 and 2010. We trim (that is, drop) the top 5 percent and the bottom 5 percent of the observations to ensure robustness to outliers. Many firms did not report sales in 2008, and there were serious differences in this across countries. Growth figures must therefore be regarded as indicative only, as they may be biased by selection bias. Figure 5.10 shows the empirical probability density across the five countries. There is substantial overlap in growth experiences across the firms in the study, that is, it is not the case that most

Figure 5.10   Sales Growth

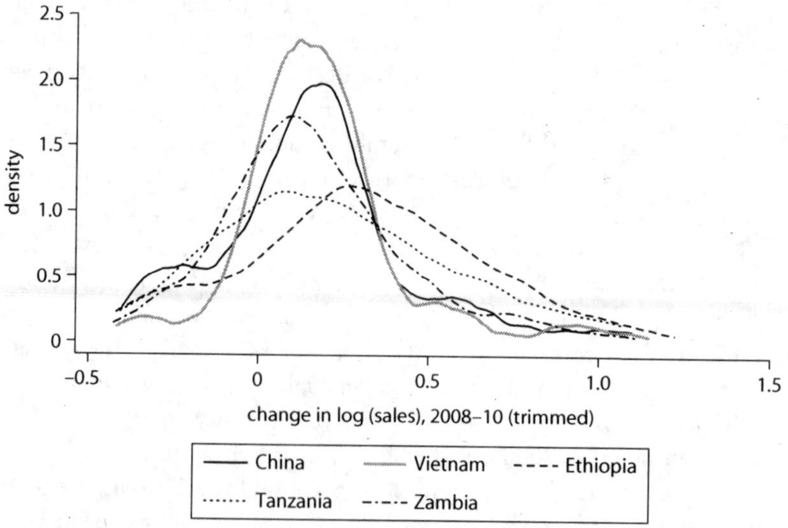

change in log (sales), 2008–10 (trimmed)

— China   ～ Vietnam   - - - - Ethiopia
······· Tanzania   -·-·- Zambia

Source: Compilation of the authors based on the Quantitative Entrepreneur Survey.

firms in China, for instance, are growing much more rapidly than firms in Africa or Vietnam.

Median sales growth is strong across all five countries and is lower in China than in the other countries, except Zambia. The main difference between China and the other countries is that average firm size is much larger, and manufacturing represents a sizable proportion of GDP. Hence, a 14.8 percent growth rate in sales has a large effect on aggregate growth. This is not true in the other countries, particularly the three African countries in our sample, where firms are smaller, and manufacturing only represents a minute portion of domestic GDP.

Annex 5.1   Quantitative Entrepreneur Survey Questionnaire

September 2010

1.	CONTROL SECTION
1.1	Firm ID code:
1.2	Name of the interviewer:
1.3	Interview date:
1.4	Interview start time:
1.5	Name of the firm:
1.6	Address of the firm:
1.7	Directions to find the firm:
1.8	Landline number:
1.9	Mobile number:
1.10	Fax number:
1.11	Contact e-mail address:
1.12	Name of the respondent:
1.13	Respondent's position in the firm:

1: Manager
2: Vice president/Deputy manager
3: Planning and statistics head
4: Finance and administration
5: Planning expert
6: Processing manager
7: Managing director
8: Sales manager
9: Department head
10: Marketing head
11: Accountant

12: Production manager
13: Deputy expert
14: Owner and manager

1.14   In which industry does this firm primarily operate?
1: Food and beverages
2: Garments
3: Leather products
4: Metal products
5: Wood products
6: Other (please specify)

2.   GENERAL INFORMATION

2.1   Is this establishment part of a larger firm?
1: Yes
2: No

2.2   Is this establishment located in an industrial zone/cluster?
1: Yes
2: No

2.3   [If yes] What were the main three reasons for this location decision:
1: Affordable land/building
2: Good infrastructure (electricity/water/roads)
3: Proximity to suppliers/customers
4: Tax incentives
5: Good central government services
6: Good local government services
7: Availability of workers security/safety
8: Others (please specify)

2.4   What is this firm's current legal status?
1: Government owned
2: Listed company (traded on a stock exchange)
3: Shareholding company
4: Limited company
5: Sole proprietorship
6: Partnership
7: Joint venture, foreign direct investment
8: Other (specify)

2.5   In what year did this firm begin operations (whether the firm is registered or not)?

2.6   What percentage of this firm is owned by each of the following:

2.6.1 Private sector, domestically owned	_____%
2.6.2 Private sector, foreign owned	_____%
2.6.3 Government/state owned	_____%
2.6.4 Other (specify)	_____%
	<u>100%</u>

2.7   Does this firm have a single owner, or multiple shareholders?
　　　1:　Single
　　　2:　Multiple

Enumerator: If the answer is "single," skip to question 2.11.

2.8   Are the shareholders members of the same family?
　　　1:　Yes
　　　2:　No

2.9   How many owners or shareholders take an active part in the management of the firm?

2.10   When the firm began operations, did it have a single owner, or multiple shareholders?
　　　1:　Single
　　　2:　Multiple

Enumerator: If the answer is "single," skip to question 2.13.

2.11   When the firm began operations, how many owners or shareholders took an active part in the management of the firm?

I now want to ask about the main owner of the firm, that is, the single owner or the person owning the largest share.

2.12   What percentage of this firm does this person own?

2.13   What is the gender of the firm owner?
　　　1:　Male
　　　2:　Female

2.14   How old is the firm owner (years)?

2.15   How long has the firm owner been living in this city/district (years)?

2.16   What is the highest level of education of the firm owner?
　　　1:　No education
　　　2:　Incomplete primary education

3:   Completed primary education

4:   Incomplete secondary education

5:   Completed secondary education

6:   Vocational/technical school certificate

7:   College/university degree (BA, BSc, etc.) from a university in this country

8:   College/university degree (BA, BSc, etc.) from a university in another country

9:   Graduate degree (PhD, Masters, MBA) from a university in this country

10: Graduate degree (PhD, Masters, MBA) from a university in another country

2.17   What was the main professional occupation of the owner's father?

1.   Farming, fishing, livestock

2.   Trader/shop owner

3.   Civil servant, military

4.   Wage worker in private sector (or commercial public sector)

5.   Entrepreneur

6.   Other

2.18   What was the main professional occupation of the owner's mother?

1.   Farming, fishing, livestock

2.   Trader/shop owner

3.   Civil servant, military

4.   Wage worker in private sector (or commercial public sector)

5.   Entrepreneur

6.   Housewife

7.   Other

2.19   Is the firm owner running the firm?

1:   Yes

2:   No

Enumerator: If the answer is "no," skip to question 2.22.

2.20   How long has this person been running the firm?

2.21   Before he or she started running this firm, how many years of
          work experience did this person have:
          2.21.1 Working in this firm?
          2.21.2 Working as a trader in this sector?
          2.21.3 Working in another firm owned by him or his family,
                  in the same sector?
          2.21.4 Working in another firm owned by him or his family,
                  in a different sector?
          2.21.5 Working as a wage employee in another firm, in the
                  same sector?
          2.21.6 Working as a wage employee in another firm, in a dif-
                  ferent sector?
          2.21.7 Working for a state-owned enterprise?
          2.21.8 Working for the government?

2.22   Does the owner own other firms as well?
          1:   Yes
          2:   No

Enumerator: If the answer is "no," skip to question 2.24.

2.23   For how many years?

2.24   Has the firm owner ever resided in a different part of this
          country?

Enumerator: If the answer is "no," skip to question 2.27.

2.25   For how many years?

2.26   If so, what was the firm owner's primary activity during that
          time?
          1:   Student
          2:   Wage employee
          3:   Business owner
          4:   Government employee
          5:   Not working

2.27   Has the firm owner ever resided in another country?
          1:   Yes
          2:   No

Enumerator: If the answer is "no," skip to question 2.30.

2.28   If so, for how many years?

2.29   If so, what was the firm owner's primary activity during that time?
    1:    Student
    2:    Wage employee
    3:    Business owner
    4:    Not working

2.30   List all of the countries in which the owner holds citizenship.

2.31   To which ethnic group does the owner belong?

2.32   What is the religion of the firm owner? (Please indicate if "no religion.")
    1:    Muslim
    2:    Hindu
    3:    Buddhist
    4:    Catholic
    5:    Protestant
    6:    Charismatic Christian
    7:    Animist
    8:    No religion/atheist
    9:    Other (please specify)

---

3.   ORIGINS AND DEVELOPMENT OF ENTREPRENEURIAL CAPABILITIES

3.1   Did the firm owner(s) contribute ideas for the creation of the firm (that is, about what to produce, where, when, and for whom)?
    1:    Yes
    2:    No

3.2   Did the firm owner(s) contribute technical expertise at the creation of the firm?
    1:    Yes
    2:    No

3.3   Did the firm owner(s) participate in financing the creation of the firm?
    1:    Yes
    2:    No

3.4   Apart from the firm owner(s), who contributed *ideas* for the creation of the firm (that is, what to produce, where, when, and for whom)? (Please tick all that apply.)
    1:    Family members and relatives
    2:    Business friends and acquaintances

      3:   Equipment suppliers
      4:   Employees
      5:   Clients
      6:   School teacher/professor
      7:   Expert/consultant
      8:   Other (please specify) _____
      9:   No one else

3.5   Apart from the firm owner(s), who contributed *technical expertise* at the creation of the firm? (Please tick all that apply.)
      1:   Family members and relatives
      2:   Business friends and acquaintances
      3:   Equipment suppliers
      4:   Employees
      5:   Clients
      6:   School teacher/professor
      7:   Expert/consultant
      8:   Other (please specify) _____
      9:   No one else

3.6   Apart from the firm owner(s), who helped *finance* the creation of the firm? (Please tick all that apply.)
      1:   Family members and relatives
      2:   Business friends and acquaintances
      3:   Equipment supplier
      4:   A bank [If yes] What percentage of start-up investment: _____ %
      5:   A nonbank financial institution (microfinance institution, credit cooperative, credit union, finance company)
      6:   Other (please specify) _____
      7:   No one else

4.   **INVESTMENT CLIMATE**

4.1   Please list all the business associations of which the firm or its owner(s) is a member.

      1:   _____
      2:   _____
      3:   _____
      4:   _____
      5:   _____

4.2   Is this firm registered with the business registry (that is, does the firm have a business registration number to appear on invoices, etc.)?
             1:   Yes
             2:   No

Enumerator: If the answer is "no," skip to question 4.4.

4.3   When was the firm registered?

4.4   Does the owner intend to register the firm one day?
             1:   Yes
             2:   No

4.5   Is this firm registered for the value added tax?
             1:   Yes
             2:   No

4.6   Does this firm hold any business licenses from local authorities (for example, to operate a certain category of business in a given area)?
             1:   Yes
             2:   No

4.7   Does this firm have an account with the electricity company?
             1:   Yes
             2:   No

4.8   Does this firm use electricity for production?
             1:   Yes
             2:   No

Enumerator: If the answer is "no," skip to question 4.11.

4.9   What is the average number of power outages the firm experiences per month?

4.10   On average, how long is each power outage? _____ hours

4.11   How many licenses, permits, and other clearances did the owner need to obtain *before* he or she could start this firm?

4.12   How many licenses, permits, and other clearances did the firm need to *renew last year?*

4.13   In the last year, did this firm need to pay any fees or penalties for operating without official registration or license?
             1:   Yes
             2:   No

4.14   Establishments are sometimes required to make gifts or informal payments to public officials to "get things done" with
regard to customs, taxes, licenses, regulations, services, etc. On
average, what percentage of total annual revenue do establishments like this one pay in informal payments/gifts to public
officials for this purpose?

5.	COMPETITION

5.1   How competitive is the market for the firm's products?
1:    Very competitive
2:    Moderately competitive
3:    Not competitive

5.2   In your neighborhood (within 15 minutes' walk), how many
businesses operate in the same sector as your firm?

5.3   For the main market in which this establishment sold its main
product, do you face competition from any medium to large
domestic enterprises (that is, enterprises with 10 or more permanent employees)?
1:    Yes
2:    No

Enumerator: If the answer is "no," skip to question 5.5.

5.4   How many?
1:    1
2:    2–5
3:    6–10
4:    More than 10
–99:   Don't know

5.5   For the main market in which this establishment sold its main
product, do you face competition from foreign imports?
1:    Yes
2:    No

Enumerator: If the answer is "no," skip to the start of the next section.

5.6   From how many different competitors?
1:    1
2:    2–5
3:    6–10
4:    More than 10
–99:   Don't know

5.7   Please list the country of your three most important foreign competitors (if they exist).

    5.7.1   Country of your most important foreign competitor:

    5.7.2   Country of your second-most important foreign competitor:

    5.7.3   Country of your third-most important foreign competitor:

5.8   Are these imported products (which compete with your firm):

    5.8.1   More expensive than yours?

    1:   Yes

    2:   No

    5.8.2   Better and more consistent in quality than yours?

    1:   Yes

    2:   No

    5.8.3   Better adapted than your products to local tastes and fashions?

    1:   Yes

    2:   No

    5.8.4   A well-known brand?

    1:   Yes

    2:   No

6.   SOCIAL CAPITAL

6.1   Do you have friends or relatives who are working as bank officials?

    1:   Yes

    2:   No

6.2   Do you have friends or relatives who are elected officials/party cadres?

    1:   Yes

    2:   No

6.3   Do you have friends or relatives who are working for the government?

    1:   Yes

    2:   No

6.4   In this country, how many friends and relatives do you have who are in business (in other firms)?

Enumerator: If the answer is "none," skip to question 6.10.

6.5   On average, are they more experienced or less experienced in business than you?
    1:    More experienced
    2:    Less experienced
    3:    About the same

6.6   On average, do they work in a larger or smaller firm than this one?
    1:    Larger
    2:    Smaller
    3:    About the same

6.7   On average, how frequently do you speak to them?
    1:    Every day
    2:    Every week
    3:    Every month
    4:    Every year
    5:    Less than once a year

6.8   Do they know each other?
    1:    All of them
    2:    Some of them
    3:    None

6.9   If "all of them" or "some of them," how did they meet? (Please tick all that apply.)
    1:    Family (for example weddings and other social events)
    2:    School or university
    3:    Religious organization
    4:    Sports
    5:    Business association and business events
    6:    Political organization
    7:    Other

6.10   Do you have friends and relatives who are in business in another country?
    1:    Yes
    2:    No

Enumerator: If the answer is "no," skip to question 6.13.

6.11   How many?

6.12   Do they know each other?
      1:   All of them
      2:   Some of them
      3:   None

Enumerator: If the respondent has indicated that he or she has no friends and relatives in business either in this country or abroad, skip to question 6.15.

6.13   Of these friends and relatives, in this country and abroad:
      6.13.1 How many are in the same sector as this firm?
            1:   1
            2:   2–5
            3:   6–10
            4:   More than 10
            –99: Don't know
      6.13.2 How many could help you to identify sources of raw materials in this country?
            1:   1
            2:   2–5
             3:   6–10
            4:   More than 10
            –99: Don't know
      6.13.3 How many could help you to identify sources of raw materials in another country?
            1:   1
            2:   2–5
           3:   6–10
            4:   More than 10
            –99: Don't know
      6.13.4 How many could help you to identify new markets for your products?
            1:   1
            2:   2–5
           3:   6–10
            4:   More than 10
            –99: Don't know
      6.13.5 How many could help you to secure external finance for your firm?
            1:   1
            2:   2–5
           3:   6–10

4:     More than 10

–99: Don't know

6.13.6 How many could help you to identify and recruit skilled workers and employees for your firm?

1:     1

2:     2–5

3:     6–10

4:     More than 10

–99: Don't know

6.13.7 How many could provide you with valuable technological information about which machinery or equipment to buy for your firm?

1:     1

2:     2–5

3:     6–10

4:     More than 10

–99: Don't know

6.13.8 How many could help you to obtain information on where to buy secondhand machinery or equipment?

1:     1

2:     2–5

3:     6–10

4:     More than 10

–99: Don't know

6.13.9 How many could provide information about how to operate and repair machinery or equipment for your firm?

1:     1

2:     2–5

3:     6–10

4:     More than 10

–99: Don't know

6.14   Of those friends and relatives in this country and abroad:

6.14.1 How many have you helped to identify sources of raw materials in this country?

1:     1

2:     2–5

3:     6–10

4:     More than 10

–99: Don't know

6.14.2 How many have you helped to identify sources of raw materials in another country?

1:      1
2:      2–5
3:      6–10
4:      More than 10
–99:   Don't know

6.14.3 How many have you helped to identify new markets for your products?

1:      1
2:      2–5
3:      6–10
4:      More than 10
–99:   Don't know

6.14.4 How many have you helped to secure external finance for their firm?

1:      1
2:      2–5
3:      6–10
4:      More than 10
–99:   Don't know

6.14.5 How many have you helped to identify and recruit skilled workers and employees for your firm?

1:      1
2:      2–5
3:      6–10
4:      More than 10
–99:   Don't know

6.14.6 How many have you provided with valuable technological information about which machinery or equipment to buy for your firm?

1:      1
2:      2–5
3:      6–10
4:      More than 10
–99:   Don't know

6.14.7 How many have you helped to obtain information on where to buy secondhand machinery or equipment?

1:      1
2:      2–5

3:    6–10
4:    More than 10
–99: Don't know

6.14.8 To how many have you provided information about how to operate and repair machinery or equipment for your firm?

1:    1
2:    2–5
3:    6–10
4:    More than 10
–99: Don't know

6.15   Is there a government agency that could:

6.15.1 Help you access land/buildings used for business at an affordable price?
If yes: please give name: _____

6.15.2 Help you to identify sources of raw materials in this country?
If yes: please give name: _____

6.15.3 Help you to identify sources of raw materials in another country?
If yes: please give name: _____

6.15.4 Help you to identify new markets for your products?
If yes: please give name: _____

6.15.5 Help you to secure external finance for your firm?
If yes: please give name: _____

6.15.6 Help you to identify and recruit skilled workers and employees for your firm?
If yes: please give name: _____

6.15.7 Provide you with valuable technological information about which machinery or equipment to buy for your firm?
If yes: please give name: _____

6.15.8 Help you to obtain information on where to buy secondhand machinery or equipment?
If yes: please give name: _____

6.15.9 Provide information about how to operate and repair machinery or equipment for your firm?
If yes: please give name: _____

7.	INPUTS

7.1   What percentage of the material inputs for your firm do you purchase from:

7.1.1	Suppliers located within 10 miles	_____%
7.1.2	Suppliers in this country more than 10 miles away	_____%
7.1.3	Suppliers in other countries	_____%
7.1.4	Local importers	_____%
7.1.5	Government agencies	_____%
7.1.6	Other (specify)	_____%
		100%

7.2   How many regular suppliers of material inputs do you have?

_____

7.3   What proportion of the value of *total annual purchases* of inputs are:

7.3.1	Paid before delivery?	_____%
7.3.2	Paid at the time of delivery?	_____%
7.3.3	Paid some time after delivery?	_____%
		100%

7.4   Please indicate the region/country of your three main suppliers.

7.4.1   First main supplier: _____

7.4.2   Second main supplier: _____

7.4.3   Third main supplier: _____

7.5   In addition to your regular suppliers, from how many alternative suppliers could you obtain similar raw materials?

Enumerator: If the answer is "none," skip to the start of the next section.

7.6   How many of those alternative suppliers do you know personally?

OUTPUT

What share of the sales of this firm go to:

7.7.1	Customers in this city/district?	_____%
7.7.2	Customers elsewhere in this country?	_____%
7.7.3	Exports?	_____%
		100%

*Enumerator: If the answer to 7.7.3 is zero (that is, if the firm does not export),
skip to question 7.10.*

7.8   In what year did this firm first export its products? _____

7.9   What are the main countries of destination of your exports?
     7.9.1   Main country of destination:
     7.9.2   Second main country of destination:
     7.9.3   Third main country of destination:

7.10   What share of the sales of this firm go to:
     7.10.1   Final consumers   _____%
     7.10.2   Manufacturers   _____%
     7.10.3   Wholesalers/traders/import-export   _____%
                   agencies
     7.10.4   Government agencies   _____%
     7.10.5   Other (specify): _____ _____%
                                        100%

7.11   What proportion of your sales are custom-made to meet
the specifications of specific customers? (Please answer as a
percentage.)

7.12   In the last six months, have you done any form of advertising?
     1:   Yes
     2:   No

7.13   What proportion of the value of *total annual sales* are:
     7.13.1   Paid before delivery?   _____%
     7.13.2   Paid at the time of delivery?   _____%
     7.13.3   Paid some time after delivery?   _____%
                                        100%

7.14   How many regular customers do you have?

7.15   Please indicate the region/country of your three main
customers.
     7.15.1   Main customer: _____
     7.15.2   Second main customer: _____
     7.15.3   Third main customer: _____

7.16   What proportion of your total sales go to your main customer?
     _____ %

7.17   In addition to your regular customers, to how many alternative customers could you sell your products? (If the answer is "many," enter "999.")

Enumerator: If the answer is "zero," skip to question 7.19.

7.18   How many of those alternative customers do you know personally?

7.19   If you shut down your firm, how long would it take your customers to find an alternative supplier?
    1:    Less than a week
    2:    More than a week, less than a month
    3:    A month or more
    4:    It would be impossible

8.	INNOVATION

8.1   How many types of products does this firm currently produce?

8.2   Give the names of the firm's three main products.
    8.2.1   Main product:
    8.2.2   Second main product:
    8.2.3   Third main product:

8.3   What was the main product when you started? _____

8.4   During the last three fiscal years, did this firm introduce any new products?
    1:    Yes
    2:    No

Enumerator: If the answer is "no," skip to question 8.11.

8.5   What prompted your firm to introduce new products?
    1:    The firm noticed a gap in the market
    2:    The firm responded to demand by its customers
    3:    The firm imitated other local producers
    4:    The firm imitated imports
    5:    Other (please specify)

8.6   Who are these new products sold to?
    1:    Previous customers in this country
    2:    Previous customers in another country
    3:    New customers in this country
    4:    New customers in another country

Results of Sample Surveys of Firms   201

Enumerator: If one of the answers is "3: New customers in this country" or "4: New customers in another country," proceed to question 8.7. Otherwise, skip to question 8.8.

8.7   Which of the following helped your firm to find these new customers? (tick all that apply)
  1:   New managers or new shareholders
  2:   New employees
  3:   Conversations with friends and relatives of the managers and owners
  4:   Conversations with competitors
  5:   A joint venture with a domestic firm
  6:   A joint venture with a foreign firm
  7:   Suppliers of raw materials
  8:   Suppliers of machinery, equipment, or vehicles
  9:   Universities/research institutions
  10: Development agencies
  11: Government agencies
  12: Other (please specify)
  99: None of the above

8.8   From whom did your firm get the technological expertise necessary to develop these new products? (Tick all that apply.)
  1:   From within the firm
  2:   Conversations with friends and relatives of the managers and owners
  3:   Conversations with competitors
  4:   A joint venture with a domestic firm
  5:   A joint venture with a foreign firm
  6:   Customers
  7:   Suppliers of raw materials
  8:   Suppliers of machinery, equipment, or vehicles
  9:   Universities/research institutions
  10: Experts and consultants
  11: Government agencies
  12: Other (please specify)
  99: None of the above

8.9   Did the introduction of these new products require additional finance?
  1:   Yes
  2:   No

Enumerator: If the answer is "no," skip to question 8.11.

8.10   Where did this finance come from?
    1:    The firm's retained earnings
    2:    New capital from existing owners (including a parent company)
    3:    New capital from new owners/shareholders
    4:    Friends and relatives of the managers and owners
    5:    Bank or other financial institution [If yes] What percentage of investment: ___%
    6:    Nonbank financial institution (microfinance institution, credit cooperative/credit union)
    7:    Joint venture with a domestic firm
    8:    Joint venture with a foreign firm
    9:    Advances from customers
    10:    Credit from suppliers of raw materials
    11:    Credit from suppliers of machinery, equipment, or vehicles
    12:    Credit from a development agency
    13:    Credit from a government agency
    14:    Other (please specify)

8.11   During the last three fiscal years, has this firm changed its production process (for example, changing the layout of machinery and equipment)?
    1:    Yes
    2:    No

8.12   During the last three fiscal years, has this firm changed the way it delivers its products to customers?
    1:    Yes
    2:    No

Enumerator: If the answer is "no" to 8.11 AND 8.12, skip to question 8.16.

8.13   From whom did your firm get the technological expertise necessary to introduce these changes to the production process or delivery system? (Tick all that apply.)
    1:    From within the firm
    2:    Conversations with friends and relatives of the managers and owners
    3:    Conversations with competitors

4: A joint venture with a domestic firm
5: A joint venture with a foreign firm
6: Customers
7: Suppliers of raw materials
8: Suppliers of machinery, equipment, or vehicles
9: Universities/research institutions
10: Experts and consultants
11: Government agencies
12: Other (please specify)

8.14   Did the introduction of these changes to the production process or delivery system require additional finance?
1: Yes
2: No

Enumerator: If the answer is "no," skip to question 8.16.

8.15   Where did this finance come from? (Please tick all that apply.)
1: The firm's retained earnings
2: New capital from existing owners (including a parent
company)
3: New capital from new owners/shareholders
4: Friends and relatives of the managers and owners
5: Bank or other financial institution [If yes] What percentage of investment: ___%
6: Nonbank financial institution (microfinance institution,
credit cooperative/credit union)
7: Joint venture with a domestic firm
8: Joint venture with a foreign firm
9: Advances from customers
10: Credit from suppliers of raw materials
11: Credit from suppliers of machinery, equipment, or vehicles
12: Credit from a development agency
13: Credit from a government agency
14: Other (please specify)

8.16   What change in government policy would make this firm consider introducing new products? (First tick all that apply, then
rank by order of importance: 1 for most important, 2 for second most important, etc.)
1: Better protection of trademarks and
proprietary designs   ____ rank ____

2: Lower protection of trademarks and
    proprietary designs   ____ rank ____
3: Assistance to identify markets abroad   ____ rank ____
4: Restricting imports of competing
    products   ____ rank ____
5: Easing import restrictions on industrial
    inputs and machinery   ____ rank ____
6: Raise minimum quality standards   ____ rank ____
7: Lower minimum quality standards   ____ rank ____
8: Provide vocational training to potential
    workers   ____ rank ____
9: Provide better training for technicians
    and managers   ____ rank ____
10: Subsidize research and development   ____ rank ____
11: Encourage foreign direct investment   ____ rank ____
12: Discourage foreign direct investment   ____ rank ____
13: Reduce the cost of finance   ____ rank ____
14: Reduce the cost of labor   ____ rank ____
15: Reduce the tax burden on the firm   ____ rank ____
16: Other (please specify)   ____ rank ____

8.17   Did this firm ever begin production of a product that had not
        been produced in this country before?
        1: Yes
        2: No

        [If yes] In what year(s)?
        8.17.1 1: _____
        8.17.2 2: _____
        8.17.3 3: _____

8.18   Did this firm ever begin exporting a product that had not been
        exported by this country before?
        1: Yes
        2: No

        [If yes] In what year(s)?
        8.18.1 1: _____
        8.18.2 2: _____
        8.18.3 3: _____

8.19   Did this firm ever begin importing an input or raw material
        that had not been imported in this country before?
        1: Yes
        2: No

[If yes] In what year(s)?

8.19.1 1: _____

8.19.2 2: _____

8.19.3 3: _____

8.20   Was this firm ever the first to introduce a new type of machine, equipment, or production process in this country?

1:      Yes

2:      No

[If yes] In what year(s)?

8.20.1 1: _____

8.20.2 2: _____

8.20.3 3: _____

9.   LABOR

Note: In this section, *permanent employees* are defined as all paid employees who are contracted for a term of one or more fiscal years and/or have a guaranteed renewal of their employment contract and who work eight or more hours per day. In this section, *temporary/seasonal employees* are defined as any employees who are not "permanent employees" (for example, employees who are hired for less than a fiscal year with no guarantee of renewal of their employment).

9.1   How many *employees* does this establishment have in each of the following categories (not including seasonal workers)?

Note: researchers to insert the relevant years here.

Category	The last fiscal year	The fiscal year before the last fiscal year	Three years ago	When the firm started operations
Professionals				
Skilled production workers				
Unskilled production workers				
Nonproduction workers (for example, managers, administration, sales)				
Total permanent employees				
Total temporary/seasonal employees				

9.2   How does this firm usually find new employees? (Please tick the most important.)

1:    Job candidates spontaneously present themselves at the firm

2:    Job postings through posters/newspaper/radio

3:    A placement agency (private)

4:    A placement agency (government)

5:    Job candidates are proposed by a school or vocational training center

6:    Other (please specify)

9.3   What proportion of the firm's employees are migrants from other cities/regions/countries? _____ %

9.4   What proportion of the firm's new employees were recommended by friends or relatives of the owners or managers? _____ %

9.5   Does the firm ever hire production workers without a recommendation or referral?

1:    Yes

2:    No

9.6   If the firm were free to hire and lay off workers at will:

9.6.1   How many of its current workers would it lay off?

9.6.2   How many additional workers would it hire?

9.7   Does the firm provide housing to any of its employees?

1:    Yes

2:    No

9.8   Does the firm provide free or subsidized meals to any of its production workers?

1:    Yes

2:    No

9.9   Does the firm provide toilets with running water for its production workers?

1:    Yes

2:    No

9.10   Are any of the firm's employees a member of a labor union?

1:    Yes

2:    No

9.11   What is the average number of years of schooling of an entry-level production worker?

9.12   How many weeks does it take to train an entry-level production worker?

10.	FINANCE

10.1   In what year did this firm last purchase machinery, equipment, or vehicles? ____

10.2   How did the firm finance the purchase? (Please tick all that apply.)
  1:    Internal funds/retained earnings
  2:    Borrowed from a bank
  3:    Borrowed from a nonbank financial institution (a micro-finance institution, a credit cooperative/credit union)
  4:    Borrowed from a government agency
  5:    Funds from family/friends
  6:    Hire-purchase/credit from the equipment supplier
  7:    Other (please specify)

10.3   Does the firm have a bank account?
  1:    Yes
  2:    No

Enumerator: If the answer is "no," skip to question 10.9.

10.4   Does the firm have an overdraft facility/line of credit?
  1:    Yes
  2:    No

Enumerator: If the answer is "no," skip to question 10.9.

10.5   What is the limit on that overdraft facility/line of credit?

10.6   What is the interest rate on the overdraft?

10.7   Did the establishment provide collateral for the overdraft facility?
  1:    Yes
  2:    No

Enumerator: If the answer is "no," skip to question 10.9.

10.8   What is the approximate value of the collateral as a percentage of the overdraft facility?

10.9   Does the firm have a savings account?
            1:   Yes
            2:   No

10.10   Over the last five years, did this firm borrow money? (Please
            record each year in which a new loan was taken and the
            source.)

Source		2010	2009	2008	2007	2006
10.10.1	A bank					
10.10.2	A nonbank financial institution (a microfinance institution, a credit cooperative/ credit union)					
10.10.3	A government agency					
10.10.4	Family/friends					
10.10.5	Moneylenders					
10.10.6	Any other source (please specify): _____					

10.11   Does the firm currently owe money for a loan?
            1:   Yes
            2:   No

10.12   Referring to the most recent loan from a bank, financial insti-
            tution, or government agency:
            10.12.1 How much time (in months) was the firm granted to
                     pay off the loan?
            10.12.2 What was the interest rate on the loan?
            10.12.3 Did the establishment provide collateral for the loan?
            1:   Yes
            2:   No

Enumerator: If the answer is "no," skip to question 10.13.

            10.12.4 What was the approximate value of the collateral as
                     a percentage of the value of the loan?

10.13   Are the annual financial statements of this firm certified by an external auditor?
    1:   Yes
    2:   No

10.14   Could the firm borrow if it wanted to purchase additional machinery, equipment, or vehicles?
    1:   Yes
    2:   No

Enumerator: If the answer is "no," skip to question 10.19.

10.15   From which source? (Please tick all that apply.)
    1:   A bank
    2:   A nonbank financial institution (a microfinance institution, a credit cooperative/credit union)
    3:   A government agency
    4:   Family/friends
    5:   Moneylenders
    6:   Any other source (please specify)

10.16   How much could the firm borrow?

10.17   For how long?

10.18   How long would it take until the funds are disbursed by the lender?

10.19   Could the firm borrow if it wanted to expand its working capital?
    1:   Yes
    2:   No

Enumerator: If the answer is "no," skip to the start of the next section.

10.20   From which source? (Please tick all that apply.)
    1:   A bank
    2:   A nonbank financial institution (a microfinance institution, a credit cooperative/credit union)
    3:   A government agency
    4:   Credit from suppliers of raw materials
    5:   Advances from customers
    6:   Family/friends
    7:   Moneylenders
    8:   Any other source (please specify)

10.21   How much could the firm borrow?

10.22   For how long?

10.23   How long would it take until the funds are disbursed by the lender?

11.   PRODUCTIVITY

11.1   For the previous two fiscal years, please provide the following information about this establishment.

Note: researchers to insert the relevant years here.

Account	Last fiscal year	Fiscal year before the last fiscal year
Total annual sales		
Other revenues		
Total annual cost of labor (including wages, salaries, bonuses, social security payments)		
Total annual cost of raw materials (including fuel)		
Total annual cost of utilities (water, electricity, telephone, etc.)		
Total annual cost of rental of land and buildings		
Total annual interest payments		
Other costs (insurance, services, etc.)		
Depreciation		
Total annual profit (before tax)		
Taxes		

11.2   What were the total annual sales three years ago? (Please indicate if the establishment was not in business three years ago.)

11.3   What were the total sales in the firm's first year of operation?

11.4   Over the last fiscal year, how much did the firm spend on the purchase of:

11.4.1   Machinery, equipment, and vehicles (new and/or used)?

11.4.2   Land and buildings?

11.5   At the end of the last fiscal year, what was the resale value of the firm's own:

   11.5.1   Machinery, equipment, and vehicles?

   11.5.2   Land and buildings?

Notes

1. Detailed results are available at http://go.worldbank.org/ASG0J44350.

2. Data are missing for 161 of the 303 Chinese respondents.

3. The proportion of missing observations is large in China; so, responses there should be regarded with caution.

4. Nonresponse may be an issue, however: of the 160 Chinese firms reporting an overdraft, only 119 answered the question about collateral, and only 68 answered the question about the interest rate.

Reference

Fafchamps, Marcel. 2004. *Market Institutions and Sub-Saharan Africa: Theory and Evidence*. Cambridge, MA: MIT Press.